CONTENTS

HOW TO SUCCEED IN THE MUSIC BUSINESS

By Allan Dann & John Underwood

Edited by Chris Charlesworth
Cover designed by Mark Lloyd

ISBN: 0.7119.9433.1
Order No: OP 49027

Whilst every effort has been made to ensure that the contents of this book are accurate and current at the
time of writing, no liability can be accepted by the authors and publishers of this book for any acts done
or advice given in reliance on the information and opinions contained in this book.

Exclusive Distributors:
Book Sales Limited,
8/9 Frith Street,
London W1V 5TZ, UK.

Music Sales Corporation,
257 Park Avenue South,
New York, NY 10010, USA.

Macmillan Distribution Services,
53 West Park Drive, Derrimut,
Victoria 3030, Australia.

To the Music Trade only:
Music Sales Limited,
8/9, Frith Street,
London W1V 5TZ, UK.

Typeset by Phoenix Photosetting, Chatham, Kent
Printed in Great Britain by Creative Print & Design Ltd, Wales

A catalogue record for this book is available from the British Library.

www.omnibuspress.com

INTRODUCTION

There are many big names in the music world who, despite all their apparent success, have come out of it with very little to show in the way of financial reward. The man in the street would firmly believe that they 'must have made a fortune', yet hasty signing of unfavourable contracts has been the downfall of many stars.-

Sometimes their problems have become public knowledge, as when contractual wrangles get as far as the courts, but many more have simply not succeeded when they could have done, or have 'succeeded' but just not made the money they should have made.

The temptation is obvious, when you first enter the business, to sign the first piece of paper thrust in front of you, just so that you can wave it about and say, 'I've been signed up, I've got a recording/publishing contract.' This is especially so when the record company or publisher often appears to be doing you a huge favour by 'giving you a chance'. The days have virtually gone when professional songwriters would sell hit songs outright for a few pounds, or important artists would make hit records for just the fee paid at the session, but it still can and does happen. The music stars who have succeeded in becoming famous AND rich, are the ones who had their heads screwed on.

This book is based on the personal experience of two professionals who between them have had more years in the music business than they care to say. It is not intended to be a definitive work on the subject (such a book would be many times this size and very difficult to read). Because of this we should stress from the outset that this book should not be solely relied upon in place of professional legal advice, for which there really is absolutely no substitute in each individual case. This book will, however, help you to find your way around the business and to know what questions to ask, and how to avoid many of the most obvious mistakes which are still, amazingly, so common. It will help you to 'have your head screwed on' in the music business.

This book doesn't presume to teach you how to write a hit song or to sing or to play your instrument (you probably don't need any guidance on this- you probably already know what you can and cannot do, musically) although there are sections giving a general guide as to how you can best sell your songs to music publishers and yourself to record companies, pointing out some of the pitfalls.

You may not need to read the book cover to cover, but we strongly urge you to read thoroughly whichever of the following sections is relevant for you. These days very few writers are not also producers and very few singers are not also writers etc. so at the very least we'd suggest that you skim through the headings in the other sections to see what might be relevant. This is certainly true for information on music on the Internet etc.

For quick reference a rough guide to royalty rates and terms offered by publishers, record companies, managers, agents etc. is included towards the back of this book.

SELLING YOUR SONGS TO A PUBLISHER

You may have signed a contract as a recording artist with a record company under which that company has asked for everything you write to go through their own music publishing outlet (most of the larger record companies have these). If at all possible you should try to give these valuable rights to a different company. So how can you go about deciding which publisher to submit your songs to?

Which publisher should I approach?

The first basic rule is to choose a publisher who is properly in the business of music publishing, and has preferably had at least one or two hits in the recent past. Unfortunately in the UK this rules out most but by no means all companies outside London (or Dublin in Eire) though cities as diverse as Manchester and Brighton do have their own thriving music scenes. In most countries the publishers and record companies are grouped fairly closely together in one area of the capital city, the USA being a notable exception with New York, Los Angeles and Nashville and other cities all being music centres (Germany is similar, with Hamburg, Munich and Berlin all being music centres). Most regional UK publishers are in fact record producers/managers/publishers with the emphasis usually not on the publishing side. For this reason if you assigned your song to even the largest and most reputable of these, the chances are that they would probably pass rights on to a publisher in the capital. So unless the local company is also doing other things for you, you might as well go direct to the 'dedicated' publisher yourself – you'll probably end up with a larger share of the earnings and may receive any royalties due to you more quickly. You'll also probably have better access to the people who are actually looking after your songs. Don't be afraid to ring the Copyright Department with a query on how and when the songs were registered and any terms of the agreement you made, or the Royalty Department with a query on statements and cheques you receive (or don't receive). They may not be able to answer instantly but you could probably expect a response within a week or so. A list of publishers with addresses is shown at the end of this section.

How best can I get to put my song across?

If at all possible, try to visit the publisher in person, but do make an appointment beforehand, even if you simply phone up asking to come in with your songs in a couple of hours. Sometimes they'll even agree to hear them straightaway but don't bank on it. Gone are the days when you'd turn up with a guitar, or ask to sit at the piano and sing something to a man with a fat cigar who'd say 'don't call us, we'll call you'. They might well be prepared to listen to your demo on CD or DAT or even cassette in your presence, or they may ask you to send something to them first (though some publishers, for legal reasons, will not accept demos through the post). At least by ringing them first you'll know the name of the person who will be responsible for assessing your demos and you'll know that you won't be completely wasting your time, as you might if you sent something out of the blue. If you do send something by post make sure you put your address/phone number on the CD itself rather than just on the case.

How many songs should I include?

Whichever way you present the songs to a publisher don't expect him to hear more than three at any one time and definitely put the best one, in your opinion, first. If the first minute or so of the first song is poor it's very possible that the others won't be heard at all. Always make a copy of your demo, in case a publisher wants to 'hang on to it' for someone else in the company to hear or in case it becomes lost or damaged. If a publisher keeps your demo for a while, don't think that he's intending to steal your songs, but don't be afraid to find out when he'll be prepared to give you a decision on them. Incidentally, don't waste a publisher's time making excuses for the poor quality of your recording or your voice before playing the songs. Most writers do this but there's really no need. If you're an aspiring singer then the publisher might be interested in passing the demo on to his record company affiliate, or some friend of his at a record company. Many of the bigger publishers have contacts with particular record labels, even if they are not owned by the same conglomerate. Otherwise don't worry – it's the songs the publisher is most interested in and unless the demo is really rough he'll see beyond your performance.

Is a home-made demo really adequate?

Naturally a studio-recorded demo, or one recorded at home and mixed down in a studio is preferable (see under 'How can I make a demo' in the next section for details) but a clear home-recorded demo is often adequate for selling a song (much more so than for selling an artist to a record company). Try to use the best quality medium you can afford. Recordable CDs are so cheap that it's really not worth presenting your demos on anything else, even if the demo wasn't recorded digitally! In any event make sure that there's no long silence before your demo starts and that there's nothing else immediately after it.

Is it worthwhile sending songs in?

If you can't get to the capital don't despair. Plenty of songs sent in to publishers from around the country have found their way onto hit records. When you ring ask for the name of the 'Creative Manager' or 'A&R Manager', or possibly 'Professional Manager' which was the old title for such people, then send the demos to him or her with a list of the songs and stamps sufficient for the return of the CD, assuming you want it back if it's rejected. A copy of the lyrics could be helpful, depending upon the clarity of the recording and the type of songs. You could send a top-line or 'lead-sheet' which is the basic tune and lyrics, but there's not too much point. Certainly don't bother to send an accompanying full manuscript or a manuscript on its own except in the concert/serious music field.

If you think the song is suitable for a particular British artist, especially one who has had a hit with one of that

...or how about this one?...

particular publisher's songs before in the last couple of years, then there is no harm in suggesting this. Publishers like to have ideas set before them as well as the songs, but be sensible and don't bother to suggest that they send the songs to international megastars, especially non-UK based ones, unless you know that the publisher has connections with a particular star.

There are magazines (so-called tip-sheets) in the UK and some other countries which you can subscribe to. These give details of which artists and their managers or producers are actively looking for new songs for a current or forthcoming recording project. These magazines can seem expensive, but it's your career we're talking about, and they can be a very useful guide to who is recording a new album, who is producing it and for which label, as well as containing other useful background information about the local music scene.

I wrote this for Yehudi – so I want you to imagine that's who I am, okay?

How can I find out which publishers specialise in my kind of music?

We have included here a list of some music publishers. As with record companies, some are more concerned with dance, garage, soul, country, folk, jazz, rock, 'MOR' (middle of the road) etc., than others, and the publisher credits on labels of records which you yourself may have will give you a guide. The publisher's name should be somewhere on the label of a vinyl 12″ single and at the top or bottom of the lyric if it's printed on the insert of a CD. Better still, printed music will have the British publisher's name and address usually on the title page at the bottom.

Remember that the absence of a publisher's name from the list in this book doesn't necessarily mean you shouldn't deal with him, anymore than the presence of a publisher's name here guarantees his complete competence and integrity etc. Finally a word about publishing subsidiaries. Most publishers have a number of smaller companies which they wholly or partly own. Some of these are simply outlets for the songs of one particular composer – that composer gets a share of the profits on his songs as well as the usual royalties. With a hit or two under your belt you might be offered such a company with one of the big publishers. Because there are so many subsidiaries we have included only a very small number of well-known subsidiaries on this list.

UK MUSIC PUBLISHERS

Amazon Music
Unit 1 Canalot Studios
222 Kensal Road
London W10 5BN
(0207 598 1184)

Amphonic Music
'Kerchesters'
Waterhouse Lane
Kingswood
Surrey KT20 6HT
(0173 832837)

Belsize Music
29 Manor House
Marylebone Road
London NW1 5NP
(0207 723 7177)

BMG Music
Bedford House
69-79 Fulham High Street
London SW6 3JW
(0207 384 7600)

**Boosey & Hawkes
Music** (serious)
The Hyde
Edgware Road
London NW9 6JN
(0207 580 2060)

Bosworth & Co
(serious)
See Chester Music

Bourne Music
2nd Floor,
207/209 Regent Street
London W1B 4ND
(0207 734 3385)

Bucks Music Group
Onward House
11 Uxbridge Street
London W8 7TQ
(0207 221 4275)

Bug Music
31 Milson Road
London W14 0LJ
(0207 602 0727)

Bugle Songs
21A, Noel Street
London W1V 3PD
(0207 439 2282)

Campbell Connelly & Co
8-9 Frith Street
London W1V 5TZ
(0207 434 0066)

Carlin Music Corp
Iron Bridge House
3 Bridge Approach
Chalk Farm
London NW1 8BD
(0208 207 6207)

Chelsea Music Pub.
124 Great Portland St.
London W1N 5PG
(0207 580 0044)

Chester Music (serious)
8-9 Frith Street
London W1V 5TZ
(0207 434 0066)

Chrysalis Music
Chrysalis Building
13 Bramley Road
London W10 6SP
(0207 221 2213)

Complete Music
3rd floor, Bishops Park
House
25-29 Fulham High Street
London SW6 3JH
(0207 731 8595)

Congo Music
17a Craven Park Road
Harlesden
London NW10 8SE
(0208 961 5461)

Deconstruction Songs
Bedford House
69-79 Fulham High Street
London SW6 3JW
(0207 384 2298)

Dejamus Ltd.
Suite 11 Accurist House
44 Baker Street
London W1M 1DX
(0207 486 5838)

Digger Music
32 Great James St.
London WC1N 3HB
(0207 404 1422)

Diverse Music
Creeting House
All Saints Road
Creeting St.Mary
Ipswich,
Suffolk
(01449 723 244)

Eaton Music
39 Lower Richmond Road
Putney,
London SW15 1ET
(0208 788 4577)

E.G. Music
63a Kings Road
Chelsea
London SW3 4NT
(0207 730 2162)

EMI Music Publishing
127 Charing Cross Road
London WC2H 0AE
(0207 434 2131)

Essex Music Group
Suite 207, 535 Kings Road
London SW10 0SZ
(0207 823 3773)

Faber Music (serious)
3 Queen Square
London WC1N 3AU
(0207 833 7906)

Fortissimo Music
78 Portland Road
London W11 4LQ
(0207 727 2063)

**Hit & Run Music
Publishing**
24 Ives Street
London SW3 2ND
(0207 581 0261)

Hornall Bros Music
Basement
754 Fulham Road
London SW6 5SW+SH
(0207 736 7891)

**Independent Music
Group**
54 Larkshall Road
Chingford
London E4 6PD
(0208 523 9000)

Jeff Wayne Music Group
8-9 Ivor Place
London NW1 6BY
(0207 724 2471)

Jelly Street Music
358 Chester Road,
Manchester M16 9EZ
(0161 872 6006)

Joustwise Ltd.
Myrtle Cott.
Rye Road,
Hawkhurst
Kent TN18 5DW
(01580 754 771)

Alfred A Kalmus
(serious)
38 Eldon Way
Paddock Wood
Kent TN12 6BE
(01892 833 422)

**Kassner Associated
Publishers**
Units 6 & 7
11 Wyfold Road,
Fulham
London SW6 6SE
(0207 385 7700)

Kingsway Music
Lottbridge Drive
Eastbourne
E. Sussex BN23 6NT
(011323 410930)

Mark Rowles Music
Cedar House
Vine Lane
Hillingdon
Middx UB10 0BX
(01895 251 515)

Marquis Music
1 Wyndham Yard
Wyndham Place
London W1H 1AR
(0207 402 2886)

Mautoglade Music
22 Denmark Street
London WC2H 8NA
(0207 836 5996)

MCS Music
32 Lexington Street
London W1F 0LQ
(0207 255 8777)

Menace Music
2 Park Road
Radlett
Herts WD7 8EQ
(01923 853 789)

Minder Music
18 Pindock Mews
London W9 2PY
(0207 289 7281)

Ministry of Sound Music
101 Gaunt Street
London SE1 6DP
(0207 378 6528)

Moncur Street Music
PO Box 16114
London SW3 4WG
(0207 349 9909)

Bryan Morrison Music
1 Star St.
London W2 1QD
(0207 706 7304)

MPL Communications
1 Soho Square
London W1V 6BQ
(0207 439 2001)

Music Exchange
Claverton Road
Wythenshawe
Manchester M23 9ZA
(0161 946 1234)

Music House
Roberts House
P.O. Box 5200
103 Hammersmith Rd
London W14 0YP
(0207 348 5800)

Music Sales Ltd.
8-9 Frith Street
London W1V 5TZ
(0207 434 0066)

Mute Song
429 Harrow Road
London W10 4RE
(0208 964 2001)

New Age Music
17 Priory Road,
LondonNW6 4NN
(0207 209 2766)

Notting Hill Music
Bedford House
88 Berkeley Gardens
London W8 4AP
(0207 234 2921)

Novello & Co (serious)
8-9 Frith Street
London W1V 5TZ
(0207 434 0066)

Oxford University Press (serious)
Great Clarendon St
Oxford OX2 6DP
(10865 556767)

Passion Music
Skratch Music House
81 Crabtree Lane
London SW6 6LW
(0207 381 8315)

Peermusic (UK)
Peer House
8-14 Verulam Street
London WC1X 8LZ
(0207 404 7200)

Perfect Songs
The Blue Building
42-46 St. Lukes Mews
London W11 1DG
(0207 221 5101)

Peters Edition (serious)
10-12 Baches Street
London N1 6DN
(0207 253 1638)

Pink Floyd Music Publishers
27 Noel Street
London W1V 3RD
(0207 734 6892)

Really Useful Group
22 Tower Street
London WC2H
(0207 240 0880)

Red Bus Music International
34 Salisbury Street
London NW8 8QE
(0207 402 9111)

Revolver Music Publishing
152 Goldthorn Hill
Penn
Wolverhampton
W. Midlands WV2 3JA
(01902 345 345)

Rondor Music (London)
The Yacht Club
Chelsea Harbour
London SW10 0XA
(0207 349 4750)

Schott & Co. (serious)
48 Gt. Marlborough Street
London W1V 2BN
(0207 437 1246)

SGO Music Publishing
PO Box 34994
London SW6 6WF
(0207 385 9377)

Sony/ATV Music Publishing
13 Gt. Marlborough Street
London W1V 2LP
(0207 911 8200)

Sparta Florida Music
(see Campbell Connelly Music)

Stainer and Bell
P.O. Box 110 Victoria House
23 Gruneisen Rd
Finchley
London N3 1DZ
(0208 343 3303)

State Music
6 Kenrick Place
London W1U 6HD
(0207 486 9878)

Strongsongs Publishing
Prospect Studios
Barnes High Street
London SW13 9LE
(0208 878 7888)

Supreme Songs
Independent House
54 Larkshall Road
Chingford
London E4 6PD
(0208 523 9000)

TKO Publishing
PO Box 130
Hove,
E. Sussex BN3 6QU
(01273 550 088)

United Music Publishers
42 Rivington St
London EC2A 3BN
(0207 729 4700)

Universal Music Publishing
8 St. James Square
London SW1Y 4JU
(0207 747 4000)

Valentine Music Group
7 Garrick Street
London WC2E 9AR
(0207 240 1628)

Warner Chappell Music
Griffin House
161 Hammersmith Road
London W6 8BS
(0208 563 5800)

Westbury Music Consultants
Suite B, 2 Tunstall Road
London SW9 8DA
(0207 733 5400)

Windswept Pacific Music
Hope House
40 St. Peter's Road
London W6 9BD
(0208 237 8400)

Zomba Music Publishers
Zomba House
165-167 High Road
London NW10 2SG
(0208 459 8899)

Most music publishers are members of The Music Publishers Association whose address is 3rd Floor, Strandgate, York Buildings, London WC2N 6JU (phone 0207 839 7779). They can advise of any change of address etc. Plenty of managers, agents and record companies also have active and successful publishing divisions, but this list covers most of the major players and the specialists in music publishing

PUBLISHERS

Music Publishers have existed for centuries, acquiring manuscripts from composers and printing them for performances at concerts or for sale to the public to sing around the piano at home. Over the last hundred years or so 'publishing' has gradually come to mean finding and then exploiting songs mainly through recording and broadcasting on radio and television and in films, commercials, computer games etc. as well as funding showcase gigs, making demos and master recordings and so on. Actual printing and publishing of music is nowadays almost a separate undertaking from most pop music publishers' business and carried out for them by specialist print music publishers, the leading company in the UK being Music Sales Ltd. However the printing, sale and hire of musical scores is still very important to so-called 'standard' publishers – otherwise sometimes known as 'serious', 'concert music' or 'classical' publishers – who are still directly concerned with these aspects of the business.

What should the publisher do for a songwriter?

Generally a publisher will not acquire a song unless he intends to do some or all of the things mentioned in the introduction to this section to try to earn money for both of you from your songs. If you don't have a top quality demo, he'll pay for one, which should be noticeably better than one you could do yourself unless you have a very good home studio. If you yourself are not an artist or producer he'll use his contacts with record companies to try to get one of their suitable artists to record your song. Bear in mind though, that in the UK this is now very difficult unless you are also a producer, in which case the publisher may be able to get you the job of producing tracks for an artist (which will probably involve co-writing with the artist). Once a record is released, he might well help the record company to exploit it. This could take the form of getting his own promotion people, if he has them, to work on the record. Or he might contribute to the cost of tour support, independent promoters or an advertising campaign of some kind. He should also arrange for the printing of a 'single edition' of your song for sale in music

shops if it's the featured track on a single and becomes at least a top 5 single in the UK (don't expect this otherwise, except perhaps as part of a songbook to accompany a best selling album).

If it is printed he will then have to deposit copies of the music edition at the British Museum library and elsewhere (the law demands that absolutely everything printed for sale in Britain be stored in a central archive). He should also ensure that royalties are collected on the song by notifying certain bodies (see later) and by having it sub-published abroad, so that no money is lost if the song becomes a world-wide hit. He should not charge you a fee of any kind for any of this, and should not deduct any of it from your share of the royalties. He takes all the financial risks, but this is what his share of the royalties is for.

Beware of advertisements from people offering to publish or record your song for a fee, or write music to your lyrics etc. Only send a song to them as a last resort if no 'proper' music publisher is interested in it but you're really desperate to see it on record or in print and you don't have the facilities to do this at home. There is nothing automatically bad or crooked about these people. They simply provide a service for a fee, but if you ever hope to make any real money writing songs you will sooner or later have to convince a 'real' publisher that your songs are worth spending money on. Remember there are plenty of publishers around to choose from, none of whom will charge you to place your song with them, nor will they recover any of their expenses from your royalties.

What should the publisher's song agreement include?

Song assignments from writers to publishers these days are usually many pages long. Although there may not necessarily be anything wrong with a shorter one, there is a good chance that it doesn't properly cover all the points necessary and if you find yourself thinking 'what if ...' then you should be slightly suspicious. In principle you'll usually be actually selling the publisher all the rights in your song in return for some initial 'consideration' which may be a substantial advance payment or a nominal sum such as £1, and always a share of all royalties the publisher receives. The actual wording of the agreements varies a lot, and these days it's quite common for a publisher to agree to a licence rather than an assignment (meaning that in theory you remain the owner of the song and just give the publisher exclusive rights to exploit it and collect the income on your behalf). This is preferable for you, though if an assignment to a publisher is only for quite a short period – say five years – then it's probably not something to make a fuss about. The royalty terms offered are the most important part – more important than any amount the publisher is prepared to pay as an advance to you, so we'll start with those. Even if you are a complete unknown, you should never be offered less than the following:

Printed music royalties – what should the agreement say?

You can expect to get 10%–12.5% of the actual retail selling price of the printed music (if it's a single song edition at £3, you'll get 30p or so). Some contracts allow the publisher to recover the cost of printing the music before paying you anything, and some provide for no royalty to you at all on songbooks or orchestrations, or uses of lyrics without music. You could obviously lose a lot of money through this, and you should insist on having any such wording removed or altered. On sales of sheet music overseas your publisher will get a royalty which he should then divide with you (this may not be spelled out, but may be covered by the 'miscellaneous income' bit in the contract).

The single printed music edition of a number one in the UK record charts will generally sell no more than about 1,000 (even less for some dance tracks), as against hundreds of thousands many years ago when sheet music royalties were a songwriter's main source of income. Even today big ballads can occasionally sell tens of thousands, but this is quite exceptional. Overseas, sheet music tends to be more expensive and sales are often even lower. Sales of songbooks, sometimes called 'folios' on the other hand are very healthy and the best of these outsell even hit single editions many times over – hence the warning about making sure you get paid on sales of songbooks. Because most publishers now appoint a specialist music sales agent to print and exploit printed music for them, this may mean that your royalties from printed music sales are not based on the retail price but are regarded by your publisher as miscellaneous income. However this shouldn't affect your royalty rate unduly. You may actually get slightly more.

Record royalties ('mechanicals') – what should the agreement say?

These are basically royalties paid by record companies for including your songs on their records. They include everything from hit singles to CDs given away with magazines and from full-price albums to cheap 30-track compilations sold at garages or in supermarkets. Even an unknown writer should get from his publisher about 70% of these so-called 'mechanical royalties'. If you are also a budding producer with a master-quality recording of the song, which perhaps just needs remixing, or are a member of a hot new band with possible record company interest you might get as much as 80%-85%, although if you expect a substantial advance royalty payment then your actual royalty percentage is likely to be lower. You may well also get slightly less on recordings secured by the publisher which you had nothing to do with. These are known as 'cover recordings' although the exact definition varies and is worth looking at closely. If possible try to exclude 'windfall' covers (ones which the publisher didn't actively go out and get). Whether you get the same rate from overseas as you do in the UK depends upon whether you have what's known as an 'at source' deal.

What is an 'at source' publishing deal?

A publisher will have or will appoint 'sub-publishers' in many countries who will register your songs in their territory, try to maximise the income and (often more importantly) make sure none goes astray. In return for that the sub-publisher usually takes about 15%-25% of the total income. If it's 25% this means that he sends 75% back to the UK publisher and if you as the writer have a 70/30 'receipts' deal (all publishing deals are either 'at source' or 'receipts') you get 70% of the 75% which your publisher gets from abroad (i.e. only 52.5% of the total). For a new writer this is still far better than the deals that used to be offered. However, if your deal is say 70% 'at source' you will get the full 70% earned throughout the world as well as in the UK and your UK publisher and his foreign sub-publishers have to share the 30% between them. If the UK is only say 10-15% of the total market for your song you will see that this can make an enormous difference to the amount you eventually earn, so you should always try to ask for an 'at-source' publishing deal.

One big UK hit single which also makes it around the world can easily bring in £500,000 and very likely a lot more, especially if it takes off in the USA. Do remember that only publishers with their own companies around the world or successful smaller ones who have very advantageous deals with foreign publishers can really offer 'at-source' deals at 70% or more. However, even on a so-called receipts deal your contract should not just say that you will get 70% (or whatever percentage was agreed) of the UK publisher's receipts from abroad. If a UK company and a related sub-publisher overseas arranged between them that the UK company receives only 10% of the total royalties from that country you'd only in theory get 70% of that, i.e. 7% of the total! Since the early Seventies, however, publishers have been obliged in 'receipts' deals to state the maximum which they will allow their sub-publishers abroad to keep, so it should always be possible for you to calculate the minimum percentage which you would get from foreign earnings.

How are mechanical royalties calculated and collected?

The amount UK record companies pay for the use of music is set by negotiations between the MCPS – Mechanical Copyright Protection Society (formed as long ago as 1911 at the time of the first really effective UK Copyright Act, which gave writers and publishers a specific right to 'record' royalties) – for the publishers and the BPI (British Phonographic Industry) for the record companies (for more on the MCPS see 'General Q&A on Songwriting'). If they can't agree then the record companies can refer the licensing schemes which MCPS is offering to a body called the Copyright Tribunal who ultimately decide what is fair.

The current rate is 8.5% of the published price to dealers (around 6% of the actual price in the shops) but the record companies have tried to get this reduced on the grounds that, as is usually the case for major retail chains, the 'actual realised price' which the companies get after giving discounts or freebies to retailers is substantially lower than their official published dealer price. All record companies pay the royalties to the MCPS or to one of their sister societies in Europe. The societies then pay the publishers who then pay you. If MCPS have the exact timings of each track from the record company then they will divide the royalty between the songs on each record strictly according to how long each one runs for, regardless of the fact that there may be just one track which is generating all the sales. If they don't have timings then MCPS divide equally according to the number of tracks.

MCPS charges about 4-5% to your publisher for collecting from the established record companies, which operate under what's known as the AP1 scheme. This means they only pay on actual sales they've made. The smaller ones have to pay on the number of records they press (AP2 and AP2A schemes), regardless of whether they sell them, as it's just too costly for MCPS to enforce the licences for thousands of different albums of which only 500 or 1,000 each may ever be pressed. MCPS charge around 7.5% for the significant 'smaller independent labels' and around 12.5% for collecting from the rest of these companies, as it costs them a lot more to collect and process the money and also to monitor the activities of companies which include really small ones who sometimes, through ignorance, press and sell records with no consent whatever. However plenty of AP2 companies do have hit records and if you're trying to work out what will be due to you it's worth remembering that if your hit is on an AP2 label then the MCPS commission will be that much higher.

How much should I actually get from sales of records of my songs?

An album on a major label which sells at, say, £13 including VAT in the big chain stores (more for retail outlets which don't enjoy substantial discounts) will have a dealer price of about £8 before VAT (this could be as much as £9 and, if so, you will need to increase the following figures by slightly over 10%). With an £8 PDP, the total 8.5% royalty would therefore work out at around 70p (say around 66p after MCPS takes its commission). If the album contains 14 tracks, each track will get roughly 4.7p (depending on precisely how long it lasts compared to the other tracks). If your deal with your publisher is, let's say, a 70/30 split in your favour, you'll get between 3p and 3.5p for every record sold (but not records sent out free for promotional purposes). So if you see that the album has been certified as having gone gold (100,000 UK sales) you should expect very roughly £3-3,500 or slightly more for your one track.

A single on an independent dance

label selling at around £4 or so will have a dealer price of around £2.60 before VAT. The 8.5% royalty will be about 22p. If you were on the same 70/30 split, you'd end up with about 15p (but remember this won't necessarily apply to 'white label' copies). If you wrote 100% of all the mixes then it won't matter how many different ones there are on the single. Your royalty will be the same. If however there is a remix on which someone else gets a writer credit (maybe because there's a sample on it) and that mix is the longest, your royalty would suffer (see 'A-side protection' in the Glossary).

If the single goes in at number 5 in the first week it'll need to sell very roughly 20-40,000 copies in the first week (though at some times of the year this could take it higher). If it drops progressively it might reach say 50-70,000 sales overall. If it goes in at number 1(even if it then drops rapidly) you might still hope for around 70-100,000 sales in the first week to get it there and 150,000+ in total (as many as 250,000-500,000 or even more for a really memorable big-seller). If the record company gives away copies not just to reviewers etc. but also to retail chains etc. to encourage sales they don't have to pay on the first 1,500 of these but after that your royalties won't suffer.

Another reason besides the advance orders why singles drop so quickly from the UK charts is their immediate inclusion on hits compilations. Because these sell so well and at a high price, the royalty is comparable to tracks on the original album from which the single may have been taken. But a compilation of older tracks on a budget label where the dealer price is only say £1 and there are maybe 30 tracks, means a tiny royalty. In the UK there is no minimum royalty per track. Compilations can make a big difference to your royalties, but don't necessarily expect more than a few hundred pounds from most best-selling budget compilations using one of your songs.

There can be substantial earnings from cover-mounted CDs on magazines etc. whether or not they're actually advertising anything (MCPS charge 6.5% of 50% of the price of the magazine under their AP7 licensing scheme for 'cover-mounts' subject to a minimum, so the amount per song per record is very low but the sales figures can be huge). MCPS collects over £2 million a year just from these.

Record royalties for songs are paid in roughly the same way in most countries. In the rest of Europe it has long been the case that the publishers' body (known as BIEM) negotiated with the record companies' body (the IFPI) and arrived at a royalty rate for the rest of Europe, though this does not have to be so and frequently there is, in practice, no such agreement in place. There the royalty rate is generally slightly above the UK one, but is then reduced by such things as packaging allowances, discounts and holdback provisions which mean that record companies can retain part of the royalty due in case a percentage of records are returned by the shops unsold or found to be faulty. The amount that reaches you can also be reduced through Central European Licensing.

How does Central European Licensing affect my mechanical royalties?

This started with a deal between PolyGram Records (which became part of Universal) and STEMRA, the Dutch equivalent of MCPS, in the Eighties and now most major record companies have a deal with just one of the European collecting societies (there's generally one society in each country). It means that the record company pays some or all of its mechanical royalties to that one society for record sales throughout Europe which is supposed to be considered one 'market'. That society then pays the other local societies in the countries where the sales actually took place, at the appropriate royalty rate, and the local society then pays the local publisher.

If it's the UK, your publisher pays you. If not, the local sub-publisher in say Germany, gets the money and pays your publisher who then pays you for German sales. This means you get the money slightly later (and on a receipts deal you get less). Also, both the society collecting who have the deal with the record company and the local society each want a percentage of the royalties as an administration fee, so this cuts down the amount you get, though under an agreement between the collecting societies and the publishers called the 'Cannes Agreement' the societies pledged to try to bring down the overall amount to no more than about 7% between them in the case of the bigger societies.

What are controlled composition clauses?

This is another phrase you are likely to hear in connection with royalties for sales of recordings of your songs. These clauses are another reason why your mechanical royalties might be less than you were expecting. This has become increasingly complicated over the years, but as briefly as possible, this is how it works. In the USA and Canada the rate is set at so many cents per track per record or a certain amount per minute for very long tracks but has been allowed to increase every year to allow for inflation- it was set at 8 cents for 2003, 8.5 cents for 2004-5 and so on up. However, this 'statutory' rate laid down by the US government was more than the record companies had been used to paying back in the Sixties and Seventies, so to compensate they began asking publishers for licences at only 75% of the new rate. This was perfectly legal provided the publisher concerned agreed to accept it. For big standard songs the answer was usually 'no', but for a new song the

publishers often agreed to it just to make sure their song was included.

Where the artist on the record was also the writer, the record companies began putting into their contracts with the artist that, as a writer, he must force his publisher to accept the 75% rate. If the publisher didn't, then the extra 25% would come out of his artist royalty instead. Gradually other provisions were added to the artist agreement too – he mustn't put more than 10 songs on his album (gradually increased to 12 on most CDs), or two songs on a single. He must force the publisher to grant a licence for promotional videos, which sometimes covers all videos by that artist, for nothing, even when the record company was being paid for the uses such as retail sales of videos or television companies paying to use them. Even worse, the record company would only pay royalties to the publisher on sales of records on which the artist was being paid. The artist contract (see next section) usually allows the record company to pay 50% of the normal royalty on many types of release, and nothing at all on some others.

Without these so-called 'controlled composition clauses', the publishers would be able to collect the full royalty on the full price of all these releases at the rate applying when the records were actually sold, instead of 75% of what the rate was when the record was first 'delivered' to the record company or else first released (only around half of the current rate for a record made 10 years ago) and maybe much less depending upon the terms of the artist agreement with the record company.

If you do decide (or the record company decides for you) to put someone else's song on your record and the publisher of that song insists on 100% of the statutory royalty, the record company will reduce the amount they pay on your own songs (or else your overall artist royalty) even further, to cover the cost to them of paying this full royalty.

This is covered in the next section, but as the songwriter you need to be aware of it.

If your publishing agreement says something along the lines of the following then you are guaranteeing to your publisher that his North American sub-publishers won't be obliged to accept controlled composition rates: 'The Writer undertakes that he has made no agreement with any third party as to the terms upon which mechanical licences might or will be available.'

If your publisher paid you a big advance, partly on the strength of your potential in the USA then this will be very important to him. If he didn't, then you don't necessarily need to accept this clause, but you do need to tell him whether his American people should accept a reduced rate or not. If they don't accept it, the difference will come out of your artist royalty under your agreement with the record company, but as you usually start getting paid more quickly under a publishing agreement than a recording artist agreement, there is an argument for refusing all controlled composition clauses which record companies try to impose.

Most USA mechanical royalties are collected by a body called the Harry Fox Agency, but they don't have the power to overturn controlled composition clauses-they just collect at whatever rate the publisher and record company agree should apply for each track on each record. Despite these complications the commission they charge is, like MCPS's commission from major record companies in the UK, roughly 4-5%.

Performing & broadcasting royalties ('PRS') – what should the agreement say?

In the UK, all of these are collected by a body called The Performing Right Society Ltd., generally known as the PRS. It was founded in 1914 by composers, songwriters and publishers to license the public performance of music and collect royalties for the use. The PRS issues a licence to every concert venue, cinema, club, pub, restaurant, record shop etc. in the country if it wishes music to be publicly performed on its premises. Even if the music is just for the benefit of the staff in an office or factory that's still a use of the writers' and publishers' property and they receive payment for it through the PRS, though exceptions include performance of music 'at home' for your own pleasure and that of your non-paying friends, and also performances in services of religious worship. Think how many places you go to where you hear music playing – all these need a licence from the PRS!

On top of this, the PRS collects lump sums from the BBC and IBA as well as cable and satellite companies for broadcasting or 'diffusing' music on television and radio and on the Internet, based on their audience or income from licence fees, advertising revenue etc. The PRS then shares out all the money collected that year from each of these licences amongst all the songs used. Generally the money collected from the BBC is divided amongst all songs used by the BBC and so forth, rather than putting all the income in one pot and then dividing it up. Having said all of that, you would expect in a territory like the USA to collect royalties for use of your songs in cinemas but the answer is no. And under their badly-named 1998 'Fairness in Music Licensing Act' there's no payment for music in bars and small and medium sized restaurants either. This law was enacted more-or-less in return for the public accepting the Sonny Bono Act under which copyright in the USA for new songs was extended to 70 years from a writer's death (same as in Europe). This was just so that US songs would get the same protection in Europe as European songs do. Incidentally- the Sonny Bono Act was named after the late highly respected US record producer/executive/politician who is still best remembered here as half of Sonny and Cher on 'I Got You Babe'!

How much will I actually get for a performance of my song?

The big money comes from television and radio broadcasts – less than £1 for a three-minute song on the smallest local radio stations to around £40 or so for national radio up to around £150 on BBC TV and around £200 on the ITV network. PRS has generally paid out slightly more if the song is 'featured' (apparently being heard by the people on the screen) than if it is 'background', but the amount has been the same for a play on *Top Of The Pops* as for a programme halfway through the morning with a much smaller audience. It would be so complex for PRS to 'weight' every single performance according to its audience that there would be no money left to distribute, which brings us to the question of 'sampling'.

Will I always get paid if my song is performed or broadcast?

The answer is no, because again it would be so expensive for PRS to identify every single performance of every single song at every single venue or on every single radio station that there would be nothing left to distribute to the writers and publishers.

If your song is broadcast on television or on Radio 1, 2, 3, 4 or 5 then you can definitely expect to be paid sooner or later, even for short snatches of music in commercials, station idents etc. The same applies to Capital Radio FM and Virgin Radio (and may from time to time include other major stations). However, with all other local radio, PRS uses a sampling system – generally they identify exactly what was played in a given week by one station and have to assume that all other stations that week played the

same. The major exclusion is locally originated music which was particular to one station. This should be analysed separately and you should receive payment, although remember it may be very small. Pirate radio stations, as the name suggests, don't pay PRS anything, so a play on one of these is guaranteed not to earn anything. PRS used to pay a small amount per year as a so-called 'unlogged performance allocation' to writers who do have earnings but are thought to have maybe missed out in the sampling process, to compensate them for this, but this has now been dropped. Unless you're very unlucky or the amounts you might have got are very small then on the basis of swings and roundabouts you'll probably wind up with roughly what you are entitled to.

So will I never get paid for the songs I play at my own gigs?

If it's not viable for PRS to analyse every performance on radio, it's obviously even less so with so-called 'general' royalties from pubs, clubs, hotels etc. PRS get 'returns' from a selection of venues of varying sizes of what music was played there, and use samples of these returns to pay out for all other uses in the same category. Of course this could tend to discriminate against minority forms of music but PRS know this and compensate by using samples from venues which play particular genres of music.

PRS also have a list of so-called 'significant venues' around Britain which include most of the major local concert halls. There are several hundred, so this doesn't just mean the NEC or Wembley etc. The county town of most counties has at least one hall and perhaps a University which would both be on the list. PRS ask these venues to tell them what's been performed, so you or your manager should tell the venue, as it's their responsibility. In practice, you yourself can tell PRS. This is especially important with a tour (most tours by 'name' artists take place almost entirely in significant venues) where the set list was the same for each night. If you're only the support act your songs will be worth as much as those of the main act unless you've had to agree in advance of the concert that the split will be different. Provided that PRS know what was performed at a concert at one of these venues then you should definitely get paid if it included your songs.

Can I collect any of this money myself and cut out PRS?

PRS is effectively a monopoly, which has huge advantages for you as a writer. Users get a licence from PRS which they know will cover all the music they'll ever play, so PRS can get a higher fee from them. The downside of the monopoly, as the band U2 pointed out in the Nineties was that, at their concerts, PRS collected the fee (3% of the money taken in ticket sales) from the promoter or venue and then deducted a fee for processing the royalties, then eventually paid the band months later. (Actually their biggest gripe was about the lack of money and very long delays from foreign concerts.) Having calculated what they thought they were losing, they asked to collect their performance fees directly from the venue.

On the face of it this seems reasonable, but of course this was for a band like U2 playing virtually all their own material to huge audiences. If everybody did it, especially when they were playing covers of other people's songs, the PRS's

licensing system would simply break down. However, PRS came up with provisions to cover this and if you think it might possibly benefit you or want to know more you should contact the PRS's Live Music team. Incidentally, the actual amount of the fees – the so-called 'concert tariff' – was set by a body called the Performing Right Tribunal (now the Copyright Tribunal) which also decides, in the event of a dispute, on the level of record royalties etc.

What if a payment I was expecting wasn't on my statement?

Remember that money does take a while to come through and be processed, so don't expect a broadcast one month to be paid out in the statement you get next month. Also remember certain statements include different types of income (the only statements you'll get in the business where this applies). By all means query your statement if you think something significant is missing or wrong, but, otherwise try not to waste PRS's time querying tiny uses. This is especially so if you believe a use would have been subject to sampling or you're not sure whether the money would have come through yet anyway. PRS will answer all queries, and they have set themselves targets as to how long you'll have to wait for an answer but they are, as you can imagine, snowed under with queries from members, so try to help them.

What about foreign broadcasting and performance fees?

Overseas there is an equivalent to the PRS in most other countries. Generally this is merged with the organisation which collects mechanical royalties as well, and the local songwriters join both organisations together. This means they collect their own shares of mechanical royalties directly, as well as their share of performing royalties. In the UK the societies have formed an alliance and work together, sharing their database information etc., but are not actually merged. Writers generally are not direct members of MCPS. However most writers are members of the PRS (see below).

These foreign societies will pay 50%, sometimes expressed as 6/12ths (all performing right societies used to calculate shares in twelfths, and some still do) as a 'writer share' to the PRS for UK writers and will divide the other 50% between your publisher and the local 'sub-publisher' or more likely pay it all to the sub-publisher who will pay your publisher his share under their agreement. Because of the time delays involved, it might take as much as two years for foreign performing fees to reach you. If you find foreign fees you were expecting are missing you can contact PRS or else your publisher, who will ask his local sub-publisher to get the local performing right society to look into it which is another advantage of having a publisher.

Should I join the PRS?

Provided the activity on your songs warrants it (see next question) then the answer is 'yes'! If you are not a member of the PRS then the PRS will pay your writer shares to your publisher who will pay you. Ideally your agreement with him will require him to pay it within 30 days of receiving it, and he should not be able to recoup it from any advances he has paid you. It will never be less than half the total. The PRS will pay out in accordance with a registration which the publisher prepares and sends to MCPS/PRS. This used always to be a printed form and used to require the writer's signature when the normal division between writers and publishers

was 8/12ths:4/12ths. Now it's normally equal so that's how PRS and the other societies pay out and there's no need for you to sign it or query it (unless of course you think that you've had the wrong share). Most publishers still send in forms, but some now register works on-line direct to the database which gets around the backlogs which sometimes build up thanks to the many thousands of registrations which MCPS/PRS receive, many of which are for songs which will never earn anything – MCPS/PRS receive close to a staggering 10,000 registrations every single week! Even if your song is not yet recorded, it's normal for your publisher to register it with MCPS/PRS as soon as possible after he's acquired it. Some agreements will actually stipulate that the publisher and his subpublishers in all the major territories will definitely register the song regardless of earnings, though in the USA the equivalent of MCPS, the Harry Fox Agency, normally only deal with recorded works.

Can any writer join PRS?

The rules vary from time to time but basically to apply for membership you must have at least one of your songs (whether co-written or solely written by you) recorded or broadcast or else printed and performed a set number of times and likely to earn significant performing royalties. It is clearly a waste of your time and theirs to apply to join PRS if your songs are not being used, nevertheless if you are having any broadcasts and other activity on songs you should join without delay. There is a fee of around £50 to join but we would very very strongly urge any British writer to join PRS. Not only will you be paid directly by them and therefore more quickly than if the money had to go via your publisher, but also you will be paid certain royalties from abroad which not even your publisher could collect for you all the time you remain a so-called 'non-member' (most foreign societies just put non-member writers' share back into the 'pot' to be shared out amongst their members). To join PRS, simply contact the Member Relations Dept., The PRS, 29/33 Berners Street, London W1P 4AA, asking for the relevant forms, and these will be sent. Some UK publishers join not only PRS but other overseas societies too, and a few big UK writers are also members of one or more foreign societies, usually including one of the US societies, but generally a UK writer will join PRS, an Irish writer will join IMRO (Irish Music Rights Organisation), an Australian writer APRA (Australian Performing Rights Association) etc.

So should I join different collecting societies for different countries?

The vast majority of UK writers are happy for PRS to collect for them from other performing right societies around the world. There are some established PRS writers who are direct members of one of the USA performing right societies ASCAP, BMI and SESAC (thus getting their US performing royalties quicker and with slightly less commission deducted) and other societies in major territories. If you wanted to join a Continental European society, it would have to be for the world, and thus your UK royalties would end up going from PRS to Germany, France etc. before coming back to you. If you did want to leave PRS completely you would have to give the required notice before the end of any year.

Although it is not always stated in songwriting agreements, many publishers will allow you to nominate which USA society you'd like your songs to go through. SESAC is much the smallest specialising in Latin, Gospel and Country music. ASCAP is slightly larger than BMI, and has traditionally been considered better for more MOR pop writers while BMI was considered better for rock. In practice however both represent writers of all types and either could be better at any given time depending on how their current distributions are structured. The US Societies have helpful representatives in the UK who can explain to you how they work, and the relative benefits of their organisation.

As we have said, writer members of MCPS can collect foreign mechanicals through MCPS if they have no publisher but in practice very few are members of foreign mechanical collecting societies.

Can I get an advance or loan from the collecting societies?

The societies don't actually pay advances in the UK in the way that publishers do. The American performing right societies will do so, as they are in competition, and some other societies abroad will make loans to members. PRS does have a so-called 'Members' Fund' into which a small part of the income is put, but this is to help writers, usually but not always older ones, who have genuine financial difficulties. Some writers or their heirs have 'donated' the royalties from some of their songs to the Members Fund, one of the best-known being 'Get It On' by Marc Bolan, so the fund does have its own income.

How much do I lose if foreign lyrics are put to my songs?

As regards foreign performance royalties, the publisher finds himself sharing his part of these with a foreign publisher, and sometimes the same applies to the writer, who has to share his part with the writer of the foreign lyric in each country, usually to the extent of 1/3rd him, 2/3rds you. This should only apply to actual uses of the foreign lyric and these days it usually does, but this used to be a major source of irritation for British and American writers – for even though the big money in foreign countries may be earned without the foreign lyric actually being used a great deal, the lyric writer still got a share of all performances (and sometimes even all recordings!). Ideally your agreement with your publisher should guarantee that he won't let his sub-publisher 'register' local foreign lyrics with their performing and mechanical rights societies except where it is likely that a big local hit by an important local artist will take place. Once you let someone make a local lyric then if he's a member of the local collecting society he will get paid automatically under the society's rules.

It would be silly to risk losing a third of your foreign performing and broadcasting income (or even some of your record royalties) just because one local cover version which sold 500 copies was broadcast a handful of times whilst the original UK recording was the number 1 hit in that country. Having said all that, if your song is pretty well dormant in a particular country and a big artist there wants to do a local lyric version, it could completely revitalise the song, and it would be worth risking the foreign lyricist getting a bit of your money just from that country if there hadn't been very much anyway!

Can I ask my publisher for more than 50% of PRS royalties?

Yes, and these days most writers get more. However, it's unlikely that the agreement will simply say that you get 70% from PRS and the publisher 30% (if your deal is 70/30 with the publisher). Instead you will always get your 50% directly through PRS from around the world (less only any local lyric writer shares) but also the publisher will pay, in this instance, 40% of his 50% too, making a total of 70% to you in all. Remember that if the publisher paid you an advance

he'll be allowed to recoup part of it from this 40%, (but not your 50% writer share – if by chance he collects any of that he should pay it to you, in full, sometimes within 30-60 days, rather than wait till his next normal accounting to you). In an 'at source' deal you should aim to end up with at least as much from foreign performing royalties as you do from UK ones – your publisher will have to make his sub-publishers pay enough to the UK to enable him to fulfil his commitment to you.

What else does PRS do?

Once you are a member of PRS you will receive regular bulletins and reports which are well worth taking the time to read, about the work of the PRS and its foreign affiliates (information is even available on diskette) including the very readable 'M' magazine which they produce four times a year. This work includes efforts to combat piracy, protect and increase the rights of British writers in many overseas countries and in new areas of technology, as well as supporting British musical institutions, organising additional benefits for its members, sponsoring competitions etc. They hold regular 'surgeries' around the country, not just in London, and you'll receive invitations to your local ones automatically.

How often do I get paid by PRS?

The PRS make four distributions every year to writer and publisher members. These take place in April, July, October and December, though do remember that different types of income are paid in different distributions (e.g. live performances in July). PRS will send you a statement and pay the money straight into your bank account (remember to tell the Member Relations department if your account changes!)

How much should I get if my song is used in a pub/club/concert etc.?

I'm afraid it's impossible to say what you'd get for small gigs – sampling is used and those works which appear in the samples get paid, the others don't. This also applies to pubs and restaurants, outdoor festivals etc. whether it's live music or recorded music that's playing, although PRS charge a different tariff depending on the circumstances. The authors of this book recently heard a song written by them many years ago being performed live as part of a street pageant. The act performing it had been using it for many years live and in local broadcasts, and had learned it from another similar act who had also been using it for over 20 years. In all that time we had never received any performing fees for this particular work but because of the way in which sampling works, this is perfectly possible. Other songs of ours have earned more than we expected. You just have to put this down to 'swings and roundabouts' and remember that even in this day and age it's impossible to expect to be paid on every performance of every song you have written. For bigger concerts in the UK PRS's Concert Tariff, at 3% of the gross box office receipts comes into play, and there's a higher tariff specifically for classical concerts.

How much should I get if my song is used in a film?

Fees for use of your songs in films, commercials and other audio-visual media are called synchronisation fees and are usually licensed directly by your publisher, though in theory you could expect PRS to license these rights and in practice the publisher may ask MCPS to do this, for a commission. The definition of Synchronisation Fees tends to be stretched to cover radio commercials too, even though no actual synchronisation of your music with visual images takes place. The country where the actual synchronisation takes place should really be the country where the licence is made, though if a film is 'being made in the USA' then the US publisher will often license it, even if the production company is based in the UK or Mexico or wherever.

You should usually receive the same share of synchronisation income as you do of mechanical royalties or sometimes the same as you get on 'covers' when the publisher specifically 'procured' the use of the song. Fees for the use of the whole of a hit song or standard which is used in a major film are often around £10,000 to £20,000 (usually more if it's over the opening or closing credits and substantially more if the film is named after the song). If it's to be used on the Internet or the song is to be used 'out of context' in a trailer or commercial for the film then there should be an additional fee, but for all other uses the film company will want to 'buy out' all the rights in perpetuity, so don't expect any more income except for money from PRS and its affiliates worldwide when the film is shown or broadcast, and for sales of soundtrack albums.

There are no fees for the showing of films in US cinemas, so this is taken into account when setting the synchronisation fee. Remember that if the song is unknown it's possible that the film will make it a hit and in this case the fees will be much much lower, although your publisher will never actually pay anyone to put it in a film. The fees could be slightly lower if the film company agrees that your song will definitely be on a soundtrack album. If the album comes out and your song's not there, then they have to pay you a bit more at that point. If it's an unknown song then your publisher might agree to a small fee up-front and more once the film has recouped its costs or made say $5m but this is not usual in the UK. This happens more in the USA, where fees tend to be a bit lower anyway.

How much should I get if my song is used in a commercial?

Your publisher could usually get around £30,000 to £50,000 upwards for a nation-wide (networked) television commercial using a hit song + maybe another £10,000+ for a networked radio commercial, another £10,000 or so for a nation-wide cinema commercial and another £12,000 or so if the television campaign extends to Ireland. Unlike record royalties or PRS royalties, where only the duration of the use counts, here the importance of the song and how badly the film company or advertising agency want to use it affect the fees enormously. A few really big songs could be worth well over double the above figures, whereas for unknown songs or old ones which haven't seen the light of day for years, you and your publisher might be happy to let them be used for a fraction of these fees, just to create fresh interest in the song.

Incidentally, remember that in addition to synchronisation fees you will still get your share of broadcasting royalties through PRS every time the film or commercial etc. is shown or broadcast.

If a film or advertisement was made and licensed in the UK then you should get the full rate under your agreement. If the actual synchronisation of your music with the film was done (even for a commercial in the English language) overseas, then the local sub-publisher could keep his share, pay your publisher his share, and he'll pay you. If you have an at-source deal then this won't reduce the amount you get, it'll just mean you get it six months later. In any event most UK agreements state that the publisher must ask you whether you mind the song being used at all, especially if there's sex or violence in the film or if the commercial is for tobacco or alcohol.

How much should I get if my song is used in a video or DVD or SACD?

In the UK a rate was set by MCPS of £1 per minute as a 'fixing fee' but the video producer then pays royalties at rates 6-7% of the PDP of the video but reduced according to the running time of the music as compared to the total running time of the video. For a music video you should get very roughly around the same as for audio-only records. As we've said, in the case of films, the film company normally asks the publisher for a 'buy-out' of all rights in any media in perpetuity, to save him having to go back and clear additional rights later, possibly at higher rates than he had budgeted for. However, buy-out licences sometimes limit the number of videos sold world-wide to 50,000 or 100,000. If there is no buy-out then again a royalty is payable through MCPS to the publisher based on the amount of music actually used in the film which of course can vary enormously.

In the case of DVD and other audio-visual technology, MCPS and its sister societies around the world are in negotiations with producers of these to establish suitable rates, but these vary widely. MCPS again charges roughly the same as the normal mechanical royalty for DVD and SACD – 6% of PDP with the intention that it should rise to 8.5%, though if there is an audio-visual use of a song then the use of that song should, in theory be cleared first with the publisher.

Are there any other sources of income which I should receive a share of?

If your song is used in stage shows etc. (see also under Q & A 'films, musicals and plays'), your publisher will also extract fees for the use. The same applies to songs or song lyrics in books, newspapers and magazines. A use of the lyric in a best-selling pop music magazine is worth up to around £500 in total (your publisher should collect this direct from the magazine publishers). There are royalties to be had from such obscure sources as microchips in mugs, birthday cards or even items of clothing which play music. MCPS normally collects these for publishers under another of their AP licensing schemes though sometimes they're licensed in the Far East where most of the chips are produced, and at much lower royalties. There are also royalties for karaoke whether for performance in pubs etc. or for home use and the use of the lyrics on sheets or on the screen is normally licensed at 2% of the published dealer price on top of the mechanical royalty. For use of your song on the Internet and for information on mobile phone ring-tones see the Internet section.

How often should the publisher pay me?

Normally you'll be paid twice a year usually 90 days after June 30 and December 31 every year. If you've already got a track record you may get the publisher to agree to pay within 60 days, or even quarterly instead of half-yearly, though most publishers are just not geared up to do this. You might be able to get them to agree to make a payment on account within 90 days of March 31 and Sept 30 but only if your income is pretty well guaranteed to be big. Generally if no money is due to you but you had an advance then a statement should be sent, but often is not. No advance and no income usually means no statement. The actual money will normally be paid straight into your bank account if you wish, and if you're VAT registered you'll need to send an invoice for this to the publishers (this applies also to royalties from record companies). Check your statement to see that any large sums which you expect to be there are not

missing, but remember that money can take a long time to reach you from the time when it was first earned (explained in more detail in 'General Q's & A's' later on).

What if I only write lyrics?

Most songwriters can write music and lyrics but very few are really good at both. Even though the lyrics on some hits can be almost inaudible and unimportant, it's also true that a good title and good lyrics can make a hit, and this doesn't just apply to MOR or ballads. Way back in the Fifties Chuck Berry produced superb lyrics to rock and r&b songs, and today a really good rap can transform a dance track.

There are plenty of examples from the distant and not so distant past of successful writing teams – Gilbert & Sullivan, Burt Bacharach & Hal David, Elton John & Bernie Taupin, Andrew Lloyd Webber & Tim Rice – where one half only wrote lyrics. These days it's much less common, but it's still possible to be a successful lyricist.

As a rule, if you collaborate with someone right from the start then you are both treated equally when it comes to dividing royalties and fees and usually the song is registered as 'words and music' by both of you. If the work is registered as 'words by' you and 'music by' your co-writer then if there's a foreign lyric to the song, you could wind up with his share coming solely out of yours. Societies and publishers have trouble distinguishing 'music only' or 'words only' uses, and it makes life much easier if you're both treated as having written both, even though this means the music writer will get a cut of a use of the lyric in, for example, a fanzine or newspaper. It also means that the work is 'joint' for copyright purposes and will go out of copyright 70 years from the death of the last collaborator to die. It sounds like a long time but remember this is your intellectual 'property'. Something like a house would stay with your heirs (till they sold it) forever.

Could I get to write English lyrics to foreign songs?

There used to be far more demand for this than today but it's still another possible source of work and income for a good lyric writer. These days the original writer or publisher usually insist that at least the meaning is the same as the original even if it isn't a straight translation. Many of the songs we think of as 'standards' today originated in South America or on the Continent and it is the work of the USA or British lyric writer which has made some of them successful here, though in some cases the lyric-writing job will go to a writer-producer who is able to secure a recording here with a big artist.

As we said earlier, a UK writer of a complete song would lose one third of his writer's share of performing fees earned abroad to a foreign lyric writer. Thus this one-third is what you should get for writing an English lyric to a foreign song. On record royalties the usual percentage offered is 12.5%, as against 60-85% or thereabouts on a normal song writing contract, although as much as half of the total writer's share can be paid to top lyric writers. Avoid giving your lyric the same title as the original song as it is unfair to expect bodies collecting and accounting royalties to differentiate between uses of the song with or without your lyric. You might occasionally collect on performances of the original version accidentally, but you're more likely to lose out. UK sheet music royalties will usually be 2.5% of the retail selling price as against around 12.5% if you wrote the whole song. This sounds terribly low when converted into cash, but is quite normal. As we said under an earlier question, you might not want a foreign lyricist writing a local lyric to your song in case they get paid accidentally on the original so if you were to find a foreign song and want to write a lyric they might not want you to do it either and simply say 'no'.

Will I collect on all uses of my lyric to a foreign song?

Sadly no, not even if you changed the title. In a few countries your lyric will still be disregarded when it comes to making mechanical (record) royalty and performing royalty distributions. Unlike the PRS and MCPS, most foreign societies are governed almost entirely by local authors and composers who for many years have defended their vested interest in maximising the income for local lyrics at the expense of the original writers. As a consequence even if you know and can prove that records reproducing your lyric have sold in a particular country the person actually receiving the 'lyric writer share' may be the author of the local language version though this situation has improved over the years.

If a lyric in the language of that country hasn't been produced you stand a better chance, because the publisher on the spot will receive in effect 100% and provided that he has acquired rights to your lyric from your publisher then astute accounting can result in your receiving your share. You will appreciate however that in the first instance the original publisher, (let's say for example it is a French song to which you have written a lyric) may have given rights to all sorts of publishers in various countries none of whom have direct relations with each other.

The British publisher who acquired your lyric may have rights for the UK and Eire only, so its use in Germany is by a contract between the French original publisher and the German sub-publisher and it's difficult to fit you into that scene. In theory the rights to your English words will go to the German publisher via the original (French) publisher, but so will the rights to Italian, Spanish, Swedish etc., etc., lyrics, hence the easy way out – assume always it is the local version. One way of tackling this is for you, the lyric writer, to withhold from the British publisher rights to your lyric outside the territory for which he has the rights. If he's only got the music for UK and Eire, then only give him your lyric for UK and Eire if you can, then you'll be free to try to do a deal with the original foreign publisher.

How long will the publisher keep the rights to my songs?

Until around the mid-Seventies it was quite normal for writers to assign songs to publishers for the life of copyright (see the next section). There are many writers of hits from that time who are still getting honest and regular statements from their publisher, who is still trying to create new interest in some of their songs. They may or may not want to change publishers, but what they would definitely like to be able to do is renegotiate a better rate from now on. Some are actually doing this, but they have no clear and definite right to reclaim their songs or negotiate better terms.

These days a new writer would probably be asked to assign a song for maybe 10-15 years. If the publisher wants it badly he may accept as little as three years. Hit songs tend to come back into favour about 10 or so years after the first success, so the publisher will want to try to benefit from this almost inevitable revival and if he's paying a big advance and high royalty rate then it's not unreasonable. If not, then try to get the song back within 10 years, so you can re-negotiate better terms with your publisher or give it to another one who will be paying you a better rate if and when the song is a hit the second time around. Remember that there will usually be a 'post-term collection period'

of one year, possibly unlimited (see Glossary of terms).

Will the publisher want the rights for the whole world?

Actually he'll probably want the whole Universe, or at least the Solar System. This may seem ridiculous, but satellite broadcasting and space travel do mean that there is a possibility that a contract just for the world won't always mean 'everywhere'. It's very rarely worth asking your publisher to accept a smaller overall territory than the whole world/ universe. It might be possible for a writer to collect all his UK fees by joining PRS and MCPS and acting as his own publisher, but elsewhere the benefits of having someone on the spot exploiting your songs or simply checking the accuracy and completeness of local royalties that come in are sufficient that even successful writers usually don't think twice about passing on all the rights to a publisher (see 'Do I need a Publisher?')

What if someone else claims to have written my song?

There will be a clause in which you guarantee that the song is 'all your own work', or to the best of your knowledge and belief it is. As you are technically selling the song (if it's an assignment) to the publisher in exchange for a sum of money, however nominal, the publisher has the right to take you to court if he ends up out of pocket because the song was in fact not all your original work. In practice of course the publisher is on your side, but it's a good reason to make quite sure that your songs really are original and that if you bring him a finished master recording, you tell him if it contains any samples (see 'Sampling' in 'General Q & A').

If faced with a counterclaim from

another writer or publisher, your publisher would normally be perfectly entitled to suspend payment of royalties to you until the matter was sorted out, though ideally he shouldn't be able to do this unless he's actually being faced with legal proceedings. Even then, if they are dropped, or as soon as they are settled, he should pay you your share (with interest). The agreement will also state that the publisher is appointed to act for you should someone else try to claim your song, infringe it, or use it unlawfully. It should be at his expense but he should be entitled to reclaim all his legal fees (but not a fee for his own time or in-house expertise) from your royalties. For this reason you will want to make sure that he has to consult you before and during any action he decides, at his discretion, to bring against someone else for infringement of your song.

Can the publisher make alterations to my song?

The publisher usually has the right to have new lyrics made in foreign languages. There are good reasons why you might not want this, so even this should be with your prior written approval. He should certainly need your approval to make any substantial changes to your English lyric (or whatever language you wrote the song in) and to the music (see also 'Moral Rights' in the next section). Changing the beat or the vocal or instrumental arrangement is generally less contentious than changing the words or music, however small the changes.

If a publisher really thinks your song needs a bit of reworking at the start then he should tell you before you even assign the song to him. He would normally ask you yourself to rewrite any parts he felt needed improvement before resorting to anyone else, but he may suggest that you get together with another writer signed to him. This could be a way of getting you to give up part of your song. However, it's

more likely to be a completely genuine attempt to create a song that will earn everyone some money out of one which may be just not quite good enough, and if the co-writer he suggests has had hits before, or else is a hit artist (even if his songwriting is awful!) then all the more reason to agree to it.

Can I stop an individual making alterations to my song?

If your song is used in an interactive game/on a website etc. where sounds and images can be manipulated by the user at home then of course you have no control over this once you've said yes. At present there is no set guideline for fees for such uses but it shouldn't matter provided that the individual doesn't try to release on record or otherwise exploit what he's done to your song, and if he does then hopefully you can track him down and then take action to stop him.

Should I ever give up part of my song except to a co-writer?

Despite what we've just said, there is no reason why an artist, producer or remixer should necessarily get a piece of your song unless you agree, in all good faith, that they really have made a noticeable improvement to it. If you do feel that you are being pressurised into cutting someone else in on a song for no good reason then create a fuss and if necessary consult your lawyer as this could be very important if the song becomes a hit. Don't just leave it and hope the problem goes away!

Your publisher may tell you that he can get a major artist to record your song on condition that you give up part of the writing credits and royalties. It's quite likely that your publisher will have to give up part of his share as well, as the major artist will probably be signed to another publisher who will want to control his share. A better arrangement if possible is for your publisher just to give up a share of the mechanical royalties on the major artist's own records, without getting a credit as a co-writer. However, if they insist, then it's ultimately up to you to tell your publisher if you're prepared to allow it. As we said earlier in this section, someone who simply makes an arrangement of your song can't claim a share automatically in the UK, though this used to be common on the Continent where the collecting societies' rules allowed it

What about the other small print in the publisher's agreement?

There are a few points you should ask for:

a) You get your songs back if your publisher goes into liquidation.

b) Your publisher won't be allowed to do a sub-publishing deal overseas just for your songs as distinct from the rest of his catalogue. He's not obliged to tell you what sub-publishing deals he has, though they should be 'arms-length' meaning that if they're with his own companies, the terms are normal in the business.

c) He should use his best endeavours to collect money from his sub-publishers, whoever they are ('best endeavours' is quite a strong phrase, and means he really should do almost whatever it takes to get the money).

d) He should use at least reasonable endeavours to promote your songs (see also 'Reversion Clauses') unless your agreement with him is what's known as an 'administration deal' where you've already got the activity and exploitation and you just want the publisher, in return for a small percentage – say 10-20% at source worldwide, to collect the money.

There will also be an audit clause (see General Q & A) and a clause covering moral rights (again see General Q & A).

COPYRIGHT (FOR SONGWRITERS)

This began centuries ago as simply the right to make copies for a limited period. Since that time it has been expanded to include the right to perform a song in public, grant permission for its use in films etc., make records of it for sale to the public and so on right up to the use of it on the Internet. In the UK the Copyright Acts, in 1911, 1956 and 1988 form the basis on which most of a songwriter's rights rest. By various international agreements, notably the Berne Convention and the Universal Copyright Convention, your song, whether written in the UK or elsewhere, is protected to a greater or lesser extent in almost every other country of the world. In Europe the EU has attempted over the years to bring most of the laws concerning copyright into line in all countries of the European Economic Area. Most countries have, like the UK, also passed various Copyright and other Acts over the last hundred years or so, updating the law to try to cover the new technologies as they have come about.

How do I copyright a song?

In Britain you don't have to do anything to 'copyright' a song. As soon as it actually exists outside your mind in some 'tangible form', that is once you have written it down or made a recording whether amateur or professional, then technically copyright begins from that moment. It is the same in most other countries. In the USA it used to be necessary to 'register' songs in the Copyright Office in Washington and to pay a fee of a few dollars. Registration is no longer necessary, but it does however help in bringing certain legal proceedings in the USA (e.g. against illegal Internet sites). Your publisher should ideally agree to register, at his expense, any song which has been commercially released in the USA.

The international symbol of copyright is a 'c' in a circle '©' and if you are sending or taking around manuscripts or lyrics with tapes of your songs you should write, at the foot of the first page of any manuscript or lyric © copyright by ... (your name and address).

In the UK even if you sell your song to a publisher, you are the first owner of the copyright, and in some Continental countries you always remain the owner or you assign the copyright to the collecting society when you join, just as UK writers

do to PRS with their performing and broadcasting right. In effect you then only license the publisher to do certain things for you i.e., print, license uses, collect royalties etc. The only exception in the UK is if you were actually employed by someone else to create the song, as a newspaper reporter would be when writing an article, in which case the employer is the first owner and the song is known as a 'work for hire'. Most film music over the years has been written under such agreements, and if you want to make a really different arrangement of someone else's song you may be asked to assign the copyright on a 'work for hire' basis, meaning that you effectively agree that you were employed to do it and therefore have no rights in the new material you've added. This sounds tough, but if you've used someone else's recording/song and it's given you a hit recording as an artist then it's a small price to pay.

How long does copyright last?

The exact time of creation of each song is not important in the UK, as copyright lasts for the whole of your lifetime and for 70 years from the end of the year of your death. If two of you wrote the words and music of the song together then, as we have said, copyright continues for 70 years after the death of whoever dies last. This is not too likely to worry you, but might concern your heirs. Thanks to the international agreements we mentioned earlier this generally applies in the UK to foreign songs as well, and your song will in turn be protected for the same or roughly the same length of time in most other countries too. Copyright in the USA used to last for two periods of 28 years then an extra 19 making 75 in all and then only if you 'registered' and 'renewed' it. However, from 1978 new songs received life + 50 years' protection, since extended to life + 70 (though not without challenges from music users) so that US works would get the same protection as European works in Europe where life + 70 is granted and it became no longer necessary to register works.

What if someone steals my song?

If you heard a song in the charts that sounded exactly like one which you wrote say a year ago and you discovered that it was written after you wrote yours, then you would have to prove that the writer of the hit 'had had access' to your song (i.e., he'd had the opportunity to hear it, and then copy it) if you wished to make a claim against him. If you kept your song to yourself and the only copy was in a self-addressed registered envelope, or in a Solicitor's or Bank Manager's safe keeping, which are two processes often suggested to new composers, then 'access' would be impossible and the similarity in songs would be regarded by the courts as coincidence. By sending a tape or manuscript of it to yourself in a registered envelope left unopened and intact, you could at least prove that you hadn't stolen the hit, by establishing that you had written your song long before you could possibly have heard the hit, but now no publisher would be interested in it and you'd have to write

it off as very bad luck. If you really thought a song of yours that had had 'exposure' had been stolen, and, perhaps surprisingly, it happens very rarely, then your publisher would take up the matter for you. George Harrison's 'My Sweet Lord' way back in the Seventies is probably still the best-known example of an 'infringement' of one song by another song which has been successfully challenged in the courts.

Do remember that virtually everything you write has been written before in some form or other, no matter how original you (and even your publisher and record label) think it is. If you think someone has infringed your song, it probably isn't worth making an issue of it unless you know of a link – e.g. a backing vocalist on the demo of your song is a member of the band who've just come up with a song that sounds just like yours – or else the similarity to yours, musically and lyrically is so strong that your publisher thinks it's worth taking it further. If someone claims that you have infringed their song, then try to find another earlier song that sounds like theirs and yours. This is known as 'prior art'.

It's often quite obvious, listening to a new song, where the writers got the idea or the sound or the instrumentation and even some of the words or tune, but once a musicologist (expert musician who will compare one song with another) gets hold of it then unless a substantial part of the actual tune is identical the chances are that his report will declare it not to be a plagiarism and no-one will consider that you have a case. Musicologists charge several hundred pounds for a 'report' but it's worth getting a report from a good one if you seriously think your song has been 'ripped off'.

Is even the shortest musical work protected?

It's been argued from time to time that some pieces of 'music' (e.g. one long

BLANKET WRITING AGREEMENTS

Most publishers who think your songs have any promise will want to give you a 'blanket' songwriting contract for a period of years, so that if they've spent a lot of time and trouble and money trying to promote your earlier efforts, they're guaranteed your entire output at least for a while once you've started writing hits. The British Courts of Justice don't look too kindly on 'exclusive' agreements for long periods which appear heavily loaded in favour of the publisher. They say that they could be restricting the development of your career, and for this reason any British publisher trying to sign you up for more than five years or giving himself options to do so without paying you a large sum of money as an advance for each option is probably making his contract unenforceable should you wish to take your songs elsewhere for any reason.

Why sign a blanket agreement anyway?

You may well ask what is the benefit to you in agreeing to write exclusively for one publisher – why not leave your options open to write for whoever offers you the best deal? The usual inducement is money. The publisher may offer an advance payment which he can recover from your royalties but which he can never make you pay back even if, at the end of the contract, none of your songs has earned a penny. Another reason to sign is that it may encourage him to make much greater effort in promoting and developing your career if it guaranteed all your songs for a certain period, as he has a vested interest in a part of your future. If he simply suggests that it's normal and that he isn't interested in you if you don't sign exclusively, then beware.

These days many publishers have recording studios or access to them, and can use their contacts and their money to try to get you a recording deal, which is the best reason of all to sign with anyone in the music business. Remember there's no particular benefit to you in being able to say 'I've been signed up by a music publisher' unless you're all agreed on what he's going to try to do for your career, or unless you simply want him to collect royalties for you, for a small percentage, while you or your manager, or even your lawyer, do the legwork, which is perfectly OK.

Should the royalties be higher under a blanket agreement?

Not necessarily, as it depends very much on how much advance you want and how long the publisher wants to keep the songs – these considerations, together with the royalty rates, are the three basic 'commercial terms' which have to be offset against each other.

You can certainly ask for a higher royalty on all songs you deliver to the publisher in the second and third periods than in the first. But don't expect him to agree to increase the royalty on 'first period songs' during the second year or once they've earned a certain amount of money. He may possibly be prepared to do this, but it's much harder for his administrative people to handle correctly and there's a chance you'll wind up being underpaid accidentally.

How long should I sign to a publisher for?

The most common blanket agreement will be for one year with two options for the publisher to renew it, each for one year or until you've had a certain number of songs released on record (usually, if you're also a recording artist, until your next album is released). If the agreement extends till the albums are released, then there should be a so-called 'long-stop' date (usually after one or two extra years) which will be the date on which the agreement terminates (or he has to exercise his option) even if the album never did get released within that time. Without this, it's possible you could be signed to the publisher for ever!

By signing a blanket agreement, you will be giving or agreeing to give to the publisher all the songs that you write during that time. Obviously not all your songs will be included on your albums or 'covered' and any that aren't should come back to you (see 'How can I get my songs back?' in the next section).

What advances can I expect?

The publisher will usually pay an advance on signing. For a typical new band with no record company interest yet, you might get say £10-20,000 'up-front' + you may get up to say £500 worth of your solicitor's bill for negotiating the deal also paid as an advance by the publisher. You could try to get him to swallow this as a non-recoupable expense, but most publishers won't. The actual cost to you of a solicitor negotiating your deal will be anywhere from £500-£700 up to about £3,000, but £1,000 is not unreasonable, particularly if your solicitor is the one who recommended you to the publisher in the first place, which is quite common.

You could ask for 'development money' by way of say another £2-5,000 for travelling, recording equipment or demo costs during the first year. Other points at which more might be payable are when you actually sign a recording agreement, when the recording is completed and finally when the first album is released in the UK, USA or possibly another major territory. With an out-and-out dance act this is more likely to be linked to the release of singles. On

release of the album the publisher might pay perhaps another £10-20,000. That brings you to the end of the first 'year' although if the album is not released in that year then the first period of the agreement will probably continue until the 'long-stop' date or until it is released.

Around four to six months after the album is released, the publisher should have to pay, let's say, another £20,000 to take up his option to sign you for the second contract period in which you undertake to try to ensure that another album is released. The four to six months is to give him time to see how well the first album does, and is quite normal. When the second album comes out, the publisher would, in this instance, probably pay another £20,000 or so. The same would apply to the third period and the third album, but with the figures increased yet again.

You could also ask for chart bonuses. The normal definition of a 'bonus' in the music business is a sum of money which is not recoupable by the publisher, record company or whoever, but here the sums will probably be recoupable from your royalties. You might ask, for instance, for an extra £10,000-£20,000 if your album makes the UK top 10, or if any singles make number 1.

Suppose I already have a record deal?

The above figures are based on a brand new writer/producer/act with no record deal as yet, where the publisher is risking that you won't even get a record deal, never mind have a hit. If however you're already signed to a recognised and respected record company then you may be able to put a nought on the end of most of the above figures. A lot depends upon whether you can induce a 'bidding war' between interested publishers. If you do, you will need to beware of leaving it too late to sign with one or other – if you wait until the release of your first single or album and sales are only mediocre then you could lose all the interest. Do remember that you'll possibly never have quite the same long-term relationship with a publisher who you are treating rather like a bank (not that the publisher will be complaining!) and the more he pays you the better he'll expect his percentage to be and the longer he'll want to keep the songs.

Is the publisher bound to pay the advances in the agreement?

For the first period the answer is yes, until the album is released. At that point he will probably have expected you to write say 90% of it, allowing for one cover-recording or a couple of co-written songs on a 10-track album. The percentage 'target' will be stated in the agreement. If you write less, then probably the overall advance for the first year will be reduced accordingly. The same will apply to chart bonuses and to the payments on release of the second and third albums. This 90% is part of your release commitment and it's obviously a lot less valuable to the publisher if the albums end up being written by outsiders, though if you know in advance that this is likely to happen, the target (and the advances) can be set lower.

The target will probably be the aggregate of your shares of songs, so if you actually wrote the 10 songs on an album equally with another writer, your aggregate will only be 50% of the total album, and you'd only get 5/9ths of the advances specified in the agreement.

Can I give any rights at all to another publisher during the term of the agreement?

Generally the answer is no, or not without the publisher's prior written consent. You might be able to exclude any music you're commissioned to write for films or other audio-visual productions. The commissioner may only want the right to use the music in his production anyway, in which case all other rights could still be given to your publisher. If you're in a fairly strong bargaining position and this is a possibility then you should ask for it.

If you also write books or poetry for a book publisher, be sure that the wording of the music publisher's contract leaves you free to do this without having to ask for the rights back to give to a book publisher if necessary.

How would I get out of a blanket writing agreement?

The first thing you do is simply write to the publisher asking for a release. He'll probably be quite prepared to do this if he's having no success with your songs, or if you have any justifiable grounds for being discontented with him, or if you really have virtually stopped writing. If he paid you a large advance royalty sum which shows no sign of being recovered by him, he may offer to release you from the contract provided that you refund to him part of the advance. This is perfectly reasonable provided he gives you back the rights to the songs you wrote under the agreement if he expects you to pay back all the remainder of advance which he hasn't already recovered.

If he won't release you, check through your royalty statements for accuracy and regularity. As we have said, the contract will normally provide for these to be sent every six months, within so many days after June 30 and December 31. If they are not being sent on time then write to the publisher demanding that he keep to the terms of the contract. If he continues not to comply with the agreement, then you have grounds for termination. Some older agreements only required royalties to be sent to you 'as soon as possible' after June 30 and December 31, but this should still not be more than about three months after each of these dates, though of course no-one can actually say what's 'possible'.

Also check any renewal. If he hasn't exercised an option on time, then you're almost certainly free (unless the agreement contained a provision that if he hasn't renewed then you have to write to him asking, effectively, if he wants to renew and has just forgotten, which is increasingly common). Two things that would stop you would be if you had been continuing to give him songs as though the contract were still in force or if you were required to give him notice that your option was due and you failed to do so. If you feel you need to start writing 'threatening letters', then get a solicitor to do it, but always start with the friendly reasonable approach, and remember that one default in sending royalty statements on time is not grounds for you simply to go elsewhere – the default must be persistent. Incidentally there's no point in attempting to deceive him by writing for another publisher under a pseudonym. You'll have to tell PRS if you want your performing fees and they'll say 'Sorry we can't register this. If you're really Fred Smith then you're under contract to so and so'. They don't take sides, but they do have all this information stored up.

Remember also that your agreement probably says that the publisher will have 30 days from the date of your letter in which to correct your complaint (it might be 60 but shouldn't be more than that).

Can I cut out the publisher and collect all the money myself?

If you have the contacts and time to fix recordings and promotion on your own songs, or if you've already got a record deal, you may well wonder why you should give any of your earnings to a publisher. Obviously you will need to be a member of the PRS to collect your performing fees but most writers are anyway. You'll also need to be a member of MCPS in order to collect all the various forms of mechanical and audio-visual royalties. MCPS collects money from UK record companies and many other users of music on 'sound carriers' (unlike the PRS who collect from users of music being broadcast or performed). They also license television companies and the like in respect of the actual synchronisation of music with their programmes. BBC and ITV are covered by blanket licences for use in their programmes in the UK as are some satellite and cable channels, but pieces of music on Channel 4 and 5 are licensed separately at around £70-100 per 30 seconds of music used.

MCPS will prosecute users if they don't pay and it conducts regular audits of them to ensure that they are paying correctly. MCPS will, if asked, also license and collect fees for songs used in commercials and feature films and other audio-visual media including music being downloaded from the Internet. It also performs a host of related tasks such as charging record shops royalties for importing records, prosecuting bootleggers etc., all of which as you can imagine is an enormous task. MCPS then pays out the money it has collected to the appropriate publishers (or composers) after deducting its commission. The commercial record rates are mentioned in the first section of this chapter.

MCPS can also, all importantly, collect for a writer (or publisher if he wishes) royalties from overseas, but has to charge a higher rate (20%) for this. This enables a writer to cut out the publisher completely if he wishes, although an alternative for a writer with titles earning reasonable money abroad would be to offer a UK publisher a 'collection deal' at say 15% or 20% at source. The publisher will avoid the 20% collecting commission by having overseas royalties paid straight to him by his sub-publishers, and this means there will also be someone in each territory to query and chase up the local collecting society in a way that MCPS with the best will in the world simply cannot undertake.

Satisfying a demand for printed music is simpler, as companies like Music Sales Ltd. in London who specialise in this, will undertake to print and distribute your music for you and pay you a royalty in respect of it (though remember that sales of single editions of music are very low, so don't expect anyone to print what they know they're unlikely to be able to sell unless they're doing it directly on your behalf and at your expense). The combination of personal attention and, usually, some form of advance royalty payments, means that very few writers do actually 'go it alone' though of course once your 'catalogue' is big enough you could form your own publishing company with its own creative and administration staff (one of each to start with) and try to acquire songs from other writers. In any event, without a publisher you will need someone to field the many queries which you will get from potential users of your songs if they're successful, but it is possible to go it alone, and some writers have gone down this road. Some of today's important independent publishers were started by writers who decided to 'go it alone'.

GENERAL QUESTIONS AND ANSWERS ON SONGWRITING

How can I get to write for radio, TV and films?

The producers of many programmes, particularly in the children's, religious and chat show fields, are always in search of new songs and music for use in their shows and you can send in demos and ask for an appointment just as you would to a music publisher. Addresses are given in Section 6. The names of individual producers can be found from *Radio Times* and *TV Times* or similar magazines or from screen credits.

As well as different regional television companies plus breakfast television, cable and satellite, more and more programmes are being made by independent film and production companies who have contracts to supply programmes to the television stations, and here again music is certain to be used to some extent. As it can be costly for producers of these programmes to use existing successful songs in them, this is an incentive for them to commission new specially-composed music. It is now possible to produce a competent video on quite a low budget, suitable for some local television slots, and this sort of thing could provide a good opportunity for a new songwriter, though inevitably, unless you already have a reputation, it's largely a question of who you know. Some publishers, including some with 'production

music' libraries, specialise in supplying music for audio-visual productions, and they will have the contacts you don't, if you can convince them that you can take on a commission (which means being able to produce a broadcast-quality recording of the music as well as writing it)

What will film and television companies pay and what rights will they want?

This depends very much on what instrumentation is required. If they expect a full orchestra they'll pay a lot more than a track composed on a synth, albeit using sampled sounds from an orchestra. Even a new writer should get a three-figure sum per minute of music, but there really are no hard and fast rules. The broadcasting fees can be much more than the commissioning fee, so this is the main consideration. If you are successful in interesting television or production companies in some of your music, they will wish to acquire world broadcasting rights in it. This is so they can sell the programme all round the world without prior reference to, or permission from you, although you would of course still get broadcasting fees in all the places where the programme was shown or heard. Some will want you to assign all the rights to their own publishing company, but others will be content to accept just broadcasting rights from you, leaving you free to assign all the remaining rights, performing, recording, printing etc., to a publisher though the film company probably has its own affiliated record company and will expect you to agree not to refuse to license the recording for a soundtrack album and to accept controlled composition provisions when it's released in North America

Can I or my publisher stop anyone recording my song?

As a preface to this answer, remember that if you have assigned the copyright in your song to a publisher, then although he may wish to consult with you, the song is nevertheless legally his property. Prior to the 1988 Copyright Act, only the copyright owner had the right to try to stop a new recording, and then only the first recording. Once one version had been 'published' it was technically a free-for-all. The 1988 Act abolished the old compulsory mechanical recording licence and since then, in theory, the copyright owner's permission is required before anyone records and releases a song unless it's almost a carbon copy of a previous release.

You can ask MCPS not to issue a first licence, so that your own version of your song can be released before anyone else's. However, the author's moral right, which the 1988 Act introduced into the UK, puts you personally in a much stronger position in saying that you don't want a particular cover version to happen at all. This is the right of integrity, discussed elsewhere in this book, and your publisher can advise on whether you or he has the power to stop a particular recording of your song, if necessary by taking out an injunction against the record company concerned. The position is much stronger again where someone has used a 'sample' of your song (even if it's not a sample of your own recording) in a new song (see 'Sampling' under General Q & A).

Can I or my publisher stop anyone else performing my song?

As regards performances it is virtually impossible to prevent people performing your song before a certain date once they have been able to get hold of some material (sheet music, demos etc.) from which to learn it. Once the song is well-known then a performance can only be prevented if, for instance, it is a parody or is included in a film or show without having been properly licensed. In most cases an unwanted performance is of no great consequence. Only in the case of a song contest entry where all the songs must be entirely new and unheard by the general public is this likely to become important.

Can I or my publisher stop anyone else printing my song?

Anyone wishing to print the song in any form will have to apply for permission to the publisher, although British Copyright Law does provide that very small extracts may be 'quoted' in books, magazines and newspaper articles (though not in advertisements), without a payment or credit being made. It is of course impossible to say exactly when a small extract becomes a 'substantial' one, but generally three or four lines is the most that would be likely to be regarded as permissible without your publisher expecting some form of payment and a credit to you (although three lines of a well-known chorus would be considered more 'substantial' than the whole of a little-known verse)

Can I or my publisher stop anyone making a parody of my song?

The answer is yes, although this does sometimes happen without your prior knowledge. Generally parodies do not really 'damage' a song, even if the parody is used in a big television commercial extolling the virtues of toilet rolls. A parody should be cleared specially with your publisher by the user before it is used, and the parody writer should never receive a written credit or part of the royalties. Few writers complain (unless they consider their songs to be highly poetical) as recorded parodies are often big sellers.

In the USA, however, it was ruled that rap artists 2 Live Crew's parody of Roy Orbison's song 'Pretty Woman' did not need the consent of his publishers provided royalties were paid, even though in that particular example the parody contained bad language. To stop a parody in the USA it is now necessary to have it considered a 'derogatory treatment' of the song.

What happens if my songs are included in musicals and plays?

The living stage rights ('dramatic performance in costume') in a musical are termed 'Grand Rights'. Unlike all other performing rights, these are licensed directly by the publishers to the producers of the show, in return for a percentage of the box office receipts, and PRS are not involved. If a producer commissions music for his show he may want the Grand Rights, but all other rights (so-called 'small rights') may remain with the writer, be assigned to a publisher, and be licensed by PRS in the normal way.

A musical show which contains songs which already existed and weren't written specially for it is known as a 'compilation show'. PRS claim the right to license these, but in practice the amount they can charge under their Tariff T (theatres) is laid down by the Copyright Tribunal and generally works out at only about 1%-3% of box-office receipts. So they will allow the publishers if they wish to try to negotiate a higher rate – generally between about 3-6% depending on the total percentage of the running time of the show which is music. Most publishers would regard it as petty and uncharitable to exact a fee for the use of a song or two in a local primary school Christmas pantomime, but the fee for their use in a big West End production could be tens or even hundreds of pounds per song every week, and some shows run for several years, so the income can mount up. PRS charge a small administration fee for granting a so-called '7(f)' notice to the publisher and he may deduct that from your royalties.

If I write a song with someone else how is the money divided?

It is hard to overemphasise how important it is to agree from the outset who are the writers and the percentage splits between them. Two writers of the Fifties hit 'Why Do Fools Fall In Love' who had never been paid and credited at all won a case nearly 40 years later in the USA, only to have it overturned on appeal because it took them so long to bring the case. The time limit was set at just three years. This is extreme, but in recent years there have been more and more legal battles, sometimes years after the song was a hit, over exactly who wrote the song. The band Spandau Ballet famously fell out over a claim that, because the others had contributed to the songs during the course of recording them, Gary Kemp should have given them a share of the songwriting royalties. You may not want to be seen to mistrust your co-writer by asking for something in writing, but you should decide as soon as you've written a song, if not before, how you'll divide it. If you're both/all signed to the same publisher then by signing an agreement/confirmation letter with him you are putting in writing your agreement to the split. If not then money could be held in suspense and the lawsuit to establish your rights could cost you a fortune. Be warned!

Beware of studio musicians, producers and remixers and divas who seem to expect a share of the song. If you think they've done a great job in turning your song into a hit (which they frequently do) or if you'd agreed on a split from the start then fine, but make it crystal clear what you think they should get, and avoid saying anything on impulse. Production teams quite often agree with the singer on one of the productions that she (usually she) can have a share of the royalties on the song and once she and her publisher have put in a claim for 10% or whatever it's a serious nuisance getting them to withdraw. It's easier later to increase their share than reduce it!

Most songwriting 'teams' divide songs equally, even where one wrote all the music and two others wrote the words, for example. In the UK the music and lyrics are regarded as separate copyright works, which is why it makes life easier to credit all the writers with words and music. Make sure your publisher knows if you're both or all signed to him and the split is not equal, or he'll usually assume that it is. Also, if you think you might have trouble from a co-writer who is signed to another publisher, ask your publisher to register the share that you claim with the societies as soon as possible. Getting in there first definitely helps. Incidentally, under a blanket writer agreement you will be asked to try to persuade your co-writer to sign his share of the song to your publisher. There's no harm in agreeing to use

'reasonable' endeavours to do so, but it shouldn't be worded any more strongly than that.

What do I get when my music is rented or hired out?

This will generally come under the 'miscellaneous' section of the contract, and you will usually get the same share as for mechanicals of whatever the hire fees amount to on printed editions or manuscript copies of your music (generally only serious music, symphonic works, classical pieces or the scores of musicals are hired out and for these this is very big business). It took the British government years to get round to giving rental rights to copyright owners of recordings, videos etc. With regard to the songs used in these, MCPS generally administers these rental rights (other than printed music and manuscripts) on behalf of publishers and writers, but of course the major potential source of 'rental' income is from renting out records and videos etc. and this is likely to wane as music becomes more readily available on a direct-to-home basis via the Internet, cable and satellite etc.

Can I use bits of other people's songs in mine?

No. Unless the song you use is out of copyright then this is an infringement of someone else's copyright and he could sue you. It used only to be jazz musicians who would work a snatch of one song into another, usually live, but now of course it is commonplace. However it's very rarely worth it (see 'Sampling' in General Q & A).

Will I be paid on my versions of existing songs?

This depends upon whether or not the existing song which you want to rearrange is 'traditional' (described as being in the public domain or PD). If the song you've arranged really is traditional then your new arrangement of it, even if you've hardly changed it at all, becomes a new copyright expiring 70 years after your own death and you'll be paid on it just as if it were all your own work. However, as we've said elsewhere, if you're 'arranging' a PD song that was recorded in the last 50 years or so then it's likely that you're infringing the copyright of someone else and you need to be very (very) careful to make sure that your 'arrangement' doesn't include any part of theirs, i.e. you need to go right back to the original song or else credit the act whose arrangement you've adapted.

The PRS used to have a committee which assessed people's arrangements of PD songs and graded them to reflect the amount of new words or music which had been added. If it was very little, only a quarter of the total royalties that an original song would have earned might be paid. A few foreign performing right societies (but not mechanical societies) still do this though most have changed. If your song 'is based' on a PD work, and it's not crucial that you keep the original title, then change it. The other reason for doing this is that when it's performed or broadcast the societies won't have the problem of identifying whose arrangement of the PD work was used, and you're more likely to get paid.

How many old songs are actually traditional?

Quite a large number of songs including the likes of 'Greensleeves', 'Camptown Races' etc., are widely known to be traditional (all the ones that used to appear in beginners' guitar tutors!), but our advice is to check up if you are at all uncertain about the copyright status of a piece of music. If someone wrote a song at the age of twenty and died at the age of

eighty it will be 130 years before that song 'becomes PD' in the UK. Some songs which never saw the light of day during the writer's lifetime get a further period of copyright from the date they were published, regardless of when they were written.

This inevitably means that there are even old Victorian music hall songs which are still copyright. The children's songs 'Happy Birthday To You' and 'I Know An Old Lady Who Swallowed A Fly' and several well-known Christmas carols are still copyright. Most spirituals are PD, as are many well-known folk songs, but many, like the Steeleye Span song 'All Around My Hat' contain so much new material that anyone using them today would be almost certain to be including someone's copyright work and would have to apply to them for permission. So if you are going to 'borrow' a PD song then try to be sure that you go back to the original and not the fairly recent hit version or you may well be infringing someone's copyright.

How can I find out whether a song is traditional?

The MCPS and PRS will be prepared to answer queries on whether a song or piece of music is copyright. You can write in to them (addresses in the list of 'useful addresses' at the end) but remember that they are extremely busy, so try not to query more than a title or two at a time, and try to give them the original composer's name if you can find it. This is a help to them as they have many different songs by different composers but all with the same title, including around 500 different songs all called 'I Love You'! Your publisher can also advise as to whether or not certain songs really are traditional in the UK.

If I record a brand new arrangement of someone else's recent hit, can I claim a share?

If you wish for any reason to record a song which you know very well to be a recent work then, as we've said earlier, you should send a copy to the publisher of the hit and ask if he or the writer has any objection. They may well allow it but subject to your not making a claim to any of the royalties and, as we've said, they may ask you to assign any new material you add to it as a 'work for hire'. You may have added a whole new rap verse or suchlike, but unless the publisher of the hit is prepared to give you a piece of the action, you should not expect any. This became a contentious issue after a court ruled in the early Nineties that KWS were entitled to claim that a separate copyright existed in their version of KC and The Sunshine Band's hit 'Please Don't Go' when it was copied.

Are there any subjects to avoid in song lyrics?

Ten or twenty years ago this was a highly awkward subject. Records could be withdrawn or banned by the BBC for seemingly the most trivial reasons. In the present permissive age there is far less to worry about, but it is still advisable not to go too far on certain subjects, these being, use of brand names, sex, wanton violence, sheer bad taste (so-called sick songs), religion, royalty and public

figures plus, of course, anything libellous not already covered in that list

Other countries sometimes have stricter standards than the UK. Back in the Sixties and Seventies Ray Davies of The Kinks was forced at the last minute, due to a ban in the US, to change 'Coca-Cola' in the song 'Lola' into 'Cherry-Cola' and the same happened to The Rolling Stones over 'Let's Spend The Night Together' which had to become 'Let's Spend Some Time Together' for the USA. Times have changed, but even now violent lyrics are blamed for fans' suicides and gun culture and in some countries albums must have warnings if they contain bad language or violence. They're also more likely to be banned by broadcasters, as are violent or explicit pop videos. The BBC now adopts the view over brand names that if they are words like 'Rolls-Royce' or 'Cadillac' which are instantly recognisable and are really the best words for the job in the lyric, then this is permissible. Otherwise not.

However it is actually possible to do a deal with manufacturer of a product which you have mentioned in one of your songs if you're successful enough. The success of 'Pass the Courvoisier' by Busta Rhymes in 2002 actually resulted in a big increase in sales of the drink itself (though the writers didn't do a deal in advance in this case). You could take it one step further and offer to call yourself Joey 'Cadillac' Smith in return for one of their cars, but we don't know of any

Nice! Just tone down the bits about the Queen, the Pope and the shop steward and we're onto a winner!

examples of this! There are no real titles to avoid, but, out of interest, of all the songs that have been hit singles in the UK, the following are the commonest titles: 'Crazy' 13 + 'Crazy For You' 4; 'Tonight' 11; 'Star' 10 + 'Stars' 5 ; 'Stay' 11 + 'Stay with Me' 9; 'Heaven' 10; 'Heartbeat' 10; 'Freedom' 9; 'Don't Stop' 9; 'Everyday' 9.

Is there any formal body looking after the interests of songwriters?

Yes. These exist in many countries. The society in the UK is called the British Academy of Composers and Authors. There is a yearly subscription which you can arrange to be deducted directly by PRS from your royalties. The 'pop' element of this (formerly known as BASCA) have for a long time produced standard publishing contracts for the use of members and can give valuable advice generally on songwriting and the music business. They also produce a regular newsletter for members and writers' workshops where new writers have the chance to have their work assessed by hit writers. This is also the body which has for many years, formerly under its old name of the Songwriters' Guild, presented the Ivor Novello Awards annually to the best or most successful British song, writer, or piece of music in various categories. You can also enter songs in the British heats of the Song For Europe through the British Academy of Composers and Songwriters. You don't have to have achieved any particular level of income or activity to join, and you can write or phone for more information (address in list of 'useful addresses').

The writers' organisations work together with the publishing fraternity to promote and protect music copyright in the UK and abroad under the umbrella of an organisation called British Music Rights (address also in our 'Useful Addresses' section).

Can I use as many pseudonyms as I like?

There is nothing to stop you, particularly on songs which are printed in books but which you are not expecting ever to be broadcast or recorded. The PRS does ask, however, that you use not more than two different pen-names as it can become highly confusing, so if in doubt stick to two. You can always change a pseudonym if you really want to. Always tell your publisher etc. your full real name, even if it's not nearly as hip as your stage name, or you'll almost certainly miss out on royalties due to you.

Can I write a song with the same title as an existing song?

Broadly speaking the answer is yes, as there is no copyright in titles. Nevertheless you would probably lose out if you wrote songs with the same titles as big standards, as any money which your songs earned might be credited in error to the owners of the well-known songs. It is also best to steer clear of very distinctive and long titles like 'Tie A Yellow Ribbon Round The Ole Oak Tree'. The PRS will tell you, if you write to them, whether a certain title has been used before, but if you haven't heard of it it's probably OK for you to use it too. There's also no copyright in ideas, although again you should steer clear of 'borrowing' the entire plot of an existing copyright song.

What are reversion clauses?

These days all songwriting agreements, even single song assignments should provide that if nothing happens to your song within say two years (or a year or two from the end of a blanket agreement) you can ask for it back. The publisher usually has three months to prove that a record was released or it was used in a film or commercial or (sometimes) printed. If not, then it reverts to you.

A publisher has what is called a 'fiduciary duty' to at least try to exploit your songs, although it would depend how big a percentage he is getting. Unless he's spent a lot on you by way of advances, demo costs etc. then he may let you have back anyway a song which he thinks he can do nothing more with.

Some publishing agreements provide that if your publisher has assigned your song to sub-publishers overseas, perhaps as part of his overall catalogue, then those publishers get to keep it even though he himself doesn't. This could apply even if the sub-publishers are under the same ownership as your UK publisher. They will now have to pay you rather than your publisher, but can still keep their agreed share. Try to ensure when first assigning your songs that when the agreement ends or when the songs revert to you, you get them back for the whole world. If the sub-publisher paid an advance to your publisher which he hasn't recovered, which is quite possible, then he may be very reluctant to start paying you!

Can I get my song back if the earnings have dried up?

If a song has ever earned money, however long ago, then the chances are there will be nothing in the agreement to say you can have it back. If it's been inactive for many years a publisher may be happy to reassign it. Otherwise he might well ask for any advances he's paid you, or any demo costs to be repaid (and you will get to own the demo). Any song that's ever been released, especially a single which had airplay, stands a chance of being 'picked up' and reactivated. If he says no, you could always ask for a higher royalty on any new recording that you yourself can 'fix'. If, of course, you think your publisher may have broken the agreement then you may be able to reclaim the songs anyway. As a result of litigation between Aaron Schroeder Music and the songwriter Tony Macaulay back in the

Seventies it became necessary for publishers to agree to give back to their exclusive writers any songs (upon request) that they'd done nothing with after a certain period (but don't expect to get back the rights to any demos of the song which the publisher made and paid for unless you repay him).

How do co-publishing and administration deals for writers work?

As we've said, if you are in a strong position you may be able to ask for one of these situations, rather than just assign your songs to your publisher. Co-publishing usually means that the publisher will form a new jointly-owned company with you. Otherwise you might invent a trading name for yourself, so that the publisher and your 'company' (Fred Smith doing business as Fred Smith Music) will own the songs equally. The publisher will collect and account for all the royalties – part to you as a writer, part as a share of profits. Do remember that demo costs, printing and anything else specifically done for your songs will come out of those profits.

If you actually form Fred Smith Limited it becomes a separate legal entity and you'd have to assign your songs to your company before the company could pass rights to the publisher.

The publisher collects and pays the royalties to your company. This can be structured like a normal blanket writer agreement (1 year + options on payment of advances) and with the publisher retaining the songs you wrote during that time for say 12 years from the end. Alternatively it can all end after a straight three year period. For megastars, publishers have even done deals like this where they don't keep anything at all (the bank interest on money they collect + the prestige of handling the songs makes it just about worthwhile).

The splits between your company and the publisher would be roughly similar to a blanket writer agreement, but established writers could command 80/20 at source or better, especially if they don't want an advance.

What are Moral Rights?

As mentioned earlier these are rights which a UK writer has under the 1988 Copyright Act (Continental writers had these rights for many years before). They are a right of 'paternity' and a right of 'integrity'. Paternity is the right to be identified as the writer of a song. You have to 'exercise' this by informing your publisher – the assignment usually covers it. Obviously you'll be aware that writers of jingles for commercials are never 'identified' though film credits increasingly credit songwriters.

Integrity is the right not to have your work 'messed about with'. It's not clear where a 'cover version' becomes a 'derogatory treatment' (if you chose to see it that way) but you should be approached before anything more than minor changes are made to your song, regardless of the precise wording of your assignment to your publisher.

Some assignments require you not to waive your moral rights, but to exercise them if the publisher asks, so that you and he can use them against infringers etc.

Who owns the demos my publisher makes?

Generally he does, unless, as is advisable, your agreement with him covers this even if in theory he was recouping the cost of them from your royalties (record companies work in the same way). However, he can't do anything with them without your approval, just as you can't do anything with them without his approval. He'll own the physical master tapes, but if you've got a CD or DAT then this can be used to press from if necessary, provided you and the publisher agree.

These days demos and master recordings are almost intertwined and a demo can always be remixed and improved on to make a commercial track . Some publishers will actually issue white labels of your recordings as a promotional tool to try to secure you a record deal, though if these are sold rather than just given to DJ's etc. then you should have a separate form of 'artist' agreement with the publisher, saying who will get what (frequently a 50/50 split of any profits).

When should I renegotiate a publishing deal?

The usual re-negotiation, as with record deals, is to offer another album's worth of material in return for an increased percentage for you from the songs on your current successful album, and maybe bigger advances from now on. If your single or album is high in the charts or about to break in the USA you'll obviously get a better deal than if you wait too long and the record begins to drop. Also, remember (and a lot of people don't) that you can also negotiate downwards if you think a publisher is basically doing a good job but your first album flopped, by accepting a smaller advance for the next option period, rather than being dropped by the publisher.

GETTING A RECORD CONTRACT

Perhaps more than anything else for a singer or musician hoping to be a star, the idea of getting a recording contract is his great ambition, and in the eyes of his friends and relatives once he has been offered a contract he will already have 'made it'. Unfortunately this may be a very long way from the truth, if the contract is a bad one.

Which company should I approach?

The reason behind most people's choice of record company is that they know someone who knows someone ... In a business where it's not what you know but who you know this has some merit, but if the company is unsuitable then it's really a waste of time. Even the major companies have different labels, sometimes separately run and specialising in different types of material. Most of the independent labels ('indies') are to some extent specialised, so aim first for one which is successful with your type of music. If, for instance, you are a rap artist, take a look at the rap records which you or your friends may already have and look to approach these companies first. The only time when this might not be advisable is if you model yourself on one particular distinctive artist. A company is less likely to be interested in signing you up if it already has an artist just like you but who is already successful

How can I make the best impression?

In the final analysis, unless a talent scout from a particular record company comes looking for you, you will just have to hawk your demo CDs (or yourself) round until someone expresses interest in you. If the first few companies don't, remember you've lost nothing, and don't despair. Many famous artists, including The Beatles, were turned down by very

knowledgeable, and successful, people in the music business before finally being signed up.

If you do want to take some demos along to a record company for them to hear, make them as near to professional quality as possible (no piano/vocal demos on cassette recorders made in your sitting room to budgerigar accompaniment). It's not that a good A&R man can't hear through a bad demo but he is used to hearing a lot of very good recordings of mediocre acts, and what's more a good recording shows you have confidence in yourself which is half the battle.

Do bear in mind that if your demo is constantly rejected by record companies it will probably not be because they are unimpressed by the poor recording quality, but because they are unimpressed by your performance or just as likely the material. If you play your first demos to all of the major companies and not one of them likes your first effort you'll be less likely to succeed with your second one, as the people listening will be expecting something mediocre and it will take something pretty dynamic to get over this in-built prejudice.

If you change your name (not really practical if you already have a big local following) or else leave it for say a year before you try a second time, however, you may find that the people listening are entirely different from those who heard your demo. Faces change quickly in the music business and you'll again have the advantage of being an unknown quantity.

Where can I get help in getting a record deal?

Rather than go it alone, you would be well advised, with this crucial step in your career, to get help, and there are five main sources: publishers, lawyers, managers, producers and mutual friends. Most acts these days write their own material, so it has to be good. Most, though not all, artists in the charts are there because they wrote, or had access to, good songs. Noel Gallagher of Oasis said that it was more important to be a good songwriter than a great musician and he was absolutely right. A Band need a good songwriter, so if you can impress a publisher first, then he will use his contacts to try to get you a record deal. As we've said, he may even make masters of you to license to a record company.

The downside is that you'd have got a better publishing deal if you'd already got the record deal, but it is a chicken and egg situation and this would be a small price to pay for a good record deal.

Is it really worth entering a television 'pop star' type competition?

In the early years of the 21st C this sort of television programme became big business in terms of audience ratings and general popularity, particularly with the revived market for singing/dancing but non-musician artists which first really emerged with 'doo-wop' groups of the late Fifties and 'Motown'- type acts in the Sixties. First point to remember is that it doesn't hurt to be a member of a 'put-together group' as winners of a talent show. Stars, whether they wrote, or co-wrote, their own hits, have always tended to come out of successful bands. In fact this goes right back to people like Frank Sinatra who started off by singing with dance bands. It really didn't harm Robbie Williams' career that he was once in Take That, and Geri Halliwell and Melananie C. etc. were successful with their solo albums despite (or because of) the fact that they were members of the all-conquering Spice Girls. So don't worry if it's a 'band' talent show or 'put-together' act or a solo one- if you're really good and/or really good looking and really pushy then it's quite possible that you'll be successful. It doesn't matter if it's *Pop Stars*, *Pop Idol* or whatever, if you think you're good at that sort of thing (and of course it is just a particular section of the market) then apply. They can only say no, in which case you just try for the next one!

What do I have to sign to be in a show or put-together act like that?

There's obviously always someone behind these shows and put-together acts, and you could reasonably expect them to want to manage you, and for their production company to record you and, if by any chance you are offered the chance to co-write any of your songs, to publish you for a normal period of three years or so. This would be a pre-requisite of your entering the competition and provided that you know that the company and/or the competition is run by a reputable television production company then you'll appreciate that they won't want to be seen to be ripping you off and you'll get a reasonable deal – maybe not the best but then OK, you can live with that. What not do to is to enter a 'talent competition' run by some local organisation without very seriously checking that they're not going to tie you to some very dodgy or simply amateur and inexperienced management/recording/ publishing organisation if you win.

Suppose someone offers to put one of my tracks on a 'promo' CD?

There are companies which produce CDs of unsigned artists and send them around the business and put them on the Internet in the hope that someone will hear something they like and sign it. These companies make their money either by charging the artists to be on the CD or by asking for a royalty on the artist's first album etc. This is a perfectly legitimate way to get noticed but, as with the Pop Idol-type talent shows, it's very important to ensure that anything you sign doesn't have the potential to give away any long-term rights or rights (e.g. to the best track you've written/recorded so far) which you might need to give the company you eventually sign to.

Can I expect a lawyer actually to go out and get me a record deal?

These days a music business solicitor will often act almost like a manager in using his contacts to get you a deal. He'll also, obviously, be able to negotiate the best terms. You will need a lawyer anyway at some point. The downside is that his close contacts may be more limited than a publisher or manager, and he'll charge you by the hour. It can easily cost £1,000 or substantially more to negotiate a record deal for you, though he might do it on a contingency basis (meaning that he'll take a percentage of your earnings rather than a fee per hour which will probably be much more expensive if you're successful but then, if you're not successful no-one makes any money anyway). It's possible that, as with publishers, he can persuade the record label to pay some or all of your legal costs anyway!

Wouldn't I be better off with a manager?

A really good manager will have contacts galore and would be the best person of all to get you a deal. He can also advise best on presentation of you and your songs, organising showcases etc. The downside is that you're more likely to attract a good manager once you've already got some record company interest (chicken and egg again). Most managers will take commission on all your income from the music business, but if you did already have the record deal all wrapped up, your manager might well be prepared to reduce his commission from record income. Dance acts may well only have one hit single (+ lots of uses of their track on compilation albums) then disappear, maybe to reappear under a different guise a year or so later. However rock acts, who will need more investment to make them successful, tend to sign record (and publishing) deals for longer and it's much harder to convince record companies and publishers to invest in them, hence a persuasive manager is more helpful. In all cases record and publishing companies now pay new artists/writers far higher shares of royalties than they used to which is good for the artist/writer but only if they can get signed in the first place, which, as you'll appreciate, applies to less and less artists and writers.

Won't a record producer only get involved once I'm signed to a label?

Not necessarily. Although this is the usual way round, it is possible that you could interest a producer who you feel understands your music and who you can work with. These days more and more acts, especially dance acts, more-or-less produce themselves, usually with the help of remixers once a track is due to be released (see 'How could I get to be a producer?' in 'General Q & A'). But there are plenty of professional producers of all types who may be prepared to make a recording of you to take to a record company, especially if they own or have a deal with a particular studio. Many belong to an organisation called Re-Pro (address in our 'Useful Addresses' list) who could advise on which producers might be prepared to listen to you, especially if they happen to be local.

With a 'name' producer singing your praises you're much more likely to get record company interest. In return the producer will expect to be able to go on and produce at least your first album. He may even want to sign you himself and license your first recordings to the record company (see 'lease-tape deals' in 'Recording Q & A') although this is less likely.

Suppose I know someone (anyone) in the music business?

Finally, personal contacts can be extremely valuable. The cost may be no more than a round of drinks, but remember, as we've said, that the contacts your 'friend' has may be with the least suitable record company, and you increase the risk that if your contact at the company leaves, his successor may well hate your music (always an occupational hazard). It's worth asking around in local record shops, musical equipment shops and certainly in the local studio where you make your demos as to whether anyone has any contacts in the business. Do remember with all the above people that you still have to impress them so much that they'll risk their credibility with their valuable contacts on your behalf, no matter how low a royalty or advance you're prepared to accept!

How can I organise a showcase?

For a band, a showcase can open doors. With luck a manager or publisher will organise and pay for this for you. If you can get to play at a suitable venue in your nearest city (even if you have to pay to play there) it's worth inviting as many suitable record company, publishing and music press people as possible.

Don't rush into it. You may only get one really big bite of the cherry. Try to get some local press and possibly local airplay of your demos beforehand and time it to follow other gigs so you can fine-tune your repertoire and build up a fan base. You must be convinced about your material and your performance and that you're guaranteed a hardcore of adoring fans. If you can once create a 'buzz' then you could be on your way. Again don't underestimate the importance of your material. A record company are ideally looking for a minimum of three or four potential hit singles per album. Even a rock band will be expected to have some hits. If you don't honestly think you're halfway there, then work on the songs first and if necessary don't refuse help from friends or acquaintances, especially ones in the business. There's no actual law that says a band must write all its own new material.

The Music Publishers Association took an initiative in providing a regular showcase for bands signed to publishers but not yet to record labels, known as the Push Club at the Borderline Club in London and providing another possibility of being 'spotted'. It may be worth asking your publisher about this sort of thing. The ultimate showcase, of course, is television and even *Top Of The Pops* has been known to feature an unsigned (but not for long!) act, so don't dismiss this as a possibility, even at the start of your career, but remember that at any given time some clubs (e.g. The Kashmir in London) are much more credible than others and the fact that your band is playing at some is almost a disincentive for them to sign you.

How can I make a really good demo?

Studios are not all the exclusive property of record companies. Most of them are independent, and smaller ones can be hired privately for as little as around £10 per hour, plus cost of tape, diskettes etc., and incidental expenses. A competent band, who don't keep making odd little mistakes, should be able to put down three songs in a day (though mixing may take another day). If you can do it during an ordinary working day (so the engineer at the studio doesn't have to be paid over-time etc.), the total cost could be as low as around £200 for 16- or 24- track demos, though don't be tempted to add things off the cuff to use up extra tracks if you have that luxury.

Armed with this, the all-important first impression with the record companies who hear the demos is likely to be that much more favourable. The better (and generally the more expensive) the studio, the better your demos will probably be, though there's no point in wasting very expensive studio time on fairly basic demos, especially if you could have made them yourselves in a home studio. Getting a good mix is as important as getting a good recording, so don't under-estimate the time it could take to mix down the tracks once you've recorded them.

The above is all very fine for groups. A straight singer who normally sings to a combo or orchestral backing could hire or cajole a pianist to accompany him, but the hiring of professional musicians is expensive and is not worthwhile at this stage if costs are to be kept low.

Dance acts almost by definition start out with their own home recording equipment sufficient to lay down the basic tracks. A day's studio time should be quite enough to mix down the tracks and add vocals if you know the studio's capability and have planned in advance.

There are now so many studios around the country (not just in London) that a list would be enormous. Check the phone book for local ones. Obviously some outside London are large residential studios for recording your second album when the first has gone multi-platinum, but any studio will quote their rates to you on request and if you have queries, you would be well advised to seek the help of an organisa-tion called the Association of Pro-fessional Recording Studios Ltd., 23 Chestnut Avenue, Chorleywood, Herts. (Chorleywood [01923] 72907). They have their own list of recording studios who are members and will be able to advise you.

UK RECORD COMPANIES

The most important factor in selling your recording services to a record company is, of course, to know who and where the record companies are. For this reason we have included here a list of addresses of British record companies. Don't think that just because a company is not on this list it's automatically not worth signing with If by this time you have already enlisted the support of a lawyer and an accountant, both of these will know who is worth talking to and who isn't likely to be interested. There are several times the number on this list in all and new companies are being formed all the time (regrettably many go out of business after just a few releases) and it is not possible to produce a fully comprehensive list. You could also refer to current Yellow Pages, local directories and the latest Trade publications such as the Music Week directory.

Not all the companies on this list, or in any other publication, are crying out for new acts all the time. Some specialise in licensing recordings from other companies or in American or Continental acts. Or they may have more than they can cope with at a certain time, or you may not really be what they're looking for even if they admit that you're good, so if they don't want to sign you, there may be a perfectly good reason.

Many big artists and producers now have their own labels which are actually a subsidiary of one of the majors. Some will try to sign new acts, others just exist to issue records by one established act. This list includes most of those which are properly in the business of releasing records (and have had their share of hits) and for the most part have been around for a while. If there's a name you were expecting to see that's missing from the list this may be because it's part of, or run by, another company.

Ace Records
46–50 Steele Road
London NW10 7AS
(0208 453 1311)

Amazon Records
Unit 1
Canalot Studios
222 Kensal Road
London W10 5BN
(0207 460 4006)

Attitude
118 Osiers Rd
London SW181NL
(0208 870 0011)

**Beggars Banquet
Records**
17-19 Alma Road
London SW18 1AA
(0208 870 9912)

**BMG Entertainment
International**
Bedford House
69-79 Fulham High Street
London SW6 3JW
(0207 973 0980)

Champion Records
181 High Street
Harlesden
London NW10 4TE
(0208 961 5202

Charly Records (UK)
13 Bridge Wharf Road
Church Road
Isleworth, Middx TW7 6BS
(0208 232 1300)

Cherry Red Records
Unit 17, Elysium Gate
West

126-128 New Kings Rd
London SW6 4LZ
(0207 371 5844)

Cleveland City
52a Clifton Street
Chapelash
Wolverhampton WV3 0QT
(01902 838 500)

Columbia Records
(see Sony)

Connoisseur Collection
2-3 Fitzroy Mews
London W1P 5DQ
(0207 383 7724)

Cooking Vinyl
10 Allied Way,
London W3 0RQ
(0208 600 9200)

Curb Records
45 Great Guildford Street
London SE1 0ES
(0207 401 8877)

**Deconstruction
Records**
(see BMG)

Demon Records
4th Floor
Holden House
57 Rathbone Place
London W1T 1JU
(0207 396 8899)

Distinctive Records
1st Floor, Berners House
47-48 Berners St.
London W1T 3NF
(0207 323 6610)

**Eagle Rock
Entertainment**
Eagle House,
22 Armoury Way
London SW18 1EZ
(0208 870 5670)

East West Records
Electric Lighting Station
46 Kensington Court
London W8 5DP
(0207 938 5500)

Edel UK Records
12 Oval Road,
London NW17DH
(0207 482 4848)

EG Records
63a Kings Road
Chelsea
London SW3 4NT
(0207 730 2162)

EMI Records Group
43 Brook Green
London W6 7EF
(0207 605 5000)

Fellside Recordings
PO Box 40
Workington
Cumbria CA14 3GJ
(01900 61556)

Fiction Records
4 Tottenham Mews
London W1P 9PJ
(0207 237 9453)

First Avenue Records
The Courtyard
42 Colwith Road
London W6 0EY
(0208 741 1419)

First Night Records
2-3 Fitzroy Mews
London W1P 5DQ
(0207 383 7767)

Fluid Recordings
Evans Business Centre
Suite 8
Sycamore Trading Estate
Blackpool FY4 3RL
(0870 046 9647)

FM Revolver Records
152 Goldthorn Hill
Penn
Wolverhampton
W. Midlands WV2 3JA
(01902 345345)

4AD
17-19 Alma Road
London SW18 1AA
(0208 870 9724)

Glasgow Records
Lovat House
Gavell Rd
Glasgow G65 9BS
(01236 826555)

Global Talent Records
6 Little Portland Street
London W1W 7JE
(0207 907 1700)

**Gusto Records/ Gut
Records**
112a Shirland Road
London W9 2EQ
(0207 266 0777)

Hyperion Records
PO Box 25
London SE9 1AX
(0208 318 1234)

Incentive Music
PO Box 20153
London W10 5FG
(0208 960 4538)

Independiente
The Drill Hall
3 Heathfield Terrace
London W4 4JE
(0208 747 8111)

Inferno Records
32-36 Telford Way
London W3 7AX
(0208 742 9300)

Jelly Street Records
Grosvenor House
94-96 Grosvenor Street
Manchester M1 7HL
(0161 273 6522)

KOCH Inernational
87 Little Ealing Lane
LondonW5 4EH
(0208 832 1800)

Lakota Records
PO Box 4704
Ballsbridge
Dublin 4
Ireland
(00353) 1 283 9071)

Lismor Recordings
27-29 Carnoustie Place
Scotland Street
Glasgow G5 8PH
(0141 420 1881)

Logic Records
1st Floor
34-35 Berwick Street
London W1V 3RF
(0207 434 2193)

Love This International
Hundred House
100 Union Street
London WE1 0NL
(0207 928 4444)

**Manifesto Records/
Mercury Records**
PO Box 1425
136-144 New Kings Road
London SW6 4FX
(0207 7705 4200)

Ministry of Sound
103 Gaunt Street
London SE1 6DP
(0207 378 6528)

Mooncrest Records
1, Pratt Mews
London NW1 0AD
(0207 267 6899)

**Music Collection
International**
4th Floor, Holden House
57 Rathbone Plac
London W1T 1JU
(0207 396 8899)

Music For Nations
333 Latimer Road
London W10 6RA
(0208 964 9544)

Mute Records
429 Harrow Road
London W10 4RE
(0208 969 8866)

Nude Records
6 Warren Mews
London W1P 5DJ
(0207 388 5300)

**One Little Indian
Records**
34 Trinity Crescent
London SW17 7AE
(0208 722 7600)

Park Records
PO Box 651
Oxford OX2 9RB
(01865 241 717)

Petulant Records
The Cottage
Le Hall Place, Manor Road
Adderbury
Oxon. OX17 3EH
(01295 812 075)

**Play It Again Sam
Records**
338a, Ladbroke Grove
London W10 5AH
(0208 324 2500)

Polydor UK
72-80 Black Lion Lane
London W6 9BE
(0208 910 4800)

President Records
Units 6 & 7
11 Wyfold Road
London SW6 6SE
(0207 385 7700)

Prism Leisure Corp
1 Dundee Way
Enfield
Middx EN3 7SX
(0208 804 8100)

Readers Digest Assoc.
11 West Ferry Circus
London E14 4HE
(0207 715 8058)

Really Useful Records
22 Trower Street
London WC2H 9NS
(0207 240 0880)

Recognition Records
Suite 6 Piccadilly House
Londonn Road
Bath BA1 6PL
(01225 448 438)

Ritz Music Group
33–35 Wembley Hill Road
Middx HA9 8RT
(0208 733 1300) and
5–6 Lombard St. Dublin 2
(00353 1677 9046)

Rollercoaster Records
Rock House
London Road
St. Marys
Chalford
Glos. GL6 8PU
(01453 886 252)

Rough Trade Records
66 Golborne Road
London W10 5PS
(0208 960 9888)

Rykodisc
8 Kensington Park Road
London W11 3BU
(0207 229 0897)

**Sanctuary Records
Group**
A29 Barwell Business Park
Leatherhead Road
Chessington
Surrey KT9 2NY
(0208 974 1021)

See For Miles Records
Unit 10, Littleton House
Littleton Road
Ashford
Middx TW15 1UU
(01784 247 176)

Skint Records
PO Box 174
Brighton
E. Sussex BN1 4BA
(01273 738 527)

**Sony Music
Entertainment**
10 Gt. Marlborough Street
London W1V 2LP
(0207 911 8200)

Splash Records
29 Manor House
250 Marylebone Road
London NW1 5NP
(0207 723 7177)

Strictly Rhythm UK
Unit 201 The Saga Centre
326 Kensal Road
London W10 5BZ
(0208 964 9815)

Telstar Music Group
107 Mortlake High Street
London SW14 8HQ
(0208 878 7888)

**That's Entertainment
Records**
107 Kentish Town Road
London NW1 8PD
(0207 485 9593)

3 Beat Music
58 Wood Street
Liverpool L1 4AQ
(0151 707 1669)

TKO Records
PO Box 130
Hove
E. Sussex BN3 6QU
(01273 550 088)

Tommy Boy Music
3rd Floor
151 Freston Road
London W10 6TH
(0207 313 8300)

Universal Music
PO Box 1420
1 Sussex Place
London W6 9XS
(0208 910 5000)

Virgin Records
Kensal House
553-579 Harrow Road
London W10 4RH
(0208 964 6000)

V2 Records
131-133 Holland Park
Avenue
London W11 4UT
(0207 471 3000)

Warner Music (UK)
The Warner Building
28a Kensington Church
Street
London W8 4EP
(0207 368 2500)

WEA London Records
Waldron House
57-63 Old Church Street
London SW3 5BS
(0207 761 6000)

Zomba Records
Zomba House
165-167 Willesden High
Road
London NW10 2SG
(0208 459 8899)

ZYX Records UK
Unit 11, Cambridge Court
210 Shepherds Bush Road
London W6 7NJ
(0207 371 6969)

RECORD COMPANIES

In these days of digital home recording, cheaply pressed CDs, distribution of recordings over the Internet etc. it is easier than ever to call yourself a record company and 'issue' records (or at least 'distribute' recordings) to the public, and in the last few years a great many new record companies have mushroomed in the world's major music centres. Some of these are owned by managers, producers, publishers or artists themselves, hoping partly to become independent of the roughly half-dozen so-called 'majors' who have for decades dominated the market in most countries, and partly to cash in on the very large profits which can be made by issuing successful records, often failing to appreciate the very heavy costs involved in recording, pressing, distribution and, often most expensive of all, advertising and PR which is frequently wasted on records that don't make it.

What sort of advance will they give me?

It's impossible to say. It depends almost entirely on how 'hot' they think you are and on how much they like the songs that would go on your first album. It also depends (crucially) on whether they're giving you a sum of money as an advance (to live on) or whether the recording budget for your first album has to come out of that! You shouldn't expect a guarantee of millions for your first album – if you can get £100-200,000 that wouldn't be too bad, though you might be offered a lot more, and if you are re-negotiating then the sky's the limit. EMI reportedly re-signed Robbie Williams in 2002 for a staggering £80 million, working on the assumption that he would sell at least 18 million copies worldwide of new albums covered by the new deal. (See also 'who pays the recording costs?')

Will they always want to give me an exclusive contract?

Publishers won't always be looking to sign an exclusive long-term contract, but with recording this is almost always the case. A record company will not normally chance making and releasing one record to 'see what happens' without having options to keep you for a long

term if you turn out to be a sensation. This is understandable as issuing recordings can be expensive and a quite straightforward first single can easily cost from £10,000 to produce plus the cost of manufacture and marketing, even without the cost of a promo video for which you can often put a nought on the end of that figure. So you will be offered a contract, generally for one or two years, under the terms of which the company will, or should be, required to record a minimum number of tracks per contract year.

What recording or release commitment will they give me?

With dance or dance-orientated chart acts it is more likely you will be offered a so-called 'singles deal'. The first single may be one you or your publisher, manager, producer or accountant has brought to them. Although they'll usually want options for albums if you're successful, they'll only commit to releasing one, or possibly two singles.

A rock act or rock-orientated chart act (guitar-based bands and the like) is more likely to be offered an album deal or nothing. As it costs more to release an album the record company will want to be that much more certain of your potential (and thus it's more likely that

T030687

they'll reject you), but if they do take you on and start spending money, they're unlikely not to make and release a whole album. Remember a five-album deal doesn't necessarily mean that the company is guaranteeing to make and release five albums – it just gives them the option to do so on terms already agreed.

Under an album deal they will commit to making recordings (or giving you a budget to organise the recording yourself) of enough tracks for a 12-14-track album plus a couple of 'bonus' tracks and maybe two or three 'spares' if they think you haven't enough potential hits or if you've had a great idea just before delivery of the album to the company.

What options will they expect?

The company are likely to want one album per year or 18 months for up to 5-7 years or so + maybe one or two 'over-call' albums (extra live or 'greatest hits' albums to fulfil demand from the public). Most companies will re-negotiate with an artist who has had success with their first album to give the artist a higher royalty rate, bigger advances or a less tight delivery schedule in return for delivery of extra albums over a longer period. Remember touring and other commitments will soon eat into your time, and neither you nor the company wants to release a 'throwaway' album. For this reason, as with publishing deals, each 'year' will if necessary extend till a few months after the album for that year has been released (even if for some reason it's taken up to about three years since the 'year' began for the album to be released).

Surprisingly, a pop act may be 'dropped' in spite of having had a couple of sizeable hits, as each company has only so much money to go round and may have a better prospect lined up (they think). One hit, however, and of course other doors open. The press want to know about you and you can put a

nought on the end of the amount you're getting per gig almost overnight. How much of that you will see is another matter (see 'Artist Management' section).

One provision which is well worth asking for in a recording contract is that the contract terminates after say one year, unless a recording produced during that year featuring you has been included in the Top 30 or 50 of a recognised British (or overseas) chart, preferably as played by the BBC. If your record has made the charts then probably you will both wish the company to renew the contract for further periods. If it hasn't made the charts then you are simply free to go elsewhere at the end of that first year.

Suppose my record is not released, or only in certain countries?

If they really hate the album they've paid for and don't release it by a given date then they should forfeit any options, and ideally you should be able to buy back the masters. Methods of calculating the price vary and will probably include more than just recording costs.

If a major company's UK people love your album but, for example, their Italian people don't, some companies will allow you to shop the rights to other Italian companies as long as royalties flow through your UK record company. This is not likely with new artists and could be embarrassing for the Italian branch if they turned it down and it became huge in Italy on another label. This lack of overseas commitment was one of George Michael's arguments in his much publicised battle with Sony Records in the mid-Nineties.

What royalties will I get under a recording contract?

With a smaller company you may be on a form of 'profit sharing' (50/50 after all costs have been recovered, maybe 60/40 or 70/30 in your favour, especially if you made the initial recording or paid for part of it). Otherwise the amount will be shown as a percentage which used to be based on the retail price but is now almost always based on the price to dealers. The dealer price is about 2/3rds of retail so 16% of PDP (published price to dealers) is about the same as 11% of retail (less VAT of course and a host of other reductions and deductions which make it very hard to work out what you can really expect to receive). It's nice to know what you'll get in pence per single or album but never have the royalty expressed in pence as you'll sooner or later be left behind by inflation. Remember these royalties are payable for the whole life of copyright (50 years) of the record and a lot of 50-year-old records are still selling consistently.

A new artist may start with a royalty of around 16-18% of PDP depending on the buzz surrounding you and the negotiating skill of your manager or lawyer but this will only be for full price albums in the UK. This would equate, on a full-price album with a PDP (before VAT) of about £8 to £1.25-£1.30p (some companies' PDP for a full-price album may be up to £1 more in which case you'll need to add slightly more than 10% to these figures, but if your royalty is based on the 'actual realised price' which the record company gets from record stores, chains etc. then it will probably be less). Remember this is split between all of you if you're a band, so it pays to be a 3- or 4-piece and pay session fees to the horn players and backing vocalists! All other releases will be at a reduced rate, even singles usually. Other than in the case of dance music, most singles are regarded as a necessary loss-leader purely to gain airplay and promote sales of the album they're from. Although they can make big money, they're not expected to.

Note that if you have a hit at the end of the contract with a record you made at the beginning, you'll invariably be paid at the rate which applied when the recording was made. The rates for foreign sales can be lower. They may be expressed as the same rate but based on the price at which your UK company is paid, which might include more deductions. (Eire should count as UK by the way). Foreign rates may be around 75% of whatever the UK company receives from its overseas affiliates or licensees (without saying how much that's likely to be)

Will I be paid for every record sold?

You may only be paid on 90% of actual sales, occasionally less. This is to cover returns, breakages and faulty records etc. Suppose you know that your record has sold 100,000 (incidentally beware of sales figures shown in the music press, as publicity people tend to exaggerate and a high chart entry could be down to hyping). Suppose your royalty works out at £1.25p per record, then don't expect to get £125,000. Why? Firstly, the 100,000 gross sales becomes 90,000 (or less) net. Then there will be 'container charges' on all forms of actual disc or tape (even still sometimes on Internet downloads where there is no container at all!) of up to say 20% for a CD in a perspex 'jewel case' (down to 72,000 from 90,000). Then there will be no payment on albums distributed for promotional purposes (even though some of these may be sold) – down to say 70,000. (i.e. your royalty is now down to around £90,000).

All of this is for full-price albums. For almost any other kind of release, your royalty will usually be reduced as follows:
only 50%-75% of your royalty for CD singles (maybe up to a certain limit)
only 50% for CDV, CDI and the like and possibly as low as this for Internet use even though you may see no logical reason why there should be a deduction
only 50% for double-albums, soundtrack albums and compilation albums

only 50% for 'budget' albums

only 50% for TV advertised albums

only 50% for sales through mail-order and record clubs

only 50% for sales to libraries, charities, government organisations and the like.

These may be shown as a percentage of your full-price album rate or the agreement may specify that, for example, singles are at 12% PDP etc.

Then you'll get nothing at all for records deleted, records sold as scrap, promotional records solely promoting your records, coloured vinyl and other unconventional releases. Remember this could include records given away or sold cheaply to chain stores to encourage sales. As a writer you get paid on most of them, but as an artist you won't.

As budget albums are cheaper and therefore the normal royalty would in any case be low this may seem a bit tough, but it's normal. However, budget frequently means anything up to 75% of the price of normal chart albums – try to get the definition of budget in your agreement down to half or two-thirds of full price if possible and try to get them to pay you as high a royalty as possible on albums they sell cheaply to chain-stores to try to increase your overall sales. They may give your records away free, in which case you'll get nothing, but you should at least know what they're doing. Also if there's a limit to the number of TV advertised albums or CDIs at half royalty before you get the full royalty, this will usually be for each separate release, not all your singles or albums added together, and will be for sales in each country of each release, not all countries added together. These reductions are fairly usual especially for a new artist, but are not cast in stone. For a dance act with a successful single see the quick reference section.

In 2002 BMG Records, one of the major record labels, declared that they would offer a much simpler formula across the board (and Universal Records did the same, notably with regard to Internet usages) which is something for which the MMF had been campaigning for years (basically making it much simpler to work out what the artist is owed). Under the sort of agreement BMG were referring to there would be no packaging deductions, no '75% of statutory rate controlled composition clauses' in the USA, less delays before you are paid, shorter deals, no (or far fewer) deductions for budget records, TV advertised records etc. and even a set amount of recording costs per album which are not recoupable from your royalties. Don't automatically expect this 'alternative' from your record company, but it's worth asking about it, or something like it.

Needless to say the record companies are not giving something for nothing – they will expect the basic royalty rate to be lower and will regard the above as giving them the right to own your recordings for longer without the possibility of a legal challenge to their rights (something the managers' and artists' organisations have always resisted, if ultimately the cost of the recordings comes out of the artists' royalties). Also it reduces the record companies' administration costs – remember, they have to pay to employ people to work out exactly how much *not* to pay you under the normal complicated deals!

Who pays the recording costs?

This is the biggest deduction of all! Except in the above scenario, you do (or rather the record company pays them, and of course takes all the risks in doing so, but will recover them all from your royalties). If a record label pays you ₤200,000 as an advance/recording budget for a first album, using our calculations you'd have to sell around well over that number of albums before you're in credit. If you as a band managed to make the album for ₤150,000 and use the rest to live on, buy equipment etc. then it doesn't seem quite so bad as long as you don't have to survive on that for more than a year at the outside (it's amazing where the money goes). Incidentally the advance may well be split 50% on signing and the rest on delivery and/or on the date of release of the album.

However almost anything else the record company paid out specifically on your behalf, whether it be photo sessions, showcases, TV and radio advertising, independent promoters, even tour support to promote the album and the cost of company staff accompanying you, will all be added to the costs they recover before paying you (subject to precise negotiations). Do try to avoid missing engagements, sessions etc. as all the costs will be deducted from your royalties. Being a so-called 'bad boy or girl of rock' may attract publicity but can be very expensive, even without the traditional wanton acts of destruction like smashing guitars on stage or riding a Harley Davidson round your hotel room. If you're going to end up losing a fortune, don't let it be through simply not getting out of bed early enough in the morning!

Who pays for promo videos?

Again the record company pays, and this time they should generally only deduct half the cost from your record royalties (hooray!). The other half will, however, be deducted from any income (and this may be considerable) from retail sales and other uses of the video. Again the record company will continue to own it. Clearly if you can get away with an 'artistic' live video for your first single on an independent label at £10,000 or so and don't need too many takes, you'll be making money sooner than if you spend the £100,000 or so which established artists can easily spend especially if they insist on using a well-known video or film producer or an unnecessarily exotic location. If each of three videos for three singles from your album cost £100,000 then at 50% recoupable from general royalties that's another £150,000 before you see a penny (i.e. around another 200,000 copies that your album will have to sell).

If you want to make your own promo video as part of your 'sales pitch' to a record company, it's often possible to find a local art college student prepared to help you make a good basic video for a fraction of the proper commercial cost. If it turns out really well then the record company might want to use it, and you'll have saved several thousand pounds and launched his career into the bargain.

So do I end up owning the recordings?

Ah, that's the catch. Under a re-negotiation you might be able to come to some arrangement on this where you lease the masters back to the company at some time in the future, for example. Otherwise, the record company continues to own them even though in practice you've paid for them if they're successful. They will own the actual physical multi-track master tape, or computer diskettes used in making the masters, and also the separate right to remix, release and exploit these, but the owner of the actual recording doesn't automatically own the right to exploit it unless it's covered in his agreement. If you, or your manager, can do a deal where the recordings are just licensed (rather than assigned) to the record company for say 10-20 years then if the record company is in 'material' (i.e. serious) breach of its obligations to you and doesn't put this right during the 'cure' period, then you can actually get your rights back and start exploiting them yourself and they'd then have to sue you, if they really thought they had a case, rather than the other way round. Record companies are gradually relenting on this point.

Who pays the producer or remixer's royalty?

Again, the record company normally makes the agreement with the producer and any remixers and pays the costs, advances and royalties, but they'd expect to deduct that from your royalties. If the royalty is 16% and the producer wants 4% for UK, 2% or 3% overseas then your royalty goes down accordingly. If a remixer wants another 1% again it comes out of your share unless the producer allowed it to be deducted from his, which is possible. Producers will probably want a fee too, which may be an advance against their royalty, and be payable part up-front and part on completing the recordings. This is partly because the record company will have the option to reject some of the tracks and replace them with the same or different tracks by another producer. In some cases remixers may take a flat fee and no royalty, but all of this goes down as part of recording costs and normally comes out of your royalty as an artist. Even if you owned the original recording and licensed it to the record company, they would insist on owning any remixes that they saw fit to make and pay for themselves (and that's assuming the remixers themselves, if they were big names, didn't want to retain an interest in their mix).

Who chooses the producer and can I cut him out and produce myself?

Depending on the deal, and your experience, either you will ask to use a particular producer, generally one you're already in contact with or the label will recommend someone. Sometimes the label will only sign you if you agree to a particular producer. They'll probably have a list of producers who have worked for them before and who they can trust to do the job well and within budget. If so, he should hopefully be someone you rate highly already, and you should ask the label what his royalty will be – see the last question. He should be interested enough to want to hear you play the tracks live and discuss them with you before going into the studio.

If you know what sounds it's possible to get out of the average collection of outboard equipment in a studio, and have a good rapport with the studio's resident sound engineer, then you could produce yourself. The engineer will know how to get the sounds you want as long as you know what sounds you actually do want. However it's not to be recommended. Even major artists who could produce themselves and have done so, still like to use a producer, partly because it's easy to become self-indulgent or unnecessarily perfectionist, and it helps to have an expert's outside opinion.

What if I can't help missing a session etc.?

The record company should always give 'reasonable prior notice' of any sessions etc. they want you to attend. They'll usually be as helpful as possible in finding a date and time which are convenient to you although the contract will state that provided they give you reasonable notice then you must be there.

Some contracts state that if you fail to

turn up for no good reason then you have to pay, or have deducted from your royalties, the entire cost of the session booked, including cancellation fees to the studio, backing musicians, orchestras etc. If you have a perfectly good excuse for your absence then this could be grossly unfair on you. If, on the other hand, you continually fail to appear at sessions which you have previously agreed were perfectly convenient for you then of course you are being grossly unfair to the record company. They will probably lose patience and drop you unless you are a megastar, in which case they will excuse you on the grounds of 'artistic temperament'! (but the costs will still come out of your royalties).

When will I be paid?

Royalties should be paid at least twice yearly to your manager or to you at your last known address, so whatever you do make sure you tell them if you move. The contract may say that they'll pay you 'as soon as possible' after June 30 and December 31, which really is too vague. Try to make sure that it says 'within X days after ...' (sixty is perfectly normal, although it may sound a long time). Make sure that the record company will continue to pay you on records made by you which are sold by the label or its licensees after the contract has finished. Generally they should be payable for the whole of the remaining period of 50 years in which the recording remains copyright in the UK. You'd think this would be obvious, but at least one international record company has issued contracts in the past stating that the royalties cease at the end of the contract, even though they can go on selling the artist's records! Some companies will pay quarterly, or make 'payments on account' on March 31 and September 30. It's as much down to their administration as to your bargaining power.

Can they stop paying my artist royalties for any reason?

Another major company's contract allows them to withhold your royalties if you lose your voice or talent or if you die before the contract has finished. As these reasons are beyond your control this is totally unfair to you (or your next of kin) as is the withholding of royalties if you are unable, through no fault of yours, to turn up for sessions as we mentioned earlier (it's possible to insure against such things – see 'General Q & A'). If they are hit with a lawsuit by, for example, another company claiming to control your recording services exclusively, then they'd have the right to suspend payment, though they should only do so once a writ has been issued and, if you are successful, should then pay you, with interest, once the case has been tried or settled. In any event they should continue to send you statements telling you what you've earned.

What happens about photographs and publicity?

Under the contract, you give the company the right to use your name, biography, photographs etc. for publicity purposes. These should be approved by you or your manager. They may well expect to own the photos etc. which they themselves have arranged for you, or expect you to supply them with photos which they can use however they like free of payment to

Thats not me?!

SCROTTY BOYLES!

you. Try to limit their use to album inserts, posters, press advertisements etc. (i.e. only things directly connected with their advertising and sale of recordings of you). The record company will want to produce electronic press kits (something on DVD to give to the press to promote you which will include your songs, or extracts of them together with interviews etc.) and there's no reason not to allow them to do this – at the start, publicity is all-important.

Can I stop my tracks appearing on a compilation album?

Generally the record company have the right to license your recordings to any compilation company or to include them in their own compilations, whether this means a high-price current package of 20 hits currently in the charts or a very low priced collection of sometimes literally dozens of old reggae hits from the Seventies, New Romantic hits from the Eighties or whatever. If you get to the stage of renegotiating a better deal, you could ask for approval (not to be unreasonably withheld or delayed) before your tracks are used on any compilation.

What are compilation album sales worth?

The albums of chart hits may sell two or three times as well as your current hit single itself! So the royalties can be quite substantial. If your track is dance or mainstream pop it could wind up on 10 or more UK compilations and 30 or 40 worldwide, all while the single is still in the charts. If you're with a smaller company they're less likely to worry which other companies they license their tracks to, so you'll probably end up on more compilations than if you were with a 'major'. Your royalty will probably be lower on compilations by other companies than compilations by your own, but

cumulatively this can be a huge source of income. All this additional income can help to recover the recording and other costs which will be deducted before you get paid, and can make a big difference.

Having said this, just one track of yours on one very cheap budget compilation, even if it sells several hundred thousand, will probably only bring in a few hundred pounds in royalties for you as the artist, just as it would for you as the songwriter

What happens if I am part of a duo or band?

Try to establish whether the company are really interested in the group, or just one member. If that's you, then you will have to do some heart-searching and decide whether you really want to succeed without your friends.

They will probably want each of you to sign identical contracts individually, then there will be one 'collateral' agreement which deals with advances etc. You will end up sharing the total royalty equally. The individual contract may well say that the artist royalty is, in effect, '16%' or suchlike but it will then go on to say that the royalty is reduced pro rata with other artists performing on the recording who are entitled to receive royalties. The 'other artists' of course will be the rest of the group who each have identical agreements. Although this wording will also cover the record company if they want you to record with another of their contract artists, it definitely shouldn't mean that your royalties are reduced pro rata with any session musicians playing on your records.

What happens if the band splits up?

If you leave the band before it has any success then a record company will probably not be interested in you and will not take up their next option on your contract. But you'll still be under contract to them till that time. If you went off and joined a group under contract to some other company during that time then the first record company may well take legal action against you and/or the new company. So if you leave a band make sure that everyone who has a hand in your career knows of your intentions and that you are absolutely clear of one company before recording for another. It's worth asking for something in writing confirming this.

If the company want to keep you as a solo artist then your contract should make it clear that from then on in you won't just get a quarter (or whatever) of the advances and royalties the band would have got when you make your solo albums. If the band splits completely remember that unless you're very successful there's every chance you'll all be dropped. There are only so many acts any company can cope with on its roster at any one time.

If someone else joins your band, he'll be expected to sign the same agreements as the existing members. If he's already signed to another label and your company has to negotiate with his to get him free, it's likely you'll all end up having the legal costs deducted from your royalties, plus any percentage of future earnings that the new company has to pay to his old label (for further information on band names see the next section).

Is it right that some bands don't play on their own records?

It used to be very common. Standards of musicianship are improving and technology makes it easier to 'drop in' and re-record over any mistakes, but it can still happen. Acts making their own albums and 'delivering' them as finished products to the label also means this happens less these days. But studio time is expensive and a band member who's perfectly OK live might have a 'block' in the studio. If by any chance this does happen to you, don't worry about your royalties – you will get your share of whatever is due under the contract regardless though the cost of the session musicians will be deducted from your royalties.

Will I have any say in album designs or notes?

You won't have the final say, but the label should take your views into consideration. You shouldn't end up like Spinal Tap, being shown their 'none more black' album cover as a *fait accompli*, but remember though that the design is a major selling factor and the record company should know best. It's the kind of point which can be changed in your favour on re-negotiation, but remember you wind up paying out of your royalties for any complex holograms, computer graphics and the like, and if you're too self-indulgent then your sales and your royalties might suffer. If you yourself can commission the artwork (the local art college being the place to look first) then, provided the record company are happy with it, there'll be less cost to deduct from your royalties and you should be able to retain the ownership of it and use it yourself for merchandising- logos on sweatshirts, posters etc. (but make sure you've paid for it and you own it outright or your art college friend could hold you to ransom in the future over the use of it).

The record company would expect to spend £1,000+ on the artwork (recoupable from your royalties) for your album and they would definitely own it if they commissioned it, so it's worth trying to come up with something yourself.

Should songwriting and merchandising be mentioned in the contract?

There should be no mention in the contract of your songwriting services. Even today some companies try to pick these up in the record contract as though it were quite normal. In fact it's nothing of the kind, and if you were already signed to a publisher as a blanket writer and you then signed a record contract with this in it you'd end up in the middle of a legal wrangle! If your songs are published by your record label's publishing company, it should be under a totally separate agreement with that company.

Some record companies' contracts also allow them to market goods such as T-shirts with your name, image or logo, but you should try to limit the label to records, tapes and videos only (see 'What should I know about merchandising?' in the next section) as the label will probably pay you a fraction of what your manager could get for you. They'll also be able to offset the income against your recording costs etc.

Who decides what songs I should record and what gets released?

The record company will have the final decision, but it's only really MOR acts who are more or less told what to record. Country acts frequently record other people's songs, but these days they're usually new songs chosen by the artist or producer. Newly-signed acts will be expected as a matter of course to write or at least co-write almost all their own material, even, to be honest, if writing isn't their strong point.

The producer may bring in some songs from contacts he has with writers or publishers, or he might be a writer himself. With dance acts or 'boy/girl' bands this is that much more likely. Don't dismiss ideas for outside songs if the label or producer suggest them, but equally if you really don't like them, do say so!

If they want you to re-record a track you did a few years back for a previous label, check to make sure your agreement with that label doesn't prevent you. About 3-5 years from the date your last deal ended would be the normal length of time which has to elapse before you can re-record a track. Much more than that would probably be a restraint of your trade and they couldn't stop you, but the copyright people at your new company will usually be prepared to check old agreements if necessary to ensure you're OK to do it.

The record company will also have the final say as to which tracks go on the album and which are released as singles, but again they should consult you.

How do the records get promoted?

Record labels have promotion budgets for all their releases. Majors have internal promo departments but still sometimes also employ outside independent promoters. These usually ask a set fee per week per record plus big bonuses if the records reach a certain chart position. Even if your label won't commit to spend a certain amount, try to ask for your records to be A-list priorities or that the label will use its 'best endeavours' to promote them.

You or your manager or publisher can employ promoters separately, though try to ensure that they work with the label rather than imply that the label's people can't or won't do the job properly.

Independent promoters are not cheap. Good ones can even expect to get a royalty of say 1% of PDP on sales of the record their promoting, but they are well worth the money because media exposure is all-important. One hit can change your life and you and they both know that!

Is there any alternative to the normal recording agreement?

It's possible these days to try to negotiate an agreement under which you and the record company jointly own your masters. One major act from the Nineties recently re-signed to a major label on the basis of a deal under which the artist would bear a substantial part of the huge marketing budget for their new album in return for huge (over 300%) increase in their potential earnings (percentage-wise) from the label for the new album. It would be exploited in all media to the maximum reasonable extent and the artist would get the rights back sooner rather than later and certainly the label wouldn't acquire the rights, as normal, for life of copyright, subject to possible reversions for inactivity.

You should certainly get back your own master recordings, though not necessarily the multi-tracks to enable you to remix them, within a few years if you are re-negotiating or you have any kind of a track record at all. Even for a boy/girl band and pop/dance records on the basis that the record company takes a share (say 50%) in a jointly-owned company with you which then also negotiates the publishing of your songs, manufacture and distribution of merchandise/streaming of live concerts etc. The idea would be that the record company would pay you an advance (though not a fortune) but would then help to negotiate these other deals and would share in them (i.e. recoup their advance to you from their share of income from them) and thus be prepared to sign you to an album deal when they otherwise might not have

bothered. It is still to be seen how successful this formula is, but it's worth discussing if it might be on offer.

How would I get out of a recording contract?

Ultimately of course a record company can't make you go into a studio and record. If you've hardly earned anything from your records, and don't expect to, then you won't be bothered with any threat to withhold your royalties. However, the best way out of a recording contract, as with a publishing contract, is by mutual agreement, although you should expect to be asked to pay back any advance payment that the record company has given you which they haven't yet recovered from your royalties. Of course there are occasionally instances where the record company itself is happy for the deal to end, to save having to pay you further huge advances which it promised you but now can't be sure of getting back (only likely to happen after a re-negotiation, it must be said). Thus Mariah Carey was famously paid no less than a reported $28 million as part of an agreement whereby her recording agreement was terminated early.

Have the record company exercised their options on time?

They may not have taken up one of their options to extend the contract. This may mean waiting till a certain date and hoping that the letter of extension doesn't arrive. If it doesn't then write to them straight away telling them politely that you note that they haven't taken up their option to renew and in view of this you intend to place your services elsewhere. Do remember though that if you carry on recording for them for some time after the renewal date, even though the contract was not properly renewed, then your position becomes less strong. You may be required to tell them that the option is due to give them a chance to exercise it. Also they may have sent it to your old address because you failed to tell them you'd moved. This would really undermine your case, although normally they'd also have to have sent a courtesy copy of this sort of correspondence to your lawyer, so he'd be aware of it.

Have the record company failed to account to you properly?

Secondly, they may have failed repeatedly to send royalty statements to you at the times set out in the contract, usually twice a year. If the contract says that they are not obliged to send a statement when there is little or no money due to you then this is probably the reason if you have had no statements for a while. Otherwise the statements should have arrived even if no money was due. If it has been over a year since you last received a statement, write pointing this out and asking for one. After a few weeks write again (politely, not threateningly), and if you again receive no reply you have probably been sufficiently reasonable and the company sufficiently unreasonable for you to rescind (i.e. simply declare yourself free from) the contract.

Have the record company failed to record or release what they promised?

Thirdly, it may be that the record company has failed to record or release the agreed number of tracks with you during the current term of the agreement to enable them to renew (obviously you will have to wait until the end of the current term before you can say this for certain). Even if they're only committed to record the tracks, not release them, if they didn't release them within a certain period after 'delivery' or 'completion' this could be a restraint of your trade. If of course you just haven't met your delivery dates because you never got round to doing final mixes or some such reason then you can't blame them for not releasing on time. Make sure you know what's expected of you.

Do consult your lawyer, even if it's only a brief phone call, before putting anything in writing when trying to get out of an agreement. He'll always try to estimate what his charge is likely to be if he has to get involved, although he won't of course be able to tell you very precisely until he knows exactly how you stand. If you are wanted by another record company they may put their business affairs people onto the case for you. In your particular circumstances there may be some other way of getting free, but the power that record companies inevitably have over their artists is well-publicised thanks to the likes of George Michael's epic court battle with Sony and 'the Artist' appearing once at the UK Brit Awards with 'Slave' written across his face.

Will I be completely tied to the company?

Your services will be exclusive to the record company, so make sure you ask them first if you want to do even one session for another company (they'll very often go along with this provided they get a royalty and credit on the record). If a record company wishes to sign you up, but you're playing regularly on sessions elsewhere, you may be able to get them to sign you exclusively under your own name, but leave you free to work elsewhere unnamed or under pseudonyms. There's no limit to the number of these you can have as an artist.

They'll require you not to re-record for another company any song which you recorded for them for a number of years after the contract has finished as we mentioned in the last section. Incidentally until recently the USA record companies were trying to regard their artists, in legal terms, as people who just happened to be employed by them (under 'contracts for hire') to come in and make records as employees. Happily this came to court in 2002 and the artists won.

Should I sign with an independent record production company?

Independent producers are very often management/publishing concerns or established record producers who are prepared to invest in the making of masters speculatively sometimes rather than 'to order' from record labels, especially if they have studio facilities on tap. Unlike most of the record companies, good independent producers are not restricted to London or other major music centres. It's possible you could be recording a demo in a local studio to find that they are so knocked out that they're prepared to give free studio time if they can have the recording to sell to a label.

They lease the records to the label in return for a royalty of well over 20% (a lot more than you could expect to get as an artist) of PDP out of which they should pay you as an artist roughly what you'd have got if you'd signed directly to a label either as, say 17% of PDP or as say 66.66% of what they get (more in the case of production companies that are part of management companies trying to do an all-in deal with you – see Management section). They will want to sign you up for a total of several years just as a record company itself would, because the record company they lease your records to will expect options on further singles or albums. There is no reason at all why you should not sign with an independent producer but you should know or find out exactly what his track record is, and what he intends to try to do for you. Try to make especially sure that your agreement with an independent

producer gives you some protection in case nothing happens at all.

If you're signing exclusively to an independent producer, rather than just making a single or two to 'see what happens' then he should guarantee to record a certain number of tracks just as a label would. What he can't of course do is guarantee that they will be released. And here is the problem. The most straightforward royalty split will be a straight division between you of all royalties he gets in, less the recording and any other direct costs which are agreed. However until he's found an interested label and done the deal, neither of you knows what the overall royalty to be split will be, or how many options over how many years the label will want. It's another chicken and egg situation. A label may be interested in you but may insist that you sign with them direct rather than through the independent producer. In that case he may be prepared to let you, provided that the label pays him a separate royalty ('an override'). If he's prepared not to sign you till he knows all this then fine, but you can't expect him to leave it, as he's guaranteeing your services to the label. It could be that he'll have a deal to make the first singles and album and then you'll sign directly to the label for any future options. If so, this will be covered in the inducement letter.

Will I have to sign an 'inducement letter'?

The record company itself will probably ask you to sign a small agreement called an inducement letter directly to the record company. Under this, if you and your independent production company split, or he goes out of business before the end of his deal with the record company, then you have to record directly for the record company for the rest of the duration of that deal. If the inducement letter states that you will, at that point, sign the record company's standard artist agreement or a similar phrase then ask to see it, as it may contain certain clauses whereby you end up with less than the royalty the independent producer was paying you! Again, read and try to understand everything you are asked to sign.

Should I let them record me before I've signed anything?

It does happen, more often than you'd think, that a company will pay to record and release records prior to getting the artist or producer to sign an agreement. This certainly avoids having to pay an advance before release, and you may not be able to dispute their ownership of the recordings later if you co-operate now on an *ad hoc* basis.

However this should ultimately be to your advantage, since if the first release is successful they'll want another and will have to offer you more by way of advances, royalties, promotion etc. than you'd have asked for before you'd had the first hit. If they don't offer it, some other company will, and they'll have trouble stopping you leaving, even though they may try to make it awkward. Some companies offer 'development' money or studio time to record you prior to taking the plunge and signing you. This is quite deliberate and you could walk away from it, but they hope that it'll buy them some time to assess your potential while making you feel beholden to them. If you do leave, they may be prepared to sell you the recordings, but they'll have no right to release them without your permission, and you could go off and re-record the same songs elsewhere immediately if you wished.

GENERAL QUESTIONS AND ANSWERS ON RECORDING

Could I make my own records?

If you're thinking of starting your own label because no-one else will release your records, think about your act's personnel, your material, your demo's and your general image first. If you're still convinced you're right and they're all wrong (unlikely but it's always possible- it has been known!) then start looking for finance to go it alone. In recent years many independent producers, including many outside London, have taken to pressing their own records in small quantities and getting someone else to distribute them. Some of these small labels have become very successful, usually with a specific type of music, up to the point where they've been bought out by one of the majors. Some are actually owned and run by a band or artist themselves, who have had some money behind them but were unable or unwilling to get a deal with an established record company. These are not to be confused with 'labels' which some record companies give to their established stars who think they've discovered someone else amazing (which really does happen e.g. Diana Ross 'discovering' The Jackson 5, Madonna signing Alanis Morissette to her own label etc.). Further down the scale from this is a one-off album or single recorded and pressed by a semi-professional act to sell at gigs or for charity (see next question).

As we said in the songwriting section, it is possible, especially with dance or mainstream pop to make a credible recording on home studio equipment. More and more people own digital all-in-one studios or have computers with software such as Cubase or Protools together with CD burners and they really only need studios for mixing down and adding the outboard effects they can't afford to buy.

It's then perfectly possible to take your finished master recording to a pressing plant and have CDs produced from it. For dance/pop recordings, before you can ask for vinyl to be pressed, you need a 'stamper' from which the pressings can be made. For vinyl these are made from lacquered discs which have to be 'cut' from the master recording. At this stage certain frequencies can predominate and make a big difference to the sound of the finished discs so you should supervise the cutting rather than leave it to others.

The minimum sensible quantity you can expect to have pressed up is normally 500 (plus or minus around 10% as they can't always stop the machine exactly at the required figure) although it's a lot cheaper per pressing to have 1,000 and so on. The pressing plant can advise on printing of labels and sleeves/cases if necessary and on the likely cost. Around 1,000 CDs of a 40-minute album should still cost £1 each or less and 1,000 12″ vinyl singles would be about 40p each, though with mastering, labels, sleeves and artwork/reproduction costs for labels etc. you'd be looking at about £1,500-2,000 in total. You obviously wouldn't have any artist royalties to pay on sales if you're the artist, but if your songs are handled by a publisher then he would have to allow MCPS to collect mechanical royalties on pressings, even though the bulk of the royalties would eventually find their way back to you. MCPS liaise with the pressing plants, so they'll know which songs you've recorded and if you call them they'll help you with the straightforward paperwork. Incidentally, beware of giving away free gifts ('widgets') with copies of your record if you're hoping that it will make the charts, as there are rules about this and from time to time records are disqualified for having an unfair advantage over their competitors through some add-on or giveaway.

How can I get my records distributed?

If you're selling them at gigs or distributing white-label 12″ singles to DJ's and specialist record shops yourself then fine, but assuming you've managed to get some airplay, even just locally, it's no use the public going to record shops to buy it if the dealers have never heard of it and don't know where to order it. At this stage you really need professional distribution.

The distribution companies used to be owned and run by the majors record companies, but they have since sold them off, no doubt looking to the future of digital downloading or streaming. However most music is still sold in the old way and the distribution companies are still there. They will charge around 25-30% of PDP to distribute for you and they will want you to agree to distribute all your follow-up recordings through them for a given period (if you sign to a major record label in the meantime this will probably override that provision, but check!), especially if you were so 'hot' that they gave you an advance on the strength of it, which is possible. They may require you to supply 'dealer mailings' to be sent to all the dealers in Britain or they may include you on theirs. Some will be more amenable to one-off or small numbers of releases than others. The one thing you should ensure is that you remain throughout the actual owner of the recording.

It is possible to put new recordings on a web site on the Internet. Record companies, publishers and others have these and you could arrange your own, or use the services of a company which for a small charge makes recordings available

for downloading at a pre-set fee by the public who will go to that site looking for good new material. This is an exciting prospect, but the market is still relatively limited for this and you'd probably do this in addition to pressing up copies rather than instead of it (see the separate section on the Internet for more details).

If you want to stand a chance of making the charts you'll have to register your 'label' with the chart compilers (the current compilers' name and address will be listed in the trade magazine *Music Week*). Incidentally you should check any P&D deal you have to release your records to see whether they intend to charge you (or offset against the amounts they owe you) for publicity or advertising which they organise.

Is it any different with charity records?

If an established artist wishes to appear on a 'Live Aid' type record or video his or her record company will usually have no problem. If you want to release your own charity record you'll need to go through the process of recording, manufacture and distribution mentioned in the last two questions. If you can persuade any of the people involved to do it for nothing, or at least for no profit or at a discount, so much the better, but just because the local Dogs' Home is very deserving doesn't guarantee that they'll say yes, any more than that the local radio station will play the record. As we've said, the publishers who own the songs can't waive their right to let MCPS collect the royalties on their behalf, but they might well be prepared to pay their share and the writers' shares if they're agreeable to it straight to your charity once they've received the royalties from MCPS.

Who owns the copyright in my recordings?

In principle you own your recordings but you assign all rights to your record company when you sign to them, though you might be able to negotiate to get them back after a period of 10, 15, 20 years or more. Just as there is a copyright in a song as soon as it exists in 'tangible form' (i.e. a recording or manuscript) there is also copyright in the recordings themselves, even though they may of course contain someone else's copyright, namely the song. Copyright in the recording in most countries now lasts 50 years from the end of the year when it was first 'published', in other words first released. If a track is remixed and re-released years later then the copyright in that mix starts from the first release of the mix. Even a cleaned-up re-mastered version of the original recording will have 50 years from the date of its first release too. There is also copyright in television programmes, films etc. which in turn will usually contain both copyright recordings and also copyright songs, so if you video'd them you'd be breaching at least three different copyrights.

All this makes clearance of rights by audio-visual producers and multi-media companies so complex that they frequently resort to commissioning their own music to ensure they're not exceeding the bounds of the licence they've been given for an already existing recording or song. This makes everything from feature films to computer games a potential source of new commissions for music writers and producers.

A record company will put a P in a circle plus the year of first release of the recording on each of their records, together with the company which first produced or now owns the master recording. Right from the start the copyright in the recording belongs to the label and not to you unless you made it at your own expense and only leased it to the label. Otherwise if the recording was organised and paid for by them, then they own the copyright in it. They will also own the phonographic performance right in it (the right to broadcast or perform it in public) and the rental right, and all

other so-called 'neighbouring rights' which exist in recordings, although you as an artist or producer now have legal rights to a share of the income from these too.

Is anything payable when a record is broadcast?

Yes. As well as the PRS collecting from broadcasters for use of the songs, sums are also collected by an organisation called 'Phonographic Performance Ltd'. This is then paid equally to the record company, provided it's a member, and the artist separately. Many artists collect their shares through an organisation called PAMRA to which PPL pays their money and there is another organisation called AURA which was set up by the Music Managers' Forum to do the same thing. Since the time that this right was granted directly to artists by law, it has taken years for PPL to work out precisely who played on which records. They have even had a team of highly respected producers and session musicians such as 'Big' Jim Sullivan and Herbie Flowers meeting to try to recall who played what on a particular track which may have made the top 30 in 1966! All the musicians and singers in theory should be credited and receive a share whenever the record is broadcast, albeit a very small amount. The total to be divided up amounts to several million pounds a year, so don't think this isn't worth bothering about.

Your record company can tell you what you need to do, or you can contact PAMRA or AURA, or PPL directly (addresses in our 'useful address' list). If your record is getting airplay then you should be assured of these fees provided the organisations know who and where you are. If you're a 'featured' artist, i.e. generally your name, or the name of a group of which you are a regular member, appears on the record label then you'll get more than if you were just a session musician. There's also an organisation called VPL (Video Performance Ltd.) which performs the same function when music videos are broadcast. PPL have introduced a database called CatCo which enables its members (3,000 or thereabouts) to register their catalogues of recordings directly on-line to PPL and in theory most recordings should be there, together with vital information regarding the artists, helping to streamline the payment of PPL royalties.

If I'm offered a royalty or session fee which should I take?

If you are not signed exclusively to one record company, but are a musician playing on sessions for various companies or a diva singing 'guest' vocals on records for various producers, there may be occasions when you will be offered either a session fee or a royalty on a particular recording. Generally if you are a 'featured' artist (i.e. your name will appear on the record label) you should choose the royalty just in case the record becomes a hit. There have been a number of hits over the years which made the national press because the artist only got a session fee. Obviously if you really need the ready money and you don't think the record stands an earthly chance of selling, or if you really don't trust the company to account royalties to you properly, you'll have to decide the case on its merits.

Is it a good idea to give my writing and recording services to the same company?

Not necessarily. The majors run their publishing arms as entirely separate operations and shouldn't try to cross-collateralise your royalties from recording and publishing. However, some artist/writers feel, sometimes unfairly, that when checking up on royalty accountings etc., you may get less assistance from the company's own publishing associate than from an entirely separate publisher.

What should I know about recording sessions?

You probably already know what goes on at a professional recording session even if you have never actually taken part in one yourself. The two vital people at a session, besides the artists themselves, are the Producer and the Engineer. The producer decides what sound he wants the instruments and vocals to have and whether anything needs to be re-recorded and at what point the recording has been satisfactorily completed. The engineer sits at the mixing desk in the control room and actually achieves the sounds which the producer wants. The two tasks overlap considerably. Most producers used to be engineers, and could do the whole thing themselves if they were familiar with the equipment of the studio being used. In fact these days almost everyone sits in the control room, as most instruments are direct injected into the mixing desk. The live room is reserved for vocals, horns etc. and the occasional live drummer (something of a novelty for a lot of studios).

Thankfully these days the keyboards can be programmed in advance and put down from the computer, and each other instrument can be recorded separately, though you should still expect to play through some tracks numerous times for the engineer to obtain the right sound before he even attempts to take it. Professional session musicians will expect to be given a copy of the music specially arranged for their instruments and will simply read this off, though if you're lucky and explain yourself well enough they'll hopefully ad lib whatever you want them to play. Bands should have 'routined' the song sufficiently beforehand so that there is no question of them forgetting it if they can't read music or have no music.

A session traditionally lasts three hours but other than in the world of film music, classical music etc. sessions just take as long as needed, usually as long as

you've got, and you can't get very much down in three hours these days, so you'd expect to hire a studio by the day. Ever since the days of The Beatles it's been quite accepted that a band can record complete tracks without ever meeting each other in the studio. Professional session musicians will be expected to arrive with their instruments. For large instruments the musician should receive an additional fee called 'porterage'. A group should ask beforehand whether their instruments and equipment will be wanted on the session. The producer and engineer may think it necessary to hire better equipment or there may be some at the studio already.

What should I expect to pay for studio time?

If you're signed to a label with its own studios, check to see whether they can charge you a 'standard' hourly rate for your sessions and offset this against your royalties. A smaller independent studio will usually do a deal for a 10-12 hour day for perhaps as little as £200-300 for a 24-track or for 'downtime' when they're otherwise empty or for a 'lockout' where you hire the studio for 24 or 48 hours or more. If the desk is new and computerised and there's plenty of outboard

equipment which you otherwise might have to hire in, then the cost will escalate but probably be worth it to you provided of course that you know what it can do. Because of this it's as important to know what 'toys' they have as to know what the basic recording equipment is.

Some studios have their own programming suites which are compatible with the studio and can be hired at much lower rates. Of course if you can do the programming at home then you can save even more.

If you're recording onto tape then the studio will supply the tape, but unless you've paid for it, expect them to retain the master tape (though not, of course, the right to exploit it without your permission). They can run off CDs and DATs or other copies for you, but if they let you bring your own CDs or DATs then they'll be a lot cheaper than 'buying' them from the studio. This applies to reels of 2″ tape as well, though it's harder just to lay your hands on a reel of 2″ tape these days. Even seemingly gratis refreshments put out might be charged to you, especially by larger studios, so it's worth making enquiries, especially if you're paying the bills up-front (rather than just out of your royalties).

A smaller studio may do a deal whereby they don't charge you the full rate in return for an override royalty on your records, but don't expect it. They have to make a living and if they wanted to gamble they'd probably get better odds on the horses, no matter how great you try to persuade them you are.

What should I be paid if I'm asked to produce a record?

As we've said, name producers would expect around 4% royalty in the UK (maybe more) around two-thirds of that overseas, together with fees, part up-front and part on delivery of the recordings. They may be able to choose the studio they work in, or this may already be decided (most producers have preferences for certain studios, as much for the ambience sometimes as for the equipment). A producer with no track record may be offered around 2% royalty or even just a flat fee and if it's your own record or your own band's record that you're producing then don't necessarily expect anything extra, even if you're clearly saving the record company money.

The record company will generally do the negotiations and the paperwork and will sign you directly. They will some-times, but by no means always, only pay the producer royalty once they have recovered not only his advance but also the costs of the production of the record. Naturally this is a very good incentive to you as the producer to keep the costs low. Some freelance producers can earn large sums by way of fees plus royalties and there are even companies acting as agencies for producers, finding them work and negotiating fees.

Of course many producers of dance tracks and a lot of dance-orientated pop tracks are, in effect, the artists, just using a session singer on lead vocals and doing all the rest themselves. In the past pro-duction teams such as Stock, Aitken and Waterman, the Bee Gees and the Motown and Memphis Soul teams used to pro-duce records which would invariably come out under the name of the singer, though the producers would usually be using their own songs and playing some of the instruments and might also either have a share in the ownership of the recordings or else be on a royalty. If you are a producer/artist then you should receive at the very least half the total artist royalty, and hopefully all of it (if you can get the featured vocalist to agree to a session fee). You wouldn't necessar-ily be signed by a label as an exclusive artist/producer, but some larger compa-nies would want to do this (sign you under that artist name for anything up to five or more albums) because this is their company policy, even though their A&R person signed you on the strength of just

one rather good dance track! Some divas who feature on such records have a big enough name to command a high artist royalty in their own right and the record company might want you to guarantee that she'll be singing on the follow-up singles and all these albums too, which both you and she are most unlikely to want to do. In such circumstances you, the producer, should try to decide in advance how much of the royalty you really want to give away on what is basically your record. If it was always envisaged that the track would be released as xxxxx (producer name) featuring zzzzz (lead vocalist) then it will be easier to negotiate the lion's share of the royalty.

What should I be paid if I'm asked to re-mix a record?

Unless you have a big name as a DJ or remixer then you'll probably be offered (usually directly by the record company) a flat fee of a few hundred pounds and maybe a royalty of 0.5%-1% which may come either out of the artists' royalties or the original producer's royalty. If you have a reputation you could receive several thousand pounds per mix. You'd usually expect to go away and do them yourself but if studio costs were expected to be high then the record company might well pay these too.

Is there any organisation representing record producers?

There is an organisation called Re-Pro to which a large number of professional record producers belong. They even have a standard form of agreement for producers to use in respect of their services (though generally such agreements are similar in form to the agreement signed by the artist the producer is working with, though somewhat shorter). Re-Pro's address is in the 'Useful Addresses' section.

What might I get if I'm in a stage show which is recorded?

You will appreciate that a record company will not want to place the entire cast under contract. They probably would not be able to anyway, for many recording artists supplement their income by appearing in stage shows even though they may otherwise be under contract to a record company other than the one which intends to record the show. What generally happens is that each member of the cast receives a session fee for the recording and separately the record company pays an Artist Royalty at the going rate to the Actors Union, Equity.

What might I get if my record is included in a film?

This is completely open to negotiation and varies enormously, but a hit record in a new film with relatively small budget, say £4m or less should bring anywhere from £5,000-£15,000 in all, usually the top end of that for a full usage of say three minutes, and not a lot more even for a blockbuster big budget epic, though it would be a great deal more for a really big song by a big artist. If it's a music film and you're guaranteed to be on the soundtrack album then it may be less, especially as there will be more songs and records for the film company to pay for.

The film company will usually want all media in perpetuity for the territory of the Universe for this, or they just won't want to use your record, though they might pay a bit extra as an option for new media and will usually pay extra for 'out of context' trailers advertising the film. If you're actually asked to appear in the film, a new artist might get around £3,000 or substantially more but as a part of a 'package' with his or her recording and song, while a top artist appearing in a film performing their record could be worth an all-in fee of tens of thousands.

It's such good exposure for you, or

your record, or your song to be in a successful film that the fees are sometimes surprisingly low unless you're already so big that you're helping to sell the film. Unless you started out as an actor (in a 'soap' for example) then this could launch you on a whole new career (if you can act!). From Al Jolson and Bing Crosby in the Twenties and Thirties through the likes of Gary and Martin Kemp from Spandau Ballet, Phil Collins and Madonna right up to the present day, fame as a singer/musician can be a route into straight acting.

MANAGEMENT CONTRACTS

Public entertainers of all types have long been reliant for guidance in their careers upon professional managers. There comes a time in most semi-professional singers' and musicians' careers and even those of non-performing songwriters and producers when they are simply too busy to worry about the business side of things, or when they feel that they are not busy enough and would like somebody to be hustling on their behalf.

Do I need a manager anyway?

This depends upon how busy you are as a performer, how much money you are making, and above all how much money you want to make. It is possible to exist as a semi-professional or even a professional singer or musician for years without a manager, but if you really want to succeed then you really do need a manager- and a good one. In the meantime you can get by with an agent to secure engagements for you, plus an accountant to ensure that you pay as little tax as possible and a solicitor to write the odd letter to any agency or venue which failed to pay you – if the uncollected fee is likely to be greater than the solicitor's charge, of course.

You can even employ your own publicist, and secure your own recording and publishing contracts particularly if you enlist the help of your solicitor or accountant (the relevant sections of this book explain what to do and what to sign). Nevertheless a manager worth his salt should be able to secure better royalty rates and terms than you could get on your own or, even more importantly, a deal with a more suitable company. Indeed he might be able to get you a deal, purely on the strength of his reputation, with a company that would otherwise have turned you down. Bear in mind that some managers who are wizards at securing good live work for high fees may be a lot less well connected and knowledgeable when it comes to recording and publishing.

Record companies and publishers will expect you to have a manager and some, especially record companies, won't sign you without one. They'll even suggest potential managers, even though they know that the one you pick will then start negotiating on your behalf against them! That's how important they think a good manager will be to your career.

Should I have a manager if I'm not a performer?

There are still quite a number of songwriters with no serious aspirations towards being recording or performing artists. Writers, with the aid of their lawyers, usually negotiate with publishers themselves and they would have no other immediate need of a manager. Recording artists on the other hand are usually primarily performers and thus their managers who look after the 'live performance' side of their career usually deal on their behalf with record companies too. This is why the songwriting section of this book is somewhat longer than the others.

However there are people who act in the same sort of way for songwriters as literary agents do for novelists. They try to set up publishing deals, monitor the income, look for work such as film and television commissions etc. in return for a manager's commission. There are also managers working almost exclusively or primarily for record producers and remixers, again using their contacts and knowledge to secure work at good rates for their clients.

How much control of my career will a manager want?

You should thrash this out with him as precisely as you can before signing anything so that it is clearly understood what you both want. In a sense he is 'employing' you and at the same time you are 'employing' him. These days, even if the contract doesn't actually say so, you are usually in practice employing him, and the position of a music manager can be almost as precarious as that of a football manager. For this reason, although a successful management company who have agreements already with other artists will probably have a sort of 'standard' contract, agreements with managers vary enormously. A form of management contract is included in the Contracts Section with notes showing what sort of provisions you may hope to get. However you should definitely get legal advice before signing anything with a manager. Sometimes a one-page agreement is actually worse for you as many aspects are not properly covered, so don't think it's not important. Some acts have been so badly burned by management agreements that they've just given up on otherwise really promising careers, so be warned. If you don't get legal advice, you may be able to overturn an unreasonable agreement by taking legal action against the manager, but do you really want to spend your time trading insults in a court when you could be filming your new video in the Caribbean or headlining on a major European Tour?

What should I look for in a manager?

The first essential is commitment and genuine interest in you and your music. It's harder to sell something you wouldn't buy yourself, and even if the manager believes in you, if he doesn't also like your image and your music then you're better off elsewhere. You may be approached by a big-time management company who will ask you to sign a contract which puts you and your career completely in their hands for a number of years. On the other hand you may find a decent local man or woman (there are quite a few women in management) with a few good contacts to 'manage' you. A manager may be convinced that you'll only succeed if you change your musical direction or buy a lot of new backline equipment (perhaps because he has a friend who deals in this) or wear frilly lurex shirts onstage. He may well know best, but if you really have no desire to do any of this, don't sign with him. Above all, if you're happy at a certain level of success, don't sign with a manager who won't rest till you're a megastar, but do remember that most managers will tell you and everyone else how great you are, and will be hoping, if not expecting, to make a good living for both of you sooner or later (in his case, sooner, in case you go off him and fire him!).

If you already have an agreement, even a verbal one or a scrap of paper, with a small-time manager or just a friend whereby they're supposed to get a cut of your earnings, make sure that you write to them making it clear that you consider it terminated, if it hasn't already lapsed, before signing with a professional manager. You could end up giving so many rake-offs to different people who have helped you at various times in your career that you're left with nothing yourself (except law suits). If you're remotely unsure, take legal advice from someone in the business. This is possibly the single most important point in this book!

Will all my income go through the manager?

A proper manager will usually collect all booking fees, record royalties and songwriting royalties from publishers (though he may not collect PRS royalties, if you're a member of PRS) plus royalties for you from the merchandising of goods bearing your name, image or likeness, fees for television appearances, even opening fetes and supermarkets. What he shouldn't get is a percentage of your income from any source, as this would include money you may earn or be paid completely outside the entertainment business or perhaps in other aspect such as acting (even in theory such things as lottery winnings or legacies from rich relatives!). It's worth asking before you get to the draft contract stage what he considers the 'music' or 'entertainment' business to include. If you're offered a part in a West End musical you'd probably expect him to take his commission. But an acting part in a Hollywood film or a few weeks as a Children's TV presenter? Yes, probably, particularly if he was in any way instrumental in getting you the work. Writing a column for a music magazine or a book about the music business? Again the answer is probably yes, but these are the grey areas which you should not be afraid to discuss, and if you don't like to do it yourself then ask your lawyer to do it for you. Most management agreements will cover these activities unless you agree that they should exclude them

It should depend really on how much of this work he actually secured for you. As all enquiries after a while will go to him, it may be difficult to find out. In general if he negotiated (or re-negotiated) an agreement for you, whether for live work, publishing, recording, filming or whatever, then he should get a cut of all this income including money from songs you wrote or recordings you made, concerts you played etc. under those agreements while he is your manager and quite possibly beyond (see below). If you already had a particular deal before you signed to him he'll probably still expect a share of your income under that deal but possibly only income that's earned while he's actually your manager.

How long will the management contract be for?

The usual period these days is three years. It might be for five years, which wouldn't be unreasonable, though any longer would be – especially so if the agreement said five years + until any money advanced by the manager had been recouped by him, which of course might never happen. In some cases, especially with bands, the agreement might be expressed as 'until x months after the release of the third (or fourth) album' which might well be a lot longer than three years but wouldn't necessarily be unreasonable, if the manager got you the album deal with a record company within say a year of you signing to him and if there's a long-stop date when the recording agreement ends whether the next album is released or not.

What percentage will the manager take?

The manager will probably take 20% of your earnings from the music or entertainment business. With some of this money he could expect 20% of the gross amounts. With others it should be the net profit. You may never make any actual profit from touring. When you're small you have to pay to get onto the tour. When you're big the cost of the sound system, lights, personnel etc. could eat up the whole of the five, six or seven figure fees you get. However some management agreements would give the manager a share of the gross income from those huge fees even if the tour (which he helped to set up and budget for) actually made a loss and even though he might be on a lower percentage – say 10%. His commission on live gigs should be at the full rate, but only on net income, not gross. Most managers should be perfectly happy with this

His commission could be on a sliding scale so that once you're earning £100,000 a year he isn't still getting as high a percentage as he was when you were earning £1,000 a year. If you are in the 'big time' then he will probably collect all your earnings himself and pay you your 80% or whatever at regular intervals. Similarly potential agents, record companies and so forth will know that they must approach him if they wish to make a deal with you. Until you reach that stage you will often be approached by these people direct, and your contract will require you to put them on to the manager, even though you may be tempted to deal with them directly. If any money is accidentally paid directly to you, you'll be obliged to pass it over to the manager (though he really should have to put all this income into an account controlled by him but in your name, out of which his commission and agreed expenses should then be paid at regular intervals). If that's the case you're sort-of paying yourself. This may seem a bit silly from your point of view but he's the one checking up on whether you've been paid properly, so it would only confuse things to go behind his back and keep the money that should have gone to him on your behalf.

What about record company advances that include recording costs?

Your manager should be perfectly entitled to his commission on any

advance paid to you by a record label for your own personal use. He might well have been paying you money to live on for some time already, and can at least now get some of it back. However he shouldn't be able to commission money that's clearly going to be needed to make your first album, so when you get the advance, which he'll probably have negotiated for you anyway, you and he should agree immediately, if not beforehand, how much of this is living expenses on which he can genuinely take a commission, and how much is likely to be needed to record the album, on which he shouldn't take anything.

Will he ever want more than 20%?

Some management companies are effectively publishing companies and independent production companies as well, and in that case they may take anything up to 50% of your overall income from these sources quite legitimately. However you should only agree a deal like that from a company that's already done such a deal for someone who has become a major star (and still is).

How would this work in practice?

Effectively the management company or subsidiaries of it would acquire your exclusive songwriting and recording services then 'license' them on to 'proper' publishers and record companies and in some cases, especially if the manager is acting as an independent production company, making your records and then licensing them to a record company he can get better deal than you would as an artist signing direct – higher royalties and shorter retention period. Remember however that he'll be taking a higher cut of these earnings and also that he will actually own those songs or recordings he makes unless there's a provision for you to get them back once the management agreement has finished (or a few years after) or unless there's some sort of an agreement for you and he to jointly own them.

Isn't 50% a rip-off?

If the agreements are all reasonable and you were properly advised when you signed them, then no. Any manager with this much control of your career, even through separate companies which he has a hand in, is however in danger of falling foul of the law in the UK. The managers of Tom Jones, Engelbert Humperdinck and Gilbert O'Sullivan back in the Sixties and Seventies were sued by Gilbert O'Sullivan for what boiled down to the fact that his agreement put his entire career far too much at the mercy of the managers, who effectively controlled his recordings and his songs, and that they had been taking advantage of this fact. Elton John was another star who eventually sued the organisation which first signed him for management, recording and publishing because he believed it was taking advantage of the fact that his career was too much in their hands. In both instances the companies were thought to have failed in their 'fiduciary duty' to the artist/writer. They hadn't acted in good faith in the artist/writer's best interest as his representative.

Had the recording and publishing deals been for a clearly limited duration and on 'arms length' terms – in other words about as good as anyone could reasonably expect at the time – then this total control would have been seen as pretty much OK provided the term wasn't excessively long and the companies were not just putting recordings and songs on the shelf and doing nothing with them.

Another factor that would have put the artist or writer in a worse position would have been if they had already re-negotiated the deal (however bad it was first

time around) and had been properly advised during the re-negotiation. This was a problem which George Michael had in his well-known legal battle with Sony Records in the Nineties

Who pays for what?

If you're signing with a professional management company the chances are that they'll initially pay for everything, although the contract will make it clear that ultimately it will be you who pays. They'll pay all your travelling expenses plus an allowance to you of so much per week while you're struggling. They won't pay you anything more than that until they have recovered from money earned by you all the money they've specifically expended on you. This won't include their office expenses and overheads but will include for example the cost of a personal manager going on tour with you to check that everything's OK, and staying in the same five-star hotel as you. They may wish to keep you on a low 'spending allowance' per week for some time after you've started to be worth big money, until they're sure that their expenses will not for a long while exceed the income, leaving them out of pocket again.

All this is fine, and it's nice to know they have such faith in you. Obviously a lot of management companies lose a lot of money this way as they should never actually make you pay any of the expenses back, unless perhaps to buy yourself out of the contract. The biggest snag with such a large and benevolent organisation, even if it doesn't have its own agency, recording and publishing companies to which you are also signed, is that you need to make quite sure from someone independent of the management company, before you sign with them, upon what terms they'll be negotiating your recording and songwriting services, and you will have to be quite sure of their trustworthiness.

If all my money comes to me through one person or firm, how can I check up on their honesty?

Even with regular statements from your management to you and even though you know what they're paying you each week in allowances it could become almost impossible for you to work out just what they've spent on you, for you are very much in their hands. You could have hit after hit – the management may give you the money to go out and buy a Rolls or a new house, but are they still advancing you their money or actually paying you what you've earned? Keep asking questions and try not to let success go to your head (easier said than done). You can work out from this book very roughly what should be due to you from a million selling record for instance. If they're honest then regular statements (say once a month or once a quarter) should be sent to you showing exactly how much you've earned and how much they've spent on you and taken in commission. As we said, they should be arranging for all your income to be paid into a separate account in your name so that you can see at any point what's going on, but regrettably you'll still probably lose track of just how much you are owed if you become very successful. (see 'Do I need an accountant?' in 'General Q & A').

Will the manager pay me an advance?

The manager will generally see it as part of his job to get advances from other people – record companies, publishers etc. – to enable you to survive comfortably without a 'proper job' until you're earning big money. Until he's got you these deals, he'll probably – as we've said – pay for anything you need out of his own pocket. He will take his commission on advances as well as royalties that you get, so he might be tempted to do a deal with the company offering the most money up-front, even if it's not the best deal on offer overall. He should however tell you of any alternative deals on offer, even if he does attempt to influence you towards the one with the biggest advance.

How long will he go on getting his commission?

As we mentioned earlier, some management agreements will give him a share on everything you ever get from a deal which he negotiated, even years after he's ceased to be your manager. Say he got you a record deal which lasted five years, but you split with him after two. You'd be happy for him to get his share on records made and sold during those first two years, but does he also get a share of records made during those years and sold forever after, and what about records made during the other three years. He got you the deal, remember. Does he get a share of royalties from sales of those records too? The answer should be to try to limit his share to the period of your agreement with him plus, say, three years afterwards, though most managers will want a further period, maybe 10 years beyond that but at a reduced rate (usually half) of commission.

His ongoing commission should only be in respect of songs you wrote, records you made etc. actually during the term of his management agreement with you, even if you remain signed to the same publisher and record company after you break with the manager. However you might agree to pay him commission on say one more album (and the songs on it) after you split with him, and then preferably at a lower rate, to leave some margin for you to pay a new manager.

A new manager who re-negotiated these deals after your contract with the first manager ended, would expect his 20% on songs or records from then on though he might accept less initially if he's keen to represent you. So, if you're still obligated to the first manager on these, you can see how it can get complicated, and why it really is vital to have legal advice on your particular case. Especially so if you sign to a small-time manager before you've signed to a publisher or record label. If he wants commission to be payable forever then you should say 'no' or (if he insists and you're really anxious to sign) only at a very low rate of commission.

Do I really need to read through contracts secured for me by my manager?

You might like to think that your manager couldn't possibly make a bad deal and he will certainly let you think that he's an expert in everything to do with the music business. Alternatively your contract with him might say that he has the sole right to negotiate the deals on your behalf and on terms which he considers to be advantageous to you. You might therefore think either that it isn't worth suggesting alterations or that you have no right to, especially if the signing is to be a formal occasion with a photographer and reporter from the music press present.

Nevertheless you should have your own lawyer, who should not also be the manager's lawyer, to negotiate all the finer points of the deal, even if the manager has already agreed the major

'commercial' points, and your lawyer should read through the agreement with you in advance of any signing 'ceremony'. It may be a terrible deal which the manager had done mainly to impress you. Or he may have been given a big advance payment for your services, and doesn't want you to know about it (though you'd be exceptionally unlucky to wind up with quite such a 'dodgy' manager). If he's also relatively new to the business he may simply not know enough about publishing or recording. Even the most professional of managers can still agree to a 'lousy' deal because of inexperience in a particular field and some really top managers of big name acts admit that they learned about the job as they went along!

You don't need to keep running up legal bills by consulting your own lawyer every time your manager buys you a sandwich or a new plectrum, but when it comes to negotiating recording and publishing deals and particularly any deal which binds you exclusively to a company for a period, even just six months, you certainly should! As we've said it's quite normal to get record companies and publishers to pay, or at least contribute a few hundred pounds towards, your legal costs anyway.

Above all, don't give the manager power of attorney to sign any long term deal on your behalf (see 'Power of Attorney' in the Glossary).

If we're a group does he have to consult all of us?

It's normal in such cases for the manager to expect the group to nominate one member to be the 'contact' who he can ask in the case of relatively minor decisions which often need to be made quickly. Any decision which would result in contracts which the whole group would have to sign anyway, such as blanket writing and recording agreements or general agreements with agencies or merchandising companies, should however be discussed at some length by all of you and the manager sitting down together. Do spare a thought for the position of the manager if you, as a band, fall out, and try to resolve any issues amicably.

If an artist is signed to a professional management company why does he need personal manager too?

You could be signed to a large management company but still have your own separate personal manager. He would generally be employed by the company, though if he works solely for you then his salary and expenses would be paid by you or deducted from your earnings. He could be employed entirely separately by you, but this would very likely cause friction. He's there to look after you, especially on tour etc. and to be at your beck and call and to liaise with the other staff at the management, record and publishing companies. He's the one who should make sure you get from A to B on time and that the caviar sandwiches in your dressing room are always fresh, and generally act as a sort of personal assistant.

How would I get out of a management contract?

This is the most important of our three 'how to get out of' sections, since if your manager is collecting all your money and turns out to be greedy, dishonest, or simply disinterested, then no matter how honest and hardworking your record company and publisher may be, you may not get a penny.

The advice given under publishing and recording contracts also applies here. First try the friendly approach, offering if necessary to pay back part or all of any advance sums or expenses paid by him on your behalf. Then check renewals and royalty statements to see that these have all arrived on time. If you haven't become successful the manager will probably let

you go, possibly subject to his retaining some interest in your future in the form of a very small percentage of your future income for the rest of the duration of his contract. If you have become successful then he won't want to let you go and you will need to go straight to a solicitor to assess the case on its merits. He'll tell you as quickly as possible if he thinks you have a good case. If you succeed in getting out, then the solicitor's fees will be money well spent.

One suggestion your solicitor might make is that you write to your record company, publisher etc. asking that royalties be paid direct to you in future. This should at least ensure that the manager doesn't get them even if you yourself don't actually get paid, although he'll probably sue you for cutting off his income stream from these sources. Faced with two 'claimants' to royalties, record companies and publishers will generally have no option but to suspend payments until the dispute is settled. This is in case it should go to court and the winner should sue them for having already paid all the royalties to the loser. Obviously this won't go on forever. In some cases you as the actual writer or artist will be considered 'right until proved wrong' and in others you, as the new claimant, will probably have a year or so in which to prove that you should now receive these royalties, otherwise they will be once more paid to the manager.

85

AGENTS, AGENCIES, PROMOTERS, TOURING, MERCHANDISING AND SPONSORSHIP

Agents are the people to which artists (or their managers) turn to find work for them, fix up concert tours and engagements and handle the work involved. It is a specialised field and, at the top end, in view of the high costs of travel and hotel bills plus hire and transportation of amplification, lighting and sets, this can be very big business indeed, especially in the case of a top band touring the USA or Europe.

Who are booking agents and how do they operate?

The principle function of an agent is precisely to obtain work for you as a live performer. Employment 'Agents' of all kinds used to be licensed by local authorities for a pound or two a year but back in the Seventies this changed so that a performer's booking agency has to obtain a business permit from the Department of Employment. This was designed to reduce malpractice but strangely, actual 'promoters' were not required to be licensed in the same way. If you are doubtful of an 'agent', whether you are dealing with him directly or not, you can now, at least, enquire as to whether he is properly registered to assure yourself that if he collects the fee you earn, he will be likely to pay you your share. However, you should note that on a semi-professional basis you will normally collect most of the fee in cash on the night from the venue, and then it will be your responsibility to pay the agent his commission (+VAT).

Can I have more than one agent?

In theory there is nothing to stop you using more than one agency if you wish, assuming that you have not agreed, even verbally, to be exclusive to one agency. However, most people have just one agent, and frequently appoint them exclusively for a period of time and the agent will liaise with others who need acts like you for venues which your agent doesn't have direct contacts with. To start with, you'll generally have an agreement directly with the venue, who as we've said, will pay you direct, usually in cash (though if you expect cash then the agreement should say so).

If you have just one agent, and he knows that, then he'll also be aware that he needs to keep you busy and will probably get you more work than if you're not exclusive to him. He'll probably prepare cards for you to hand out to interested enquirers at your gigs which will direct them to approach him rather than you. He may ask for a list of free dates in a year and then try to secure bookings for those dates although he should let you know before confirming them and always give you plenty of notice of when and where the gigs are (you're not obliged to take them, but you wouldn't want to refuse too many unless they were hundreds of miles away or for a lower fee than you told the agent you expected – as long as the fee you expected was reasonable). So he will check with you beforehand as to whether you are free and wish, at the price, to play at certain venues. Once it is verbally agreed, he'll send you a form of agreement to complete. An example of this is included later in this book under 'examples of contracts' together with some notes about the terms.

As you wouldn't be looking to an agent

to pay an advance, there's no reason not to make your exclusive agreement terminable by you at almost any time, although you'd obviously have to fulfil (and pay commission on) any gigs after termination which he'd already got you, so you may not want him to be booking you too far ahead. He'll also want you to agree not to take bookings yourself, although for just a semi-pro act it'll probably be much more ad hoc, as we said – if you gave him a date but get yourself a booking in the meantime, so be it, but remember to tell him.

Early in your career you would normally collect the cash or a cheque from the venue after a gig and then pay the agent but for much bigger concerts and tours the venue or promoter would normally pay you and the agent your shares directly. The agent would generally collect any deposits but if he collects all the money, he should pay your share over to you within days (unlike royalties from publishing and recording where you only normally get two or four accountings a year respectively).

There's not usually a huge amount of choice of agencies in any particular part of the county or area you live in, and you probably want a local one to start with. A Club DJ won't want an agency which books mainly rock bands, but most local agencies will find work for anyone, from function bands and DJ's to fire-eating, knife-throwing tightrope walkers (now there's a gimmick that would get you noticed but for the wrong reasons!). Agents will deal with individual venues and also, once you're big enough- which usually means you've had at least one album out on a successful label- with promoters, whose business it is to hire (or buy) venues and then find acts to fill them. Concert venues, even small ones, don't come cheap, as you can imagine, so promoting concerts can be very big business and of recent years some American companies have seen this as a lucrative source of income and have bought into the UK 'market'.

How much commission should a booking agent take?

The agent's commission is almost always 15% (maybe slightly less on top of your manager's commission if he's also your agent as sometimes happens). Be aware at the lower end of the scale, that if you're collecting the cash on the night and paying him 15% of it, there is a probability that he will already have asked for a substantial deposit from the venue or person booking you, particularly with one-off gigs like weddings, parties and Masonic functions and he might well not tell you about this. Thus a £400 gig might be costing the organiser £5-600. However, the commission the agent charges you will only be on your £400.

If you have a manager, then of course he will deal with the agency or agencies on your behalf. Otherwise you can obviously deal directly with an agency, or direct with the venues themselves quite satisfactorily. Note that you shouldn't deal directly with venues which you were first introduced to by the agency for a set period – usually about two years. They'll expect you to go through them again for future engagements with that venue. A form of simple agreement between you as an artist and a venue is also included in the 'Examples of Contracts' section.

Naturally if you are contacted directly by venues you will see no point in paying either a manager or an agent a percentage of this money unless you firmly believe that the agent can negotiate a much better fee, leaving you with more even after his commission. For this reason there is no necessity to tie yourself either to a manager or to an agency if as a semi-professional you have as much work as you want already. If you are a member of the Musicians Union, then check that you're being offered at least the MU rates for gigs.

Should I pay a fee to the agent to 'sign on?'

The general answer is 'no'. An agent can't actually guarantee to get any work for you. As a semi-pro act or an act without a recording contract, you probably won't initially want to guarantee that you'll only work entirely through the agent (i.e. you might not want more than one agent but if you get offered a gig directly, you won't want to have to refer it to the agent and pay commission on it). If the agent is offering to do something very specific such as undertaking to put a certain number of minutes of your demo recordings on a general demo CD which the agent makes (at his expense) and sends out to a certain number (at least several hundred) prospective clients, then he might ask you for a few tens of pounds, but generally getting you work is his business and this is how he makes his commission, and he should do it at his expense.

Do I really need an agent if I'm only semi-pro?

Most semi-professional acts who are working regularly do have an agent, though they'll probably also get work themselves. If you're prepared to do a lot of ringing around and visiting pubs, hotels, social clubs, golf clubs (or whatever your intended 'market' is) with a demo CD and cards and posters then you'd be unlucky if nothing came of it. However remember some venues, especially social clubs and the like, book all their acts for the year, as a package, for an all-in fee from one agent. If you have a web-site with good pictures and soundbites this can help, and there are other sites which can help, such as www.partysounds.co.uk which contains details, county by county of acts playing for parties, dances etc. in Britain.

Do I need an agent as a session musician?

It's quite likely that if you're a session musician (i.e. basically very talented and you can read music) then you'll have an agent getting you work, although you may also be getting it yourself. It's possible these days to get work for sessions or tours which might suit you from your website (provided that you include soundbites of your previous performances and information as to the very best of what recordings/tours you've been involved in before). Although getting tours and sessions is very much a case of who you know (or who you knew, for older musicians) it is still possible to get work this way if you fit the bill, rather than just relying on your contacts with a session 'fixer' who knows you and would recommend you.

How much per appearance should I be worth?

This really is the hardest question of all to answer, because there are so many factors to take into account. It's where managers and agents really earn their money, as they should know exactly how much they can get for your services in every situation. Most solo pop artists start their careers with bands these days, as they couldn't possibly start from scratch employing backing musicians or buying or hiring all the necessary equipment themselves.

You'll know roughly what a PA system and backline equipment will cost, but it's worth splashing out on a decent PA and mic's or else hiring these on a regular basis. You'll obviously start out as your own roadies, but even if you're not being mixed from the back of the hall it pays to have a friend who knows what you're supposed to sound like telling you what volume and frequencies to turn up or down. Do a soundcheck if at all possible, but you won't need us to tell you that it'll all sound quite different once the place is (you hope) full.

If you're a semi-pro band and are prepared to play music to dance to and can get bookings at working men's clubs, parties, wedding receptions etc., the minimum going rate for these should be about £100 for a solo act with backing tapes, £150-200 for a duo and £3-400 for a four- or five-piece band (at which point the law of diminishing returns comes into play, so a 10-piece band won't be offered much more than a five-piece one to play at a small function). A really competent self-contained five-piece band (with own PA, lights and interval music) playing a Masonic function or big corporate party or a residency at a big hotel etc. ought to be able to get £5-600 up to £1,000 or so. You'd expect to play a minimum of two 45-minute sets, but could wind up playing up to four hours with only a half-hour break in the middle without much variation in the fees. If they do ask you to carry on beyond the stated finishing time then you should get at least an additional payment in line with the amount per hour you're getting for the rest of the gig.

Music pubs are another source of bookings. At the right pub you're likely to be able to play whatever you want to – rock'n'roll, blues, jazz, folk, Sixties music etc. as you don't have to worry about whether people can dance to it. The audience will expect a much higher standard of musicianship than for 'functions' and the venue will probably pay a lot less because there are so many ex-professional musicians doing this for fun, especially in 'rockbroker belt' areas of counties like Surrey, Sussex, Hampshire and Berkshire and the rest of the home counties. The downside of all these bookings is that you're very unlikely to be heard by anyone in the music business who might be able to further your career, and the gigs that could lead to better things frequently don't pay anything at all. You have to make the decision at some point which road to go down.

If you do succeed in getting a record deal then live work of course becomes enormously more lucrative. A straight 'pop' group with a recent hit (even a small one) should immediately be able to command £5,000 a night, much more if they consolidate their success. If they stay together, they can still be worth that long after the hit if they remain crowd-pullers. Major tours, however, frequently don't make any money as the expenses are so high, even when a major act can gross as much as $1m or so a night on US tours.

At the lower end of the scale it is worth bearing in mind that as long as the instruments and voice are in tune then sheer reliability – always turning up on time, having the voice clearly audible, avoiding technical hitches, feedback etc. – can be more important to the securing of regular well-paying engagements than real musical talent!

A group playing at social clubs, parties, dinner-dances, etc. who are prepared to play and take their breaks when asked, and to turn the volume down (or occasionally up) when asked, and to look presentable, and to set up and pack up quickly, and to vary the programme to suit the age or taste of the audience are certainly more likely to be re-booked than a bunch of brilliant but unruly musicians. For most functions it's also important to try to play songs that the audiences already know and are more likely to dance to (though you might get away with a few of your own numbers or songs you particularly like eg. blues, jazz, folk etc. and if you play these sorts of gigs you don't need us to tell you that it's up to you to assess on the night what you can 'get away with').

It is another plus for the group if they have their own stage lights and taped music to play during intervals – some small venues lack these facilities, though the club or whatever might draw the line at strobe lights, dry ice and pyroflashes. Do remember that these types of venue can only pay a certain fee for music regardless of the number of musicians in the line-up. They should certainly expect to pay much more over Christmas and especially on New Year's Eve, when demand for music exceeds the supply. Once you're big then for major concerts/tours organised by promoters it's more likely that your fee will based on a percentage of actual ticket sales (but subject to a realistic minimum fee).

They're always on time! Pity they're never _in_ time!

What happens if a venue cancels a gig?

Generally where an agent has dealt with the venue, the agent will have put into the contract a clause to the effect that a cancellation fee of perhaps 50% is payable if the engagement is cancelled by the venue less than a week before it was due to take place. If you are dealing directly with the management of the venue yourself and have made no mention of cancellation fees then you will have to regard it as bad luck and

avoid making any further bookings with that venue or management.

What happens if the management of a venue don't pay me as agreed once I've played?

In certain circumstances a 15-stone roadie might help persuade the venue management that prompt payment would be prudent! Like any other cash business, confrontations can arise and most on-the-road veterans can recount stories of 'difficult situations'. Chuck Berry is famous for refusing to play a note until he'd been paid, in cash, in full. However, provided that you arrived on time and played, or made it clear that you were prepared to play during the time stated, then start by writing polite letters followed by a strong letter from a solicitor if it's worth it. Unfortunately this isn't always the case, but you can always ask a solicitor what his approximate charge would be for a letter like this and what it would cost to pursue it through the small claims courts. If you were late or unable to perform for the length of time expected once you'd arrived, then the management of the venue, if they were bloody-minded, might deduct a portion of your fee for this provided it was in proportion to the time during which you failed to perform.

What happens if I agree to perform somewhere and am unable to turn up?

If there is a good reason then apologise to the management of the venue absolutely as soon as you know, and they're not likely to do too much with the exception of not booking you again. They could ask you to send a replacement, and some bands can provide 'deps' with no problem. However, only an agency can reasonably be expected to supply a whole substitute band. Your only alternative would be to offer to perform on another date, perhaps for a reduced fee.

Do I need to know if the venue I'm performing at is licensed for live music?

The basic answer is 'no'. It's the venue's responsibility. The venue will need an entertainment licence from the local council and a licence from the PRS. For years, the 'two in a bar' rule has been in force – meaning that a pub for example could allow a duo to perform without a licence but the moment a third person came up to join them for a guest spot then the venue would be breaking the law. However a change in the UK legislation meant that any number of musicians could play provided that the venue had told the council in advance that they wanted to have more musicians playing, and had had this provision added to the terms of their general license to sell beer, wine etc. Again, this sort of thing is the venue's responsibility, not yours and if there had been objections from neighbours about the noise then it would be the venue's responsibility (if necessary by installing a 'noise-meter') rather than your responsibility to reduce it. A crowd of drunken football supporters watching a live 'big-screen' broadcast of an international game, or a particularly raucous party could generate as many decibels as you and your local band even with all your amps turned up to 11, and with your guitarist's Les Paul Custom so loud that the audience could almost smell the 'sustain'!

Do I have to pay to perform or record other people's songs?

Singers or groups normally should never be charged for performing a song in public (even on television). The venue where the performance is taking place should be licensed by the PRS as we have discussed earlier, and if it's not, then that isn't the fault of the performer who, having been booked to appear, can reasonably assume that the place was properly licensed for live music.

If you yourself wish to put on an open air concert then for any performance to which the public has access in a place which is obviously not regularly licensed for the playing of music, permission should be sought from the PRS's general licensing department. This could cover everything from a tea party on the Vicar's lawn to Fat Boy Slim on Brighton beach as well as raves in the middle of someone's field (though these, in their heyday, were famously 'unlicensed'). You will probably also need the permission of the police and/or the local council for any such gigs. As we've said, religious services do not require a licence, although if a song of yours were to be broadcast on television or radio as part of a religious service then this would be no different from any other broadcast as far as the payment of performing fees is concerned.

If you wish to record the performance then you do need to ask the publisher of the songs through the MCPS but unless you're releasing your own records you shouldn't physically have to pay to use it. The record company will do this, and for normal CDs and other audio records it'll cost the same in royalty payments whether you've recorded huge international hits or songs hardly anyone's ever heard of.

What do I need to know about touring?

Lots of medium sized bands who've been in the business for years, and maybe haven't had a hit record for years (or even decades) but who have a following have got touring down to a fine art and can actually make money at it. This is by being as 'self-contained' as possible. They'll have the minimum road crew + a tour manager who also drives a truck and sells the merchandise. If the act is no longer big enough to make money on its own, there are an increasing number of 'package concerts' in which several acts which are similar or are from the same era each play a shortened set and attract people who wouldn't have bothered to go and see any one of them individually, even for a lower ticket price.

A rock band on tour playing a different venue virtually every night will probably need at least 30 people with them, the tour manager, road crew, lighting crew, caterers etc. On a really big tour like this there will even be a separate tour accountant, usually employed by your own or the manager's accountants, who will have worked out in advance how much everything should cost (and how much you might need from sponsors or your record company to break even) and who will collect the money from the venues/promoter, check up on ticket sales if you're on a percentage of the take and generally make sure everything is financially in order. Nevertheless if an act can sell 10,000 tickets at £25 a time on average they should make a gross profit of 50% of the £250,000 takings. Out of this the agent will expect to be able to make 15% and the promoter will expect to make at least 10-15% (depending on whether the act is on a percentage of 'box office') as he's taking the risk of putting the whole thing on. What's more it'll probably have to be organised around a year in advance or the venues simply won't be available. If a webcast is then made of one or more of the con-certs, or even a 'rockumentary' which can be sold to television around the various countries where you're well known, then there's even more possibility of breaking even. At the very top end, the figures are huge. In 2002 Paul McCartney did a 50-date tour of the USA (admittedly a long tour) and the box-office revenue alone (without merchandise, webcasts or any other spin-offs) was reported as 100 million dollars!

How could I get a sponsor for a tour?

As major tours are frequently loss-makers and are primarily to improve your profile with the music-buying public, your record company will usually liaise with your manager in finding a suitable sponsor. You should have the right to say no to a particular sponsor, especially if it's a tobacco or alcohol company and therefore possibly damaging to your image. But remember that if the record company is underwriting the tour up to an agreed figure, then the money they pay will eventually come out of your record royalties, so in general it definitely pays to agree to sponsorship. If it comes as part of a general endorsement of the product or company including press or television commercials etc. then of course you should be handsomely paid for the deal, though there are no hard and fast figures. If the sponsor wants to be involved in merchandising sold on the tour then your manager will need to work this out in advance.

The sponsors will probably want you to put their logo on your website + concert tickets, programmes, posters etc. (anywhere where the venue itself will let you, bearing in mind that they probably have their own sponsor too!). It's possible to approach sponsors directly but there are agents who, for around 10% of what you get from the sponsor (including a calculation of the value of any goods you receive), will try to find a suitable sponsor for you. If you actually like the product and are happy to talk about it and be seen eating it/drinking it/wearing it, even singing about it, then you can expect a better deal.

Like a Formula One racing car and driver with brand names plastered all over them, there's nothing to stop you having more than one sponsor – as long as it doesn't all look so blatant that your fans think you've 'sold out' (although back in the Sixties The Who actually made a 'concept' out of it on an album called *The Who Sell Out* which included advertising jingles played by them in between the songs). Your deals could be for one tour or could last for years – there are no hard and fast rules. For a lot more money you could even agree to appear in commercials for the product which you'd probably get away with provided they were humorous but not otherwise – you'd need to vet the scripts very carefully to avoid the commercials making you look greedy or just plain embarrassed.

It's worth remembering that your record company quite probably has sponsorship deals with companies too, like the deal that Sony and Pepsi Cola did in 2002 under which Pepsi would preview new Sony releases in commercials and would sponsor US television specials featuring Sony artists. If you were one of those artists, they'd obviously want you to 'go along with' the promotion of the brand where possible.

Can I get some money/free instruments by endorsing them?

On a smaller scale, even session players on tours as well as 'name' acts should be able to secure free instruments and amplification from a particular manufacturer, provided that they can be seen using it on the tour (write to them and ask). Any additional endorsements, such as you appearing in commercials, posters etc., may be worth a substantial fee, depending on the size of the act and the likely impact that their use of it would

have on sales of the product. This is particularly true of guitars and guitarists – companies like Gibson, Gretsch and Fender have, between them, produced models named after just about every famous guitarist – it's one of the ways to tell that you've really made it!

Can I get to tour as a support act?

This would usually be organised by your record company pulling strings or arranging for you to tour with a major act also on their label or who are handled by the same management/agency. Although the major act won't want any adverse comparisons with you, you should at least be playing roughly the same sort of music. If a major act really likes you they may take you under their wing and let you tour for nothing, i.e. they don't pay you, you don't pay them, but you do get to share their audience, (or at least the percentage of the audience who don't stay in the bar till the headline act comes on) and to use their PA. Otherwise you would expect to pay to join a major tour, maybe several hundred pounds a night, sometimes more. If it seems tough, remember that once you make it big you can get the same deal from support acts yourself. As we said earlier, touring is big business, especially in the USA, and with ticket sales of $1 million a time or more for some gigs you'd think it would be impossible not to make a profit, but touring is very, very expensive. It's that much more so in Europe where there are less large venues to fill and the largest country, Germany, has tax laws which at one stage required you to pay German tax on the gross box office takings, though thankfully this was later modified.

What does a tour manager do?

A tour manager is usually employed by your management. Many fairly modest tours are 'run' by the manager himself with an assistant or two, but for big tours there should be someone who is solely focused on the tour and of course the bigger the tour the more important he is. He's the one who will make sure that the whole 'show' stays 'on the road' and that you don't end up like Spinal Tap! He'll see to it that the trucks and the PA and the lighting rig all work and are replaced (very quickly indeed) if they don't, and above all will smooth out any problems with the road crew or the staff at the venues when the dressing room you expected isn't available, or at the hotel when you're all trying to get a drink and the bar is supposed to be closing etc. etc. Unless it's dealt with by a separate company he may also be the one who sees to it that the merchandise is there (still in sufficient quantity three weeks into the tour).

What should I know about merchandising?

We've included this subject in this section because the most obvious place to sell merchandise is at live concerts, but actually this subject almost deserves a section in itself as there is so much money to be made from merchandising of music (as well as sport and other 'personality') goods. As we said under the Recording section, you should ensure that your record company don't expect to control merchandising rights under your agreement with them, and in general they won't. For megastars and cult acts, merchandising can gross millions of pounds a year! If you're photogenic that helps, but luckily you don't have to be good looking, legendary and dead like Curt Cobain or Jim Morrison to sell a lot of merchandise.

Can I do my own merchandising?

Most people do, to start with, and it makes good commercial sense. As soon as you (you, in this case, usually means a

band) have enough of a reputation, it's worth organising the making of T-shirts and posters which you sign, or rather 'autograph' (ordinary people sign things, stars 'autograph' them)! If you or your friend from art college can come up with something so tasteful/tasteless/bizarre that people might wear it even if they don't know who you are, then you're really winning. You can start by giving copies to your girlfriend/boyfriend and all their friends if they agree to wear them (though maybe not to your mother). Someone walking around with your T-shirt on is a great piece of free publicity, especially if most of their friends and acquaintances haven't heard of you yet. If you've got as far as having your own fan club then they can sell them or give them away as prizes in competitions etc. Frankie Goes To Hollywood received a huge amount of PR as a result of so many people wearing T-shirts that said 'Frankie say Relax' or something similar, even though most of them were counterfeit and the band received nothing from them.

What can I expect to make per item from merchandising?

If you're doing it yourself then the profit margins will probably be high for the ones you manage to sell, but once you've actually got a record deal this starts to be big business and there are experts who can make you more money in the long run than you could yourself. It varies a great deal according to the goods, but let's start with T-shirts, posters etc. being sold at live concerts. The owners of the venues will take 25% of what the T-shirt, sweatshirt or whatever is selling for (more like 35-40% in the USA).

There are specialised merchandising companies which will organise both the making and selling of your products. They may only expect to make less than £1 profit from a £20+ sweatshirt, but will be prepared to take the risk, especially with a well-known act (even a relatively small one) provided that they can estimate pretty well the likely number of ticket sales and can be reasonably sure of at least some protection from pirated goods (see later). They'll hope for a total 'spend' of up to about £4 a head at the average rock concert. They will be much less inclined to pay big advances for a pop act with only one or two hits when they're not at all certain how well the tour will go, unless it's an act who have already developed an image in the way that the Spice Girls did, and the goods will sell anyway. You probably don't need telling that 'rock' audiences are much more likely to buy merchandise than MOR or mainstream pop audiences. Whatever deal you do, try to make sure you have some input on quality control, and, if at all possible, on pricing – better to get slightly less from a merchandiser than have your fans think you're ripping them off. On that subject it must be said that one reason why pirates on the street corner outside the venue are so successful is that the official merchandise often does seem very expensive in relation to similar goods (without of course the artist's name and logo) in normal clothes shops etc.

Suppose we pay to have the goods made?

If the act are effectively paying to have the merchandise manufactured and employing a separate company to sell it they could hope to wind up with a higher percentage of the gross. Most artists could hope to get about 25% of the selling price of the merchandise (after tax and the venue's 25% has been taken off). You could reasonably expect your manager to know exactly how much he could negotiate for you. With sales in normal retail outlets a deal is sometimes done whereby you will simply let someone else do the whole thing for a royalty to you of 10-15% of the retail price.

Can I get an advance royalty payment on merchandising?

You can expect substantial advances against royalties or profits from merchandising companies under deals where they make and sell them – as much as £50,000 or so for a big, but not huge, act touring over the course of a year and there are seven-figure sums to be made by really big acts from merchandising alone. Specialised merchandising companies will hopefully bid for the right to make and sell your merchandise as soon as they know a tour is imminent. They'll know what's likely to sell, but you won't need reminding that merchandising can be far more than T-shirts. Back in the Seventies *Abba – The Film* was accompanied by everything from *Abba – The Album* down to Abba – The Soap! (literally a bar of soap). It should go without saying that you should have the right to approve any merchandise before it is put on the market. It's worth bearing in mind that under some deals if the tour is cancelled or even if they don't recoup the advance they paid you then the merchandising company will have the right to carry on selling your goods, either at live gigs or at retail outlets etc., until they have got their money back, which may stop you doing a lucrative new deal for your next tour.

What rights do I have to give the merchandiser?

First of all he will want the exclusive right to use your name/logo on his particular merchandise. The first question he will ask is 'is your name/logo a registered trade mark?'. If you're a rock/guitar-based band then it's worth trying to design and register a good logo almost from the start. If it's not particularly good and especially if you haven't registered it then once you're big enough to do a merchandising deal you'll get a lot less money from merchandisers and you may not get a deal at all. This is because they want to be able to use their right to your trade mark to sue, or at the very least threaten, pirates. If you're worried about the number of bootleg/pirate albums or videos out there, the market for merchandise is even worse.

So can I actually make my name or my band's name a 'registered trade mark'?

Yes, you can. It's expensive, but if you seriously expect to be successful then it's worth doing it sooner rather than later. It will cost several hundred pounds just to register it in the UK and even then for specific products. In your case you want to cover recordings and probably also clothing and posters in the first instance. It will take months before it comes into effect but at least it'll then be backdated to the date when you applied for the registration. To protect your name completely you (or your agents – probably affiliates of your manager, record company or publisher) will need to do the same thing in the USA and then the rest of the major countries of Europe too, at perhaps the same sort of cost in each country. However if you're successful it will be worth it many times over! In the UK the main reason is that if you have a registered trade mark then you can ask the Trading Standards Authority to prosecute anyone you find selling 'bootleg' merchandise using your name. As we've said, if your record/management company, and their merchandising licensees, know that you're registered they'll almost certainly be prepared to put a lot more money behind you. If your manager/record company help with this it is vital for you that the registration is made in your name, not the manager's name or the record company's name (i.e. that you own the name/logo and not them).

Suppose I don't bother to try to register my/my band's name and logo?

Without this you or your merchandising licensee would be forced to sue the pirates individually and in the case, for example, of people selling your records or T-shirts on a street corner near one of your gigs, it would not be economic to start legal proceedings – it isn't and virtually nobody does – the sellers would probably 'disappear' within days or even hours. This is appalling when you think that even a high percentage of the clothing including 'brand-names' within the actual shops (not street corners) in England's most famous shopping street, Oxford Street in London, is 'bootlegged' and no legitimate writer/record company/publisher and, for that matter, fashion designer or manufacturer is getting anything at all. Laws and policing are just unable to cope. And if that's England's most famous shopping street, imagine how much you're losing in most of the rest of the world!

How else can I protect my stage name or group name?

Unless you were already successful, then you would probably be unable to prevent another act using the name and would just have to regard it as bad luck. As long ago as the late Fifties Hank Marvin & The Shadows were prevented from using their original name, 'The Drifters', by the American group, already making records, with that same name and in the Eighties the UK act 'The Beat' were required in the USA to call themselves 'The English Beat' to avoid confusion with an act who had already been successful there under that name.

If you have not yet achieved any sort of national recognition and another artist or group appears and becomes successful with an identical or very similar name to yours then there is really not a great deal of point in sticking to your name.

Members of the public hearing the name will immediately think of the other, already successful, act. If the other act were to feel it necessary, they could probably stop you using your name sooner or later if the courts of law felt that it would mislead the public, and it would be unlikely that you could reverse the process and stop them using theirs, even if you had been using yours much longer. Of course if you have had some success then you should stick to your guns and if necessary issue legal proceedings to stop the new band, even if they are successful. A good example was the band Liberty who successfully prevented the band formed by the 'flop stars' (those who nearly made it but not quite) from the television pop stars competition calling themselves Liberty – although they weren't required to change it much – "Liberty X" was considered different enough to avoid confusion.

There is an organisation called the National Band Register which not only provides regular newsletters and a lot of useful information for gigging bands but publishes a list of the names of all bands who have registered with it, as well as lists of venues where live music is played. This doesn't give any legal protection against claims of passing off by another band or give you any legal right to challenge another band using your name. However, you can at least see whether someone else is already using your band's name, though remember it obviously isn't conclusive because there are bands who are not registered. Furthermore, by registering with the National Band Register you may discourage (though it won't actually stop) anyone else from using your name. There is a small annual charge which again is well worth it and we would urge any band to join. The address to write to is in our list of Useful Addresses.

The more unusual your stage name, as long as it's not too bizarre or inappropriate, the more people are likely to remember it and the less likely it is that anyone else will already be using it. At the bottom end of the scale, the shorter your name the bigger the letters it will appear in on social club notice boards etc! There are, of course, examples of artists who have actually decided to change their name by deed-poll to their stage name. It's not enormously expensive to do this, but there's really no point unless you particularly want to.

What can I do if my real name is the same as someone famous like Paul McCartney or Diana Ross?

I'm afraid this is, as you'd probably expect, simply bad luck. Obviously if your famous namesake is still alive (especially if they're still performing/recording) then you'd be silly to try to use it, as no-one would dare book you or record you under that name for fear of audiences and record buyers thinking they were going to hear the star. In fact the manager of the well-known artist would probably take you to court over it anyway if you used the name as your stage name. A name like Elvis Costello on the other hand was fine as there was really no likelihood of anyone confusing him with Elvis Presley. A songwriter with a 'famous name' would be well advised to use a pseudonym because of the possibility of their royalties going astray. However remember, in that case, that you must tell your publisher and PRS your real name in any event and, as we said, all writers have a unique 'CAE number' so these days there's less scope for confusion.

If a group splits up, who owns the name?

Regrettably there is no straightforward answer to this question. It may be that the members will work something out between them. It may be that they themselves do not actually 'own' the name at all. If the record company or manager suggested it in the first place then there may be something in the contract whereby they reserve the right to the name, in which case if all the members of the group leave together or one by one, they can be replaced by an entirely new group with the same name. This chilling prospect is something to question managers or record companies about when signing with them. You will almost certainly be guaranteeing to them that you have the right to use the name, but not necessarily that you're the only person or band in the world using that name at that point in time. If your band name is a registered trade mark then there's even more reason to decide in advance, and, pedantic as it sounds, to put something in writing as to what will happen to the name if the band breaks up.

If you, as a band, formed a limited company, or agreed to work as a legal partnership then that will at least have prompted you to think what happens to the name if you disband or split. If you had a company you could agree to split the profits equally if you disbanded, but you ought to think about some 'formula' for calculating how much the name of the band might be worth to any of you who want to carry on using it, if it's successful (even remotely successful). If just one member leaves then the others could agree to 'pay him off' and he probably wouldn't expect to have the right to use the name if it was well-known, but you need to think what you'd do if a four piece band split in two, for example.

Can I stop anyone else recording or performing in my style or manner?

Unfortunately not, unless they are actually deceiving the public into thinking that they're really you, which is known as 'passing off'. In that case your manager or record company, if you have them, will take action against the other artist. If you come up with a 'great new sound' then the chances are that all sorts of people will copy it, and unfortunately there's nothing you can do to stop this either as long as people aren't actually sampling your records. There's nothing to stop you looking like someone else as long as you're not actually pretending to be them or deliberately trying to put doubt in peoples' minds

Is there anything to stop me forming a 'tribute band'?

A 'tribute band' can play someone else's songs and call itself a name similar to that of the stars without any authorisation. Again as long as there's no likelihood of anyone seriously thinking you are the star, or that when they buy your records or go to your gigs they're actually going to hear or see the star, then it's fine. If the original band are no longer gigging then so much the better. The grey area is with bands, mostly from the Sixties and Seventies who may have one member left out of five and still perform under the same name. Provided no-one else owns the name and wishes to stop them, then even a band with no members left from the original hit line-up can pretend to be the real band, although there should be some sort of tenuous link. It's big business of course. Many tribute bands are amazingly good copies of the original in their heyday, and the first tribute bands to 'succeed' like Bjorn Again and The Bootleg Beatles have even had hits in their own right.

USES OF SONGS AND RECORDINGS ON THE INTERNET

The Internet is not only the fastest-growing source of music for consumers of it, but is also the most contentious. In 2002 the Oxford Union debating society voted, perhaps not unsurprisingly, hugely in favour of music being free on the Internet. As a listener to other people's music, especially if you're a student and simply can't afford to buy all the CDs you'd like to, you might think this is great. However you're also someone who will hopefully, sooner or later, be earning your living from your songs and recordings, and you don't need us to tell you that free downloads and streaming of music from the Internet is bad news for you. World record sales have recently dropped by between 5% and 10% a year and a lot of that, though not all of it, is down to the Internet. If you think that the estimated number of illegal downloads is over two and a half billion (yes, billion) every month (yes, month) worldwide, then you'll realise why this is so important to you as a writer/performer.

Why has it taken so long for the major record companies to put their music on the Internet?

There's no doubt that if the majors, who control around three-quarters of all music (songs and recordings) had found a way to let people download their music from the Internet much sooner then people would have got used to paying something (maybe not CD prices, but at least something) for downloads. The first problem was that until the advent of broadband it took quite a long time to download one three-minute song, let alone a full club mix of a track or a whole album's worth, so the record labels knew that the majority of the public wouldn't bother. By the time they did get worried, Napster and Gnutella were operating their file-sharing systems. Although they were declared illegal it had to go through the courts, by which time people had got used to Napster and the others being free.

Once they were successfully sued, along came P2P services offering digital downloads effectively for free such as Kazaa, Streamcast and Grokster, doing by and large the same thing. Universal Records sued MP3.com and settled for no less than $50m but nevertheless any 'locker-room' service where, in theory, you can download the album that you legitimately bought and then access it (or of course let other members of the public access it) is likely to be extended to albums someone else bought or to albums the company itself bought, and the illegal sites are happy to take the risk of being sued.

Why couldn't they just start a kind of Internet record store?

When you go into a record shop, especially a big one, you expect to be able to buy records from all companies, not just one or two, and you'd certainly expect to buy anything from the current charts. Even experts like Paul Gambaccini couldn't be expected to know what label every single major artist is on, so if you want a record by a particular artist you shouldn't need to know the label. Because the record companies were not prepared to work together they allowed the illegal sites to flourish. Because the Internet is worldwide and copyright protection is hopeless in some countries, even quite wealthy ones, this means that as soon as one illegal site is closed down (which they regularly are, because the big ones are at least easy to find) another will open up somewhere. The major record companies were so afraid that selling downloads on the Internet would devalue their music (all music) that they refused to co-operate to set up a legitimate place where people could listen to or download music using the most user-friendly technology available.

What about the major record companies' own companies like Pressplay and MusicNet?

Even when the major record labels finally got round to making their music available on these sites, it took a while before they could all get to share anything. Pressplay was launched by Universal and Sony and allowed subscribers to download a certain number of tracks and also to stream, though not to burn, a certain number of tracks per month for a monthly fee, set according to how much access the user wanted. MusicNet was launched by AOL Time Warner, EMI and BMG amongst others but was always intended to be licensed to other businesses (Internet portals and ISP's). Others such as Rhapsody and Wippit were launched by independent companies and groups of companies. However all of these faced competition from other companies traditionally regarded as broadcasters and communications companies who thought that they, and not the record companies, should be the 'Internet record shops'. This is the reason for the merger of a company like AOL, with its communication services, Internet profile etc. with Time Warner, with it's catalogue of recordings, songs etc.

With so much competition from illegal sites you can't really blame the majors for being cautious when the authorities in the USA and the EU started investigating whether they were trying to operate monopolies (called 'antitrust' in the USA). On top of this the record compa-

nies even faced the possibility that, under the terms of their agreements, some really huge catalogue acts like The Beatles could just say 'no' if they didn't want their music used willy nilly on the Internet (the kind of thing you can do when you're that big!). In 2002 the major companies finally (mostly) got together behind Pressplay and Listen.com + its subscription service Rhapsody (licensee of MusicNet).

The major companies are also increasingly interested in trying to use foolproof (they hope) anti-piracy software for their products – so-called 'Digital Rights Management' ('DRM'). Sony and Philips reportedly paid nearly $500,000 for a company called InterTrust, some of whose business was the ownership of patents for DRM. Sony and Philips have a good track record for owning patents. They own the patent on CDs (so that all other companies or manufacturers have to pay them something for every CD made) so this was a measure of their confidence that DRM is a serious way to prevent illegal downloading, piracy etc.

So what do I actually get if my song or record is streamed or downloaded from a legal site?

In the USA the Digital Millennium Copyright Act specified your right to be compensated for uses of your music and the Library of Congress subsequently set a rate of $.07 per track for radio broadcasts which are streamed simultaneously over the Internet. AOL as a leading user is paying over $100,000 a month so it's potentially big business. The record companies, which started out with ridiculously low rates or large deductions from your royalties when used on the Internet, have now, by and large, agreed that you will be paid for downloads at the full album royalty rate (usually about 25% higher than the singles rate formerly applied) and without the packaging deductions of up to 25% which were crazy when applied to downloads from the Internet (even with the information available on the CD insert).

You should also receive at least 50% of what your record company receives when your recordings are 'simulcast', i.e. as well as a concert being heard live on UK radio, it can be listened to on the Internet on the other side of the world. You should also receive the sort of amount that a subscriber pays to make a download of your recording from one of your record company's licensee companies. Companies such as Liquid Audio have been making music available like this, legitimately, for years now, through deals with individual companies that owned the rights (though this didn't include music from the major labels and artists). As regards you as a songwriter, it's really still impossible to say in any given year exactly how much you'll get out of any particular use of your song, so don't think your publisher (or the PRS and the other collecting societies) are cheating you if it doesn't seem to amount to a lot.

What actual rights do I have over use of my songs/recordings on the Internet?

As long ago as 1996 the World Intellectual Property Organisation (WIPO) agreed a 'protocol' (international agreement to change a particular aspect of the law around the world) regarding recognition of your right to prevent other people using digital distribution of your music, where this wasn't clear already. It basically said that someone else definitely has to have your permission, or the permission of someone you've given your rights to, to use your song/recording on the Internet. This subsequently became law in the USA under their Digital Millennium Copyright Act and was directed by the EU in 2002 to become law in the European Union too.

So much for the history, what rights do I need if I want to use songs/records on my own website?

If you're an artist who performs other people's songs then you'll appreciate that you need to clear the songs with them before they appear on your site. In practice if these are 'soundbites' of 30 seconds or less most people won't worry too much (although they're entitled to), but if you're using the whole track, and you as a singer or a band or a DJ remixer suddenly become even slightly well-known, people will start downloading the tracks from your own website. Suddenly you become like a miniature version of Napster or Kazaa – a pirate, just as you would be if you pressed or burned some CDs to sell at your own gigs without permission from the people whose songs you performed, so you ought to get permission from the MCPS on behalf of the publishers and writers.

What about my song/recording getting changed in some way or put with video or other material?

In general this would be called 'interactive' use and would still be subject to your permission, or at the very least the permission of your record company and music publisher. However you should be aware that the term 'interactive' can also mean the possible use by some member of the public of a normal 'webcast' including your song/recording in which they're able to move your recording to a different slot or delete it (or others) altogether. There's still a debate over exactly what someone can do to your song or recording which they download over the Internet. However you should at least be protected, just as if someone sampled your record/plagiarised your song, to the extent of being able to stop them doing anything with it publicly (i.e. more than just in the privacy of their own homes, where you're probably not too bothered anyway).

Is it illegal to send an MP3 of a record to someone else?

If it's your own song and your own recording (made entirely by you), and you're not a PRS member (as a song-writer) and you're not signed to a record deal then probably not! Otherwise some-body somewhere will have the right to expect some payment. In practice within the music business itself people send MP3s all over the world to their col-leagues or potential customers to listen to, and no-one tries to prevent this as it's part of the business (just like music publishers or record companies sending sampler CDs to advertising agencies, film companies and others who might use their song/record). Most people/compa-nies don't own the song *and* the record but more publicity is in everyone's interest, so no-one usually objects. But if you've 'ripped' a CD and sent it as an MP3 to one of your friends, this is a bit like 'home-taping' – it's illegal (unless it was copy-protected but stated that you were permitted to send one copy to one friend, for example).

If you can and do download MP3s legally and for a fee or as part of a monthly subscription service, whether you do it at home or on an MP3 man player at a retail outlet – wherever, then it's still illegal to send it on to your friends. The record companies' ideal scenario is that any copies you make simply won't be usable by the people you send them to, through something like SDMI. The EU directive to member countries to amend their Copyright Acts included a requirement to make any kind of attempt to get around 'encryption' (DRM or electronic devices to prevent duplication of recordings) illegal. This is therefore a very serious offence. Only a really dedicated 'nerd' would have any chance of doing it anyway, but you don't really want to be guilty of downloading his free software that enables you to crack a legitimate website if you're hop-ing one day to be one of the people whose records are up there.

What is SDMI?

A good idea – the Secure Digital Music Initiative – to physically prevent music being downloaded without permission from the Internet or bought legitimately then copied indefinitely. In practice most people could find the music somewhere anyway and therefore could simply by-pass it. It also has the problem that any such system, like the ideas for preventing CDs from being copied more than once, will attract 'nerds' who will try to crack the system and invent something that makes it useless, as we said under the last question. Nevertheless, most people who can afford to pay for some music that they really want simply won't be bothered to try to get it illegally just so long as it's very very easy (and quick, which it would be via broadband) and not too expensive to download their own copy. As we've said some major record companies put very large sums of money into coming up with programmes which will prevent this.

If I'm signed to a record deal will they want to control my domain name and website?

You might already have got a good web-site up and running, possibly through friends, particularly college friends with the technical and/or the artistic expertise to do it. However there has been a move by some record companies to want to take over artist websites (or re-launch them and close down the existing ones) because they know that they can sell records and publicise themselves, as a company, through your site. As long as the record company keeps it updated, some artists are not bothered if, when people go into their site, those people find themselves at the record company site and are bombarded with information about other acts. Try, if at all possible, to resist this in your negotiations, especially if you've already got a good site. Your domain name on the Internet is worth serious money to you, if not now then certainly in the future. If this really is a 'deal-breaker' with the record company then see if you can negotiate to get it back when the deal finishes or after a given number of years.

Suppose someone else has used my name?

Bad luck but there are now a variety of suffixes you could register – .com/.co.uk/.net/.org (even if that's not really appropriate) etc. and 'cybersquatting' (using, without any reasonable excuse, the name of someone famous for a URL before that person got around to it) can be illegal. Obviously the more original your name the more likely it is that no-one else has used it yet, but the moment you start to become well-known or there is even the remotest chance of your being signed for recording or publishing then you should register your name as soon as possible.

What do I get if someone wants to use my song/record on their site?

This is very hard to say as it depends what they're doing with it, and where they're doing it from. Even within Europe, the European Directive to its member countries about the WIPO Protocol that we mentioned earlier gave 20 possible exemptions, all of which have been adopted by Luxembourg. What this means is that you could probably close down a P2P file sharing service in the UK, or France, or Germany, but a service like that could exist in Luxembourg. You'd then have much more trouble closing it down (and if that's a country in the EU, imagine how much harder it is to get at such a service based in the third world).

The only other point to make about this is that with satellite television the country from which the broadcast was 'beamed up' (called 'the upleg') was the country where the licence for the use of the music was expected to be made. In theory 'communication' to the user via the Internet takes place in the country where the user is situated and not where the information came from (so if it came from Luxembourg but was downloaded in the UK then the UK collecting societies could be entitled to collect and could possibly enforce that right against a 'pirate' company in Luxembourg). Whether this will make any difference in practice remains to be seen.

How can I make them 'take it down'?

There is something called 'Rightswatch' which was set up on behalf of the owners of songs and recordings to make it easier to remove offending sites from the Internet. The idea is that if it is quite clear that such a site is making available unlicensed songs or recordings then the Internet Service Provider will co-operate with the rights owners to have the site or the songs/recordings removed as soon as possible without anyone having to go to court, with all the expense that involves.

Is it worth letting my recordings/songs be used on a site to publicise unsigned artists/songs?

This is where the Internet did work well almost from day one – some sites allowed people, free of charge, to listen to or even download music by new unsigned artists (usually bands). It is certainly another avenue to follow-up along with sending out promo CDs, starting your own website and doing showcase gigs, but beware of signing anything which will let someone do anything more than just use your track on their site.

What about ordering actual CDs via the Internet from sites like Amazon?

This is really just an extension of normal mail-order except that instead of quoting your credit card details over the phone or sending money by post, you can do it on the Internet, and therefore it's really not part of the problem or the brave new world (depending on your point of view) that the Internet represents. In practice sites like Amazon have been hit hard by people being able to download music for nothing. If you've got the technology (and know-how) to look up a site like Amazon which obviously a huge number of people have, then you've probably also got the technology and know-how to find an illegal site and download music from it directly. There is a sort of halfway house when it comes to buying music which is the in-store digital facility for downloading and compiling your own CD.

This would be completely legitimate and of proper CD quality but you could select your own tracks and, of course, the record shop wouldn't need to stock the physical product. This is one reason why the major record labels around the turn of the century sold-off their own actual physical record distribution companies. Along the same lines is the 'digital juke box' where you can dial up almost any record you want to hear in a pub/club etc. and it will be downloaded from a server belonging to the juke-box company. As an artist or writer you should get paid, though not very much per play, whenever your record is 'used' because the computer linked to the 'server' can report on actual uses,

Is there a big market for live concerts over the Internet?

It's one more way of getting to your public. If someone on the other side of the world won't ever get to see a broadcast/video of your live concert in say London, then by streaming it over the Internet for a fee you can increase your audience. Of course they'll need to know that it's going to happen, which costs money for the publicity/advertising, but the ISP should pay money (probably to your record company) to do it. It's possible that a sponsor will even pay for the entire cost of the concert on the strength of it if he's trying to get into markets where your concert (including his logo etc.) can be seen via the Internet, but wouldn't otherwise have been broadcast. In some cases the concert is recorded solely for webcasting or simulcasting (broadcasting and diffusion on the Internet at the same time) either to an invited 'live' audience or no audience at all.

Is there really any money to be made for music on the Internet if the stocks and shares of the companies that were buying up rights have all collapsed?

Yes. The problem was that in the late Nineties there was a scramble for rights to put recordings on the Internet and it was expected that downloads would be the major source of income. Later it looked as though asking people to pay a subscription to stream music from the Internet would be the way the business would go (sort of half-way house between being able to tune a radio to exactly the track you want to hear and actually owning a CD of that track). Now Pressplay, Rhapsody etc. are licensed by the major labels it's possible to access music legally on the Internet, streamed or downloaded, and to join a subscription service to allow so many streamed/downloaded tracks per month.

So who actually gets what from a download/streaming of a song?

Artists get whatever is specified under the agreements with their record companies for use of downloads or streaming of their recordings. For streaming it may be a percentage of the company's receipts. For downloading it should be roughly the same percentage as you'd get for the sale of an actual record. As regards the songs, MCPS in the UK came up quite early with a figure of 10p per download of a complete normal length track. The record companies complained about it, but at least it set some kind of benchmark. Although there was no general agreement amongst the record companies as to how much a one track should cost a user to download, US$0.99, or maybe a bit more if you also get the artwork from the single/album, was the rough norm for the cost of a download. Under MCPS's 10p per track licence, the writer would get the same for a normal length song no matter what the user pays. At $0.99 per track, the artist would probably get roughly his normal royalty per album sold for each album downloaded.

There is also a PRS element to the use of songs on the Internet – performances are taking place and some sort of performance royalty ought to be payable. MCPS and PRS therefore came up with a joint licence which would cover most Internet sites for both 'mechanical' and 'performing' aspects of the use of music on the Internet. As well as the 10p download rate they offer a licence starting at 8% of gross revenue from the service, including webcasts, subscription services and individual streaming (though it excludes adaptations, use of music in advertising and graphic rights). It was also not aimed at business-to-business services, where separate negotiations need to be worked out in each case, or at very small sites, such as fan-club sites, selling downloads, which are covered by the equivalent of their LAP (Limited Availability scheme) for actual records.

What would I get for a ringtone download of my song or recording?

In the UK the MCPS has offered licences to operators of sites for downloading of ringtones at 10p per download – the same as the rate per track for downloading a song on record – or 10% of gross revenue of the site, if higher, and PRS licenses the site at 5% of its gross revenue, (subject to a minimum amount). It's different in other countries and it's subject to constant change, though the collecting societies in Europe and elsewhere are trying to make it easier for ringtone companies to obtain licences for more than one territory (Nokia for example obtained a licence from the Finnish collecting society to cover ringtones throughout Europe).

It's a growing area of exploitation for the record companies. An example is Sony Records' deal with Vodaphone under which some users could download 30 second soundbites of as-yet unreleased tracks from their mobiles as an incentive to buy Vodaphone's products and as exposure for Sony's records.

Downloads are big business, as you can imagine – especially as many people will change their ringtone after only a few weeks and download a new one. There is no set rate for the use of an existing commercial recording as an actual ringtone, as most people are still happy with phones which will only play monophonic ringtones (where only one note is heard at a time). If you buy a phone with commercial ringtones on it then the manufacturer will have had to pay the equivalent of the download royalty up-front on the number of phones with those ringtones already included. In Japan ringtones are such big business that as long ago as 2000 the Japanese equivalent of MCPS collected around £20 million just in the one year.

Text messaging of birthday/Valentine/New Year greeting with a 30 second soundbite of an attached music track is another rapidly growing source of income, as is identification of tracks via Shazam and also downloading of commercial tracks via mobiles which are connected to, or usuable as, MP3 walkmans. All of these can be added to the user's phone bill.

Is it possible to limit where my music is used on the Internet?

If the use is legal then yes – sort of. If one record company owns your recording for World ex. USA and Canada and another unrelated company owns the USA and Canada (reasonably common for successful artists) then the USA and Canada company can offer downloads or streaming of your recordings in its own territory, roughly. The reason it's rough is that they can take credit card information and if someone's card is from within the USA and Canada then they will assume (and of course usually they'll be right) that the downloader/subscriber really is within the USA/Canada and therefore is within their territory and therefore they're entitled to the money. It's not a perfect solution but it's the best compromise available.

Who actually owns the design of my website?

If it's really all your own work, subject to any prompts from a widely-used computer programme which enabled you to do it, then you own it. If you asked someone for example from the local art/technology college to set it up for you then unless you paid him or her, and it's very clear that you paid for all rights to it, it's possible that they could have a claim against you at some point. This is especially true if artwork or other material which was designed for your website winds up on posters or sweatshirts or other merchandising. The people who design these things do have rights automatically to their artwork just as you do to your recordings, which is why you need to acquire these rights from them. Even if you only pay them £1, that's enough, as long as it's unquestionable that you really did acquire their work outright and they warrant that they didn't steal the format/graphics from anyone else's site. You really ought to get something in writing and if in serious doubt spend a few pounds consulting a lawyer who knows about such things.

If you do have enough technical know-how and artistic flair then of course it is possible to design it yourself up to the limit of your knowledge and your flair. From other sites you've visited you probably won't need telling that the more of the important stuff you can get onto the home page, the better; the quicker something loads that's eye-catching and readable while the visitor is waiting for the rest of the homepage to load, the better; and above all keep it updated. There's nothing more off-putting for a visitor (maybe even someone in the business who might have been prepared to help you) than to read about a free offer of tickets to gigs in last year's tour.

Is it possible to sell music from my own site?

Yes, but you would need to have all the rights – performing and mechanical and the right of distribution, and if you're a PRS writer member then in theory they already own the performing part of this even to your own songs. This is something to take specialist advice on. First of all you'll need a host for your website which you can reasonably expect to be secure (if people are giving out credit card details). If your records are available elsewhere then you can always have a hyperlink to the site from which they're being sold (mail order) or downloaded, so that when people click on 'buy' they go straight to the other site (but make sure they've seen the rest of your site first).

Can I use the site in any other way to make money?

Indirectly of course you can use it to get responses from visiting fans who, if you offer them something in return, might leave you their names and addresses (see Fan Club question in the Recording section). At the very least you can make sure you know how many 'hits' your site has had, but if that's visible on-screen then start it rolling at at least several hundred, for the sake of your cred! You could also sell posters or T shirts on the site and if you get enough interest you could even try to get someone to pay to advertise on it. What is more likely is that, if you can get a sponsorship deal, even just a local one at first, you would agree to include the sponsor's logo on your site. If you are, or would like to become a session musician (or get work touring with solo artists as part of their band) then you can use your site to list your qualifications/records you've played on etc. + 30 second soundbites to try to attract work.

GENERAL QUESTIONS AND ANSWERS ON THE MUSIC BUSINESS

Is it illegal to record TV programmes or records on a CD, tape, DVD or video recorder?

Yes, especially if you were to make copies and sell them, even to friends. This would be 'piracy', unless the recording was released over 50 years ago and the writers of the song have all been dead for at least 70 years – which would seem to rule out most of the music that most people want to listen to today. Although manufacturers of CD, cassette, DVD and video recorders often seem to be inviting people to do this, it is illegal to record any copyright material without the permission of the copyright owners. As long ago as 1988, Amstrad were sued over the introduction of their new cassette-to-cassette machine on the basis that the most obvious use of it would probably be home-taping of copyright music. Amstrad won the case on the principle that their machine *could* be use for copying of personal recordings – Christmas greetings from a family to their relatives etc. and other non-infringing uses, which clearly was possible.

In the case of radio or television programmes, 'copyright owners' means the BBC or IBA or producer of the programme, the owner of the recordings and the publisher of the songs being performed, as well as any musicians or actors, script writers producers or others whose services were not 'bought out' by any of the first three.

Even the taping of records still affects the rights of both the record company and the publishers of the songs on the record. In some countries (but not the UK) there is a levy on the price of recording equipment and blank audio and video cassettes, DVDs and CDs to compensate these 'rights owners' for part of their losses through home taping. However it doesn't amount to much and the UK industry has always preferred not to have a levy so that the activity remains completely illegal – not that it's viable to go around suing individuals for making copies of recordings at home but it does mean they can legitimately campaign for better protection and can use copy-protect software to prevent records being copied without being accused of trying to have their cake and eat it. The levy also penalises the very small number of people who genuinely do only ever use cassettes or CDs for personal messages etc. and seems tough on people who use videos etc. for 'time-shifting' television viewing prior to erasing them (however the only real solution is encoding the recordings with something to prevent copies being made – something too clever for pirates to get around it).

Is it always illegal to make copies of printed music without permission?

Assuming that we are not talking about your own unpublished compositions, then there are still few circumstances under which it is acceptable to make copies of music, even for purely personal use. Many publishers subscribe to a 'code of fair practice' for individuals, schools etc. to make a few copies, usually for study. Others may permit this on request if copies are not sold or used for other purposes. In the past the publishers have had to resort to suing schools who flagrantly photocopied music without permission. It's not great PR for publishers, but the schools should really have known better. Publishers may also permit the arranging of their works for

SATB (soprano, alto, tenor and bass) vocals or some other line-up, since pop publishers will not expect to make such versions themselves. But remember that a publisher can't usually give permission for the use of a recording and a record company can't usually give permission for the use of a song.

How long must I wait for my royalties?

Royalties can take a very long time to reach you from the time when they are first earned. Using the example of overseas publishing royalties on record sales, if a song you write is a song which is a hit in say the USA in autumn of one year the American record company waits until the end of the next accounting period under which they have to pay mechanical royalties to the Harry Fox Agency (the USA record royalty collecting agent). At the end of their accounting period they account to the USA publisher, who waits until his next accounting (could be as much as nine months) to pay the UK publisher. At your publisher's next accounting (possibly another nine months) he pays you, or if you have a manager then he pays your manager, who, maybe a few months later pays you.

Most, though not all, accountings are half-yearly (though PRS account quarterly and MCPS monthly), but in many cases for every single link in the chain you might be waiting up to another six months for your royalties. It could easily be at least two years after the records were actually sold or the performance took place. Artist royalties should be accounted slightly quicker, but the problem with these is that until all your advances/recording costs/tour support etc is recouped you won't get anything at all in royalties (you'll only get any additional advances the record companies undertook to pay you). The moral of this is don't go out and buy your post-vintage sports car or 1959 Les Paul Standard the moment you learn that you have a hit song in the USA or another foreign country as you may be waiting years for the money. Don't assume also that your publisher, record company or manager are being dishonest. Just try to keep a track of where your biggest earnings should be coming from and be patient. This should be one reason why publishers and record companies ought to pay advances. They can afford to wait longer than you can for the money to come trickling in.

Where will my biggest earnings come from?

In terms of straightforward UK earnings for a UK artist/songwriter, unless the songs become standards, in which case they will go on earning enormous sums year after year, then artist royalties on hits will bring in more money than songwriting ones, but only once you've recouped the advances. These will almost always be much bigger (but take much longer to recoup) under your record deal than your songwriting deal. Over the period when you have the hits, your earnings from live appearances, provided you were capitalising on your popularity, will be even greater though not usually for a really big rock band, who may well make very little money from gigs because of the sheer expense of staging them.

The best place in the world in which to have a big hit moneywise is, as you can imagine, the USA (but as an artist you'll almost certainly have to spend months there touring, doing interviews, writing with local songwriters etc. before you take-off). Then comes Japan, where some unlikely foreign acts are really big and other huge international acts strangely fail to make it at all. After this comes GAS (Germany, Austria & Switzerland – a good market for heavy rock and 'unsubtle' dance tracks – anything slower than 200bpm+ was at one time jokingly considered a ballad), then the UK followed by France (another unpredictable market), Italy, Brazil (if you can get the money out) and other 'markets' such as Spain and Portugal, Benelux (Belgium, Luxembourg & the Netherlands), Australasia, Canada (almost always lumped in with the USA), Scandinavia ('the Nordic Countries', if all are included) and South Africa. Owing to the ineffectiveness of copyright protection and consequent lack of exploitation, large areas like the rest of Africa, India, some Eastern European countries and Russia, the Middle East, parts of the Far East and parts of South and Central America can be almost ruled out when working out where money will be coming from. It is possible to get some sort of money out of South America, where legitimate sales are huge but inflation and problems in collecting the money can reduce the income enormously.

In most of these places there is copyright protection of sorts but generally it is not properly enforced. Many foreign records are imported and sold, along with 'bootleg' and 'pirate' recordings in Europe, especially from Eastern European countries like Rumania. In the Far East things are often even worse. Decades ago, long before the average person had the possibility of making copies at home, you could, in parts of the Far East, take a record into a record shop and for a small charge have a copy made, in total disregard of the songwriters' and artists' rights and those of the publisher and record company.

There are places in the world, mainly in the poorer parts, where money may have been collected for you and put into a bank account in your name. Contracts with publishers and record companies sometimes specify this because 'Exchange Control' regulations prevent money being sent out of the country. This means that sooner or later you will have to go there to spend it, fine if it's Spain but not so funny if it means paying your fares to and from Brazil.

Isn't Anglo-American Music still dominant worldwide?

In your favour in all of this is the fact that yes, English and American pop music, in the English language, is supreme all round the world. This is borne out by the tendency for many Continental-European artists to perform local songs with English lyrics in the Eurovision Song Contest in years past, believing that this will increase their chances of success. The biggest exception is Japan, where millions of Japanese rush out to buy largely Japanese artists singing Japanese songs. To some extent the same is true in France. In some countries the radio and television stations are forced, by government quotas, to play a minimum of say 40% local language recordings, to slow down the spread of Anglo-American culture through rock and pop music.

The Americans have been prepared to put on their trade 'blacklist' countries which don't have or don't enforce copyright laws during their GATT (General Agreement on Trade and Tariffs) negotiations under the TRIPS (Trade Related Intellectual Property) section of the regulations. This is mainly aimed at piracy of IBM software etc. but in the process also covers countries which allow piracy of music. Unfortunately the 21st Century started really badly (unusually badly) as regards UK success in the USA charts, but if you're dedicated and prepared to tour there/live there then success is still possible. The charts can change remarkably quickly and it has surprisingly little to do with the particular styles of music produced in USA/UK/Continental Europe, although European dance music in general doesn't tend to make it over there (with notable exceptions).

Can I assume that a printed contract will be 'standard' and therefore reasonable?

These days most contracts are prepared on word processors. It is worth noting however that if you are offered a printed contract then the company offering it is less likely to let you have anything altered in your favour as the terms are probably pretty standard. The terms are, of course, less likely to be prepared specially to your disadvantage as they could possibly be with a typed and photocopied contract. Obviously the only real answer is to read it. It may contain a 'schedule' setting out the royalties and the duration on the outside with other important details, and contain a lot of small print on the inside, or vice versa. If this is the case then read the small print on the schedule as you go along whenever it's referred to in the main agreement. An apparently high royalty and short duration may be totally different once the small print is applied.

If the contract is altered in pen (with the alterations initialled by both parties) make sure that all the copies are identical and that the meaning of all the wording is completely certain, especially if it relates to how long you're signed for or the royalty rates. Usually there'll be only two copies, but the publisher/record company etc. may want an extra one and may prepare an extra one for you to leave with your manager or lawyer. If they're not all the same, then whoever is signing you up could try to claim, in the event of a dispute, that the real intention or wording was something different from what you understood it was at the time of signing. The intention of the parties to a contract is what the judge would be interested in if it went to court and as the company can produce a copy of the agreement signed by you this could possibly present you with problems.

What should I know about insurance?

It's perfectly possible for you or someone else to insure your voice, fingers etc. for whatever you or they think might be lost if something happened to you. It's just a question of balancing the cost against the possible risk. If you've been paid a big advance by a record company, they may want to insure you at their expense and may ask you to undergo a medical examination or Aids test. It may not be a 'deal-breaker' if you say no, but you should be prepared for this.

Some semi-pro bands do insure their equipment, but the cost is always high, although once you're making your living from music you can't afford not to have some sort of protection. People in the music business don't have a great reputation for 'stability'. Rock'n'roll fans ripping up cinema seats in the Fifties, bands like The Who smashing guitars in the Sixties and the anti-establishment image of punk bands in the Seventies right down to recent Gangsta Rappers and heavy rock bands with parental guidance warnings about their lyrics – all these have led to the feeling that we're all irresponsible drug-crazed maniacs. However, insurance is possible – at a price.

It is also possible to get third party insurance (public liability insurance) in case, for example, your PA speaker falls on someone's head. If you're a Musicians Union member then you can get public liability insurance free of charge up to a certain amount, and also a certain amount of insurance for your equipment. Major acts have to have third party insurance to cover themselves against accidents to road crew, lighting technicians and others who are effectively employed by them to run big concerts and tours. Venues will have their own third party insurance but will look to pass on the liability to you if an accident appears to have been caused by you or your entourage.

What happens if I lose my copy of the contract?

Just a general cautionary word about being methodical where contracts are concerned. Even if your manager has secured the contracts for you and has copies himself, always try to keep a copy of every contract you sign and, importantly, of every letter you write on the subject of contracts. Put the letters with the contracts. You're never quite sure when you might need to produce them. If you lose a contract you can ask the other party (publisher, record company or whoever) for a copy to be made of their copy, and most companies will do this quite readily. A crooked company could always take the opportunity to alter the terms in its favour. This isn't at all likely, but it has been known.

Should I join the Musicians' Union?

The MU has been active for decades in ensuring an increasing supply of work for musicians and at reasonable fees. They have constantly campaigned to ensure that radio stations do not play records all day, so that a proportion of the airtime is devoted to live music. They have at various times required that all musicians appearing on such television programmes as *Top Of The Pops* must either play live or, if they wish to mime, must mime to a re-recording of their record, thereby making more work for musicians and singers.

The Union lays down certain minimum rates for all session musicians, at a specific rate for a three-hour session plus extra for doubling on another instrument, extra for porterage (bringing a heavy instrument to the session), overtime, etc. If a session musician records for a commercial record, there's a sepa-

rate fee payable if that recording also gets used in a television programme etc. The record companies have agreements with the MU whereby they agree to pay MU rates for all their sessions, and you should certainly be a member if you wish to start doing sessions regularly – the Union is in any case working in your interests. This would mean agreeing not to play for less than Union rates, but this is unlikely to worry a good working musician whose interests the MU is safeguarding.

Membership also brings such benefits as several hundred pounds' worth of free legal advice (the MU lawyers will check over any agreements you may have been offered) plus public liability insurance (see 'What should I know about insurance' in this section). Each branch sends out a regular newsletter to members in its area full of useful information. Membership of the MU costs annually £50 or so upwards to a certain maximum depending upon the member's earnings as a musician. A professional musician should be a member of the MU anyway but if you're not, and you're tempted to think 'that's £50-70 I could save', or that it's only for orchestral or jazz musicians, think again. If you seriously want to make money as a performer then you need all the help you can get and the MU could help a lot. The address to write to for information is in our Useful Addresses list.

What are publicists and what do they do?

Some managers, record companies and the like make use of independent publicists (PR Companies) either to generate publicity for themselves or their artists or to release 'statements' to the press about new artists signed, forthcoming tours arranged and suchlike. Other larger organisations have their own 'press offices', to arrange the company's advertising. One feature of their activities which is much less common than it used to be is the 'publicity stunt'. These are actual events deliberately staged for the benefit of the press, rather than just over-dramatised or largely fictitious stories of stars getting married, getting divorced, moving abroad, narrowly escaping death in car crashes, denying (or admitting) taking drugs and so forth.

What can I do personally to get publicity?

If you are just a local artist or group and you wish to publicise yourselves then the possibility of your making a record (for a 'proper' record company, rather than just your own to sell at gigs etc.) is usually enough to interest the local press. The most basic piece of publicity is to have cards printed with your name and what you do plus your address or just phone number to give to enquirers or to leave at venues where you have played. A few hundred of these will cost no more than a few pounds or so and are an absolute must. As we've said, if you have a manager or agent then he will provide you with cards showing himself as the contact instead of you. Advertisements in local papers are not too expensive, though the 'entertainers' heading will mostly list children's magicians and mobile discotheques. The other obvious means of attracting publicity is through

posters, but you need to be very careful that you don't fall foul of the local authority by putting these up where you shouldn't. If you're doing pub gigs they'll probably expect you to produce your own posters and do a bit of local PR.

PR is obviously a lot cheaper than advertising, although a lot of PR comes at a price (sometimes a magazine will do an article on you but only if you take out a full-page advert). The other really good source of work/publicity is of course the Internet (see separate Internet Section for more). As regards PR you are more likely to get this if you look good and are good at, or very amenable to doing, interviews. It's only beneficial to be really antisocial and unhelpful if you're already well-known and therefore the press can paint you as today's bad boy/girl of pop.

As regards public appearances you could try to get to do a 'tour' of supermarket car-parks. On the face of it this might sound 'desperate' but as long as it's publicised locally well in advance then for pop acts a PA in a supermarket car-park usually produces very good crowd and could result in substantial local sales and media attention.

Can anyone start up their own fan club?

There have been moves to try to regulate the running of fan clubs but the basic answer is yes, and even an unsigned new band would benefit from doing so. If at all possible you need to find some friend, relative or fan who is prepared, more or less unpaid, to be the secretary. This position has no legal status but if you are going, for example, to charge £10 a year for membership in return for regular newsletters, CDs of special messages from the band, cheaper merchandise etc. then you need to be very sure that who-ever's organising it for you can literally deliver the goods. The last thing you want, even if you're only well-known locally as yet, is a scandal caused by fans

115

paying out, however little, and getting nothing or next to nothing in return.

Once you are more successful you can afford to pay to have your fan club organised on a large scale if you wish. The fan club would also probably have its own web site on the Internet and so on. Incidentally if someone you don't know wishes to start a 'You Appreciation Society' then you'd have trouble stopping them, but unless you provided them with something which fans couldn't get anywhere else, they'd be unlikely to make a very big impact.

Beware of record companies wanting to get involved in your fan club in order to sell not only your records/merchandising etc. but material by their other artists. It's also worth bearing in mind that, under the UK's Data Protection Act, you can't (not that you may necessarily want to) go selling lists of the members of your fan club to other people. You would have to get the fans to agree, or else agree not to disagree by not completing the appropriate box on the membership form or Internet site. To you such a list is invaluable, even in the early stages, as you know who to contact with offers of T-shirts, cut-price concert tickets etc. If you have a web-site then you don't even necessarily need a fan club to get the names of the visitors to your site who might then be interested in more information on gigs, merchandise and above all recordings from you, provided you give them an incentive to give you their name/address/e-mail address.

Do I really have to get my agreements vetted by a solicitor?

In the case of simple agency agreements for concerts it isn't strictly necessary and only if you have problems would you need to consult a lawyer. However for all songwriting assignments, recording and management agreements, especially 'blankets' as opposed to one-off's, you will actually be expected to have taken independent legal advice. The agreements will say, usually at the end, that they could have an important impact on your career and will either strongly urge you to take expert (legal) advice or will ask you to warrant that you actually have taken such advice.

This is to protect the publishers, record companies etc. from your going back to them a year or so later and claiming that the agreement was unfair because you did not understand what you were signing or your bargaining position was weaker than theirs. Actually with a really hot new act that's not necessarily true at all, but the press and the courts and the British public generally favour the one who appears to be the underdog, and disputes are always portrayed as big fat rich music business people taking advantage of poor struggling artists and writers. If there is no warning or warranty about your taking legal advice in your agreement and you don't in fact take any then if you want to get out of an agreement you probably have a head start, depending on other factors.

The expert advice should really come from an entertainment lawyer, not one who is more used to conveyancing, divorce or whatever. Record companies, publishers etc. could suggest three or four to you and leave you to choose, but you'll understand that they can't suggest just one in case you accuse them in a few years' time of having influenced the advice you got. In practice once he's acting for you, then your lawyer will be bound to act only in your best interests. Not only should he not be the record company's, manager's or publisher's lawyer but he should really be from a different firm altogether.

Do I always have to take the lawyer's advice?

No. You'd be silly to ignore it of course, but in the end you are the only one who knows just how badly you want to be signed up to this particular deal. You should be aware that it's not unknown for a lawyer to blow your chances with a particular company by asking for too much in advances, royalties or too many concessions in the small print. Make sure he or she knows how much you're prepared to concede, and that they're guided closely by you throughout any negotiations they conduct on your behalf. They'll do the best deal they can for you, but they can't read your mind.

What if I'm under 18?

If you're under 18 then you are technically still a minor and would find it easier to get out of any deals you make on the grounds of 'immaturity'. Therefore one of your parents or your legal guardian will have to be involved in the negotiations and counter-sign your agreements, to ensure that you're bound by what you've signed.

How binding are verbal agreements?

A very straightforward verbal agreement between you and, for instance, a publisher made in the street in the presence of a couple of independent witnesses, to give him your next composition on his usual terms in return for £10 advance, while not in itself an assignment of the copyright in that song, could nevertheless be something to which either of you may be able to hold the other. If his terms turned out to be much less good from your point of view than you might reasonably have expected, then probably he would have to improve them to what a court would regard as usual in the business before he could hold you to the contract, unless of course you already knew beforehand that his standard terms were not very good.

A verbal agreement is never good enough on its own and should always be confirmed by a written one. It is simply impossible to cover all reasonable eventualities in a verbal agreement even though you might think it satisfactory at the time. You might agree with someone over the telephone to play at his venue for £300 on a certain night from 10 pm until 1am, but what happens if he claims not to have realised that you expected a longer break than 10 minutes during that period or if it turned out that he expected a singer and you were just an instrumental band. Such snags are much more easily ironed out where a written agreement exists.

Above all, note that on any agreements at or near the bottom there should be wording such as 'this agreement represents the total agreement between the two parties and can only be altered in writing'. If the person offering you such an agreement says, while explaining it, something like 'Oh don't worry about that', 'this never happens' or 'obviously we'll up the royalty after a little while' you cannot hold him to any of this, and must ask him to have the contract altered to cover these things or else sign it at its face value.

In what ways might VAT affect me?

Value Added Tax is payable on a great many goods and services in the UK and VAT or an equivalent sales tax exists in many other countries. The only person who cannot claim it back in some way is the 'consumer' at the end of the line. Thus each member of the chain in the production and sale of a record can claim back some of the tax he has paid by collecting tax himself from the next person in the chain until it is eventually the record buyer who pays the appropriate tax on the cost of a record. The advisability of putting VAT on the cost of sheet music and books has been under consideration for many years, but records had VAT on them right from its introduction in the UK.

If you are 'in the business', say as a musician, then you can register for VAT. You can claim VAT from record companies, publishers and the management of venues at which you perform. If you are registered then the first two of these bodies are obliged to pay you the additional VAT on top of your royalties if you send them an invoice for it quoting your VAT registration number. At venues you can charge this if you ask for it initially together with your fee, but if you forget then you will be in the embarrassing position of having to go back to them and ask, or else work on the basis that the fee you got included VAT. Although all this VAT you have collected is payable quarterly by you to the government (make sure you get your returns in on time!), you can of course, before paying it, deduct (if registered) all the VAT you yourself have had to pay on new instruments, stage clothes, recording equipment – in fact almost everything reasonably necessary to the pursuit of your musical career (but don't push it too far).

All this may sound fine but it does have to be properly worked out by your accountant (you'll need to have one if you wish to register for VAT unless you have enough free time and/or you're good with figures). It is often worth registering even though your earnings don't reach the level where you're obliged to, but it may require an accountant to tell you whether in your particular circumstances this would be a worthwhile step (it would be very unlikely to be worth it for a semi-pro act).

Should I get a royalty statement even if nothing is payable?

If something (anything) was earned in the last accounting period but nothing's payable to you because they haven't yet recovered the advance they paid you, then you should still get a statement. Publishers tend not to carry forward

amounts less than about £25-£50 and much the same thresholds apply with record companies, but they should be prepared to pay you if you ask specifically. If you want to receive statements even when no money has been earned you will need to be sure this is covered in your agreements, otherwise many companies will not send them.

Do I really need an accountant?

Once you have a manager who is receiving and spending money on your behalf then you should definitely have your own accountant, preferably one who understands the entertainment business. Even if you trust your manager implicitly, it's better to have your finances sorted out by someone independent. The advice your accountant can give on tax liability could save you a small fortune. There have been a few horror stories about stars being ripped off by their accountants, but you'd be very unlucky to fall into the hands of both a crooked manager and a crooked accountant. The more questions you ask, within reason, the harder it is for anyone to pull the wool over your eyes. As with lawyers, you can ask an accountant for a rough estimate of his likely charges.

Can I audit my manager/ publisher/record company?

Your agreements with all of these should contain an audit clause (some of them run to over two pages!) which should state that you can appoint someone to audit the company, usually not more than once a year or maybe once every two years, at their normal address in normal office hours on giving reasonable prior notice. You can't expect them to let absolutely anyone look at their books, so it should be a professional accountant. It will usually say that if you don't query any royalty statement within around three years then you lose the right. After a few years, the Statute of Limitations allows them to throw away the documentation in any case, though for serious fraud your solicitor may advise that it will be possible to make claims back beyond this.

Usually if a deficit of more than 10% is found they'll be expected to pay your audit fees (your accountant can advise what they're likely to be) although they may limit their contribution to your fees to the same amount as is found to have been underpaid, which would be reasonable.

It is actually surprisingly rare for audits to be made by individual writers or artists. It's not cheap (even quite a small audit can cost several thousand pounds) and you'd normally only do it if you seriously suspected the company of deliberately underpaying you a lot of money. It is therefore likely to cast a shadow over the relationship between you and the company you're auditing, especially if it's a smaller company and you don't find much underpayment.

Incidentally the MCPS do conduct regular audits of record companies on behalf of all writers and publishers, on which they charge 10% commission, and they generally find substantial amounts owing. The societies also audit other societies abroad – they call them 'technical visits' – and again this usually unearths a large amount of unpaid earnings. Where possible the money these audits recover is paid to the songs used, but mostly it's impossible to identify them and the money is divided pro rata according to your other earnings.

What happens if my manager/record label/publisher goes broke?

This is still regarded as a get-rich-quick business, although it's actually much more 'business-like' than ever before. However there are still lots of companies in the music business which look good after a couple of hits but have completely disappeared a year or so later. The one thing you should try to ensure is that not only does the agreement terminate if they go bust (there are various phrases to cover the various stages of this) but that also you get back all the rights to any recordings made or songs written during the term of your agreement up to that point. If they wish to look remotely 'legit' then hopefully they'll agree to this. If they don't then you really could be looking at trying to get your songs/recordings back from the Official Receiver who could otherwise sell them to a third party and your rights would (sad to say) quite often be difficult to enforce against that third party – i.e. they could go on selling your records/using your songs until they in turn are sold to some other company and all this time you won't receive anything at all in royalties and won't have anyone to sue (as there'll be no-one with whom you had a contractual relationship). The smaller and newer the company you sign to, the more likely, statistically, this is to happen. That doesn't mean you shouldn't sign to a new company. Many newer companies are very pro-active and prepared to take a risk on a writer or artist who the majors would shy away from . . . but the newer they are the more insistent you should be about getting your songs/recordings back if they go under. Be warned!

Can any of my earnings be guaranteed?

It used to be the case that managers and some record and publishing companies would write into agreements that the artist was guaranteed a certain level of earnings. The only real guarantees are advance payments which a company is obligated to pay under the terms of the agreement, for example when an artist signs to a label, when an album is released, or when it reaches a certain chart position (and the only absolute guarantees are the advances they pay you on signing!). If you are offered a £1m recording deal, this usually means that the advances will have totalled £1m if, and only if, the label takes up all its options. These days if anyone were to offer a deal where you continued to be bound by it until the 'guaranteed earnings' had been reached by way of normal royalty payments, you'd be able to claim that it was a restraint of your trade, as there would be no way of knowing how long you could be bound.

What royalties should I get on sales of videos, DVD etc.

As a songwriter, the use of one of your songs in a video tape or disc will be licensed by your publisher, usually through the MCPS at a rate agreed within the industry. This is rather complex but comes out at around the same percentage of the retail price on the sale of a 'videogram' (the name for video tapes and discs) as on the sale of a record. For films, television programmes etc. which are reproduced on video there is a lower pro rata rate on the amount of music used. If the film was made before the emergence of video then the publisher's original synchronisation licence to the film company may have covered the sale or rental of videos, in which case you may miss out. Royalties on videos which are released for hire tend to be fairly insignificant. Add to this the fact that many of the street videos sold are illegal pirated copies and you will see that songwriters and artists have not been making fortunes from video and DVD.

Although there are usually no artist royalties payable on uses of promo videos, an artist should certainly receive royalties on sales of long-form videos (whether of live concerts, compiled from promo videos of your singles or compilations of videos by various artists). The royalties on videos sold by your record company alongside the records and tapes will usually be at the same rate, but remember the cost of making your promo videos will be offset against your royalties – usually half from general royalties and half from sales and uses of the video.

How are the charts compiled?

The best selling singles and album charts in the UK are compiled by a market research company on behalf of the BPI, the trade magazine *Music Week* in which they're published and the BBC who feature them on *Top Of The Pops* and other television and radio programmes, though some music papers and broadcasters have their own charts. *Music Week* also includes club charts and dance charts, as well as specialist country, rock and indie charts.

They also include charts for compilation albums, as these sometimes sell in such huge numbers that they would dominate the main album chart if they were included in it (although 'greatest hits' compilations from one artist still are). The information on sales comes from 'returns' made by a certain number of retail outlets in the UK ('chart shops') which tell the researchers exactly what they sold every week. Specialist charts are generally compiled from 'returns' from specialist shops, as it is otherwise debatable as to which category some albums fall into – were the Eagles albums in the Seventies and Eighties country or rock? They have been listed in both.

The charts are broadcast by BBC on Radio 1 on Sundays, published a day or two later in *Music Week*, then televised in *Top Of The Pops* later in the week, but it is possible to estimate the positions from the 'midweek' information which the researchers supply to the industry.

In the USA the definitive Top 100 singles, Top 200 albums and other charts are published in the magazine *Billboard*, but these are based on radio and televison airplay as well as sales. The sheer size of the market and the inclusion of airplay, means that records climb the charts more slowly, unlike the UK. The airplay is actually so important that it's possible to have a US top 10 singles hit without even releasing the single! The recording is simply given exposure and sent to radio stations etc. This is becoming more common, as record companies don't want people buying the single if they could possibly sell them a whole album on the strength of the song they've heard and liked on the radio.

How do I get a silver/gold/ platinum disc?

These can be awarded for any single or album which reaches a certain level of sales which are certified by the market research company compiling the charts. In the UK at present singles are: silver – 200,000, gold – 400,000, platinum – 600,000. For albums the thresholds are: silver – 60,000, gold – 100,000, platinum – 300,000. Most albums that enter in the Top 10 can expect to go silver after the first few weeks. An album entering at number 1 can expect to go gold more or less immediately and almost any album that's been in the charts for three months or so can expect to go platinum. Once the figures have been reached, anyone connected with the record can get one. They cost about £100 each and your manager, record company and every different publisher of a song on an album will probably all buy at least one for themselves plus possibly one for the artist or writer. However, you should be aware that nobody actually gets one automatically and free of charge. They are often awarded to such people as the act's lawyers and accountants, and the company which makes them will even make one for presentation to your granny for making the cakes you ate during rehearsals if you're prepared to pay for it.

What should I know about sampling?

The first thing to say is 'Don't do it!' That's all very easy to say and, of course, the use of a really distinctive sample, or re-recorded extract, from an earlier song, in a record can make the difference between success and failure. Imagine 'Gangsta's Paradise' by Coolio, 'Millennium' by Robbie Williams or 'Bittersweet Symphony' by The Verve without the use of the earlier song. On the other hand samples are frequently used when it would have been almost as easy to write and record something original. The vital thing to remember when you use a sample is that you're using someone else's property. They can quite legally demand a ridiculously large percentage of your entire song/record, even for a tiny sample. You don't have to pay it, of course, provided you take the sample out of your recording. If you've already had it released, then you're in trouble!

Record companies and publishers are usually not too unreasonable, but you can't assume that. They'll be guided by their artists or writers, and very broadly the less the artists/writers of the original song need the money, the more likely they are to say 'no'. In this case you won't be able to release your record no matter how much you offer, and you'll have to take it off the market immediately if it's already been released and possibly pay damages.

On very small samples the owner of the recording you've sampled may accept a flat fee from your record company to use the sample. The publisher of the song you've sampled will normally expect to become a co-owner of the copyright in your song, even if the share they've asked for is only 5% of your song. They'll also expect to collect their shares directly from the users, not from your publisher. Remember that you guarantee to publishers and record companies in your agreements that the song and recording will be 'all your own work' so you're financially liable if they contain bits of someone else's.

There are arguments as to whether some samples are too insignificant to be an infringement and the question of whether you've used 'a substantial part' of another song will be brought up. However even drum loops can be enough, so don't say we didn't warn you. There's a 'halfway' position which would be for you to use a bit of someone else's song but re-record it. Again you must ask permission first, but only from the publisher of the original song this time. If, of course, it's your record that's been sampled then the boot's on the other foot, and you and your publisher should try to agree between you how much of the new song you should ask for. You will then become a part writer of the new song.

What if the sample is only on one mix of a song?

This does make life complicated, and if it's your song that's been sampled we would suggest that if it's at all likely that the mix containing your sample will be the featured radio edit ('A-side') you try to ask for a share, albeit a small one, of all the mixes. If you don't then it's quite likely that you won't get any performing and broadcasting fees as the PRS and other societies abroad won't be able to distinguish which mix was being played. You may even miss out on royalties from sales of compilation albums too, though you can at least tell MCPS and other mechanical societies when you know it's the mix with your sample on it that's included in a particular release.

Incidentally, beware of remixers getting hold of a track of yours which has no samples in it and putting some in. You could of course suddenly find yourself losing a share of your song, possibly all of it, and possibly on all the mixes including the hit radio edit, just because of someone else's actions.

Would my career take off better overseas?

There have been quite a few British artists who have first made it in Continental Europe, usually Germany or Holland. You may well get a record deal from a major label there and be able to make a good living. There's still a mystique about Anglo-American artists on the Continent. Do remember, though, that very many records are successful all round Europe except the UK. Certain types of music such as Italian dance music and Scandinavian heavy rock do have credibility in Britain, but often your major label's UK office will either not release or else not get behind a release from one of their Continental affiliates. So if you really want to make it in the UK then this isn't always a good option. If all else fails, however, it is a possibility you should be aware of. Some artists have become huge in one or two other particular markets, such as The Kelly Family from Ireland who became huge in Germany without ever breaking in the UK.

Then there's the USA. Despite the Americans' love of 'cute' British accents, it's not an easy place to launch a career no matter what nationality you are. But it's another possibility, though even British acts who have already been big in the UK often have to go and live there permanently for a while to make any impact. Occasionally, as in the case of the London rock band Bush, UK acts do make it in the US before their home country.

Do I need a licence to run a mobile disco?

As with live bands, the venues where you play should be licensed by the PRS and PPL and if you're simply playing records then you're entitled to assume that you don't need a separate licence. If you yourself were organising a gig somewhere where music isn't normally played, then you should be licensed. Again, as with bands, most DJ's can make good steady money — £150 or a lot more – for a good mobile disco + lights working on a local level at parties and functions without having to spend a fortune on new releases every week, provided they play 'Hi Ho Silver Lining' and 'The Lady In Red' etc. It's possible to get from there to Hospital Radio and with a lot of tenacity from there to local radio and on upwards, but it won't, of course, open doors to being a club DJ.

How can I get to become a club DJ?

If you're a mobile DJ who's already buying a lot of current dance music then it's a question of being persistent in trying to find the local gigs where you can get to play what you want to play. Most top DJs built up most of their reputation in one club before 'playing the field'. The better known you get, the more freebies you can get from the record labels, especially if you co-operate in filling in their audience response forms and keep in touch with them. Having said that, even the top DJs still spend some of their own money on new releases. DJs have, of course, become stars in their own right on the club scene and you could earn up to £500-£1,500 or more per performance. Some will do maybe three clubs in one night, although some top DJs deliberately try to preserve their value to clubs by not taking all the work offered. For special nights of the year the prices rocket and you could add a nought to the fees for New Year's Eve. It's not just musicians who can make good money from appearing live.

If you haven't any ties then once you've got a reputation you could easily spend as much of the summer as you want sunning yourself in Ibiza or Aiya Napa. If you're lucky you might be able to build up a reputation by being based

there first, then start earning big money in the UK too.

Another big source of income, and means of increasing your reputation, is mixing and remixing existing tracks, some of which are re-released on an almost regular basis with new mixes. There's nothing to stop you as a successful DJ getting together with a producer and putting out records in your own names, and increasing numbers of these have made it into the main UK singles charts. Equally it's possible for music stars such as Boy George to move over to being successful DJs, especially when their roots were in the clubs in the first place.

How can I find out more about the music business?

The best answer is to read as much as you can of the music press. The predominant trade magazine in the UK is known as *Music Week*. It's quite expensive but it does have the full UK singles and album charts, including specialised charts and lists of all new releases as well as news and views within the industry and is a very good place to look for ads for jobs in the business. It also includes full club charts, dance airplay charts, alternative and urban charts relating to the dance music scene. The long-running weekly paper *NME* still contains a lot of information, as do the glossies such as *Q* and *Mojo*. In the USA the major trade magazine is called *Billboard* and this contains the Top 100 singles and Top 200 album charts as well as lots of specialist music charts.

How could I get a job in the music business?

These days this is no longer frowned on by school teachers and those giving careers guidance. There is a realisation of how much the pop music business is worth to the UK's economy and of the

UK's cultural influence through music. It's possible to take a music GCSE specialising in 'pop' music which would have been unthinkable even in the Sixties when British pop music first dominated the world.

BA courses in commercial music studies are now available at quite a number of colleges up and down the country. There is a book called the *Music Education Directory* produced by the BPI and North Glasgow College indicating the courses available at these colleges. Information is even available from the BPI's Internet pages on www. bpi.co.uk. The MPA also publishes a regular list of people seeking jobs in the business to all its members, so this is a possible avenue. Needless to say, a very large number of people working in the music business are also former professional musicians or singers. It's so popular that lots of people with honours degrees from University are still running errands and making the tea and are on much lower than average salaries compared with other businesses. Remember also that most jobs in music are actually accounting, clerical and secretarial and in many respects are therefore much the same as in any other business. But even today it's the kind of business in which many top executives started out at the very bottom, so if being in the music business is what you really want, don't be put off.

Have we made you feel that everyone is out to swindle you?

We hope not, because although you'll now know what pitfalls to avoid, it needs to be said that for every crook in the music business there are dozens of honest people. Just because someone's contract could be interpreted as giving him the right to do all sorts of evil things to you, he very likely has no intention of ever doing any of them. They may just have been thought up by his over-zealous lawyer and quite possibly he simply doesn't know how to alter them slightly back in your favour without the risk of losing all his rights. For all that, it's nice to know that the contract you've signed is a reasonable one, and also that it really does set out what you think you've agreed to. It's usually easier to create music, or anything, when you know that you'll be properly paid for it.

CONTRACTS

EXAMPLES OF CONTRACTS, WITH COMMENTS

In this section we have included some shortened versions of a song assignment, an agreement to record one single for an independent producer, a form of management agreement and simple agency and booking confirmation agreements. A full blanket songwriting agreement can run to 30 pages or more and a long-term artist/record company agreement to around 50 or more pages and space prevents us including these. You will in any event need to take legal advice before signing all such agreements and your lawyer can explain the details. Examples of royalty terms have generally been included, but you will know from our earlier comments what you could normally expect to get under such contracts in terms of royalty rates and hard cash.

Also shown is a joint notification of works form (JNWF) to the MCPS and PRS. Your publisher will complete one of these for each new work coming under his control. It is no longer necessary for you to sign this form and some publishers now make registrations on-line directly from their databases without completing the form manually. PRS/MCPS then send confirmation to them that the registration has been made. If you know your CAE number, let your publisher have a note of it. If you want to see the registrations of your songs or print-outs of the entry for your song on MCPS's database then your publisher will probably not mind providing these if you ask.

As we have said, artist management agreements can range from a scrap of paper appointing your next-door neighbour as your manager, to a multi-paged document with an international company which takes a long time to read and even longer to understand. There is no such thing as a 'standard' artist management contract but again your lawyer can explain the pros and cons. Try to think 'If I'm immediately successful, am I going to be happy to be bound by this contract'.

1. Publishing assignment for a specific song(s). *For notes and comments on the terms of this agreement see under 'Publishing Contracts' section. Songwriter/ Publisher contract for one song*

AN ASSIGNMENT made this ..... day of ..... between

.... of............ ('the Writer') of the one part and
.................of............ ('the Publisher') of the other part

WITNESSETH:

1. In consideration of the sum of £1 (receipt whereof the Writer hereby acknowledges) and of other good and valuable considerations the Writer with full title guarantee (and by way of assignment of future copyright and rights where appropriate) hereby sells, assigns, transfers and delivers to the Publisher its successors and assigns the whole of the property title copyright and interest vested and contingent and all other rights whatsoever now or hereafter known throughout the Universe ('the Territory') in the musical work entitled: '...............' ('the Work') for a period of .... years from the date hereof ('the Term') including the right to collect royalties and fees outstanding for payment in respect of any uses of rights in the Work prior to the date hereof and the right to collect any royalties and fees accruing during the Term but actually payable within one year thereafter SUBJECT to the rights of the Performing Right Society Ltd. ('PRS') arising by virtue of the Writer's membership thereof but including the reversionary interest of the Writer in such rights expectant upon the termination of the rights of PRS subject to the payment to the Writer by the Publisher thereafter of the share payable by the PRS to the Writer thereof.

2. The Writer hereby warrants and agrees:

(a) that the Work and every part thereof is the original work of the Writer and does not infringe the copyright or any other right whatsoever of any person firm or corporation and is not obscene or defamatory
(b) that he is the owner (subject to the terms of this assignment) of the copyright and all other rights in the Work and has not previously granted transferred or assigned and will not during the Term purport to grant transfer or assign any interest therein assigned hereunder to any other person firm or corporation
(c) that he has the full right power and authority to enter into this agreement and is under no disability in regard thereto
(d) that each and every part of the Work is and will at all times be capable of such copyright protection throughout the Territory as is afforded to works of UK origin
(e) that he has made no representation to or agreement with any third party as to the terms upon which mechanical licences might or will be available in respect of the Work
(f) that he will indemnify the Publisher in respect of any claims demands and expenses arising from any breach of these warranties PROVIDED THAT the Publisher will not compromise or settle any such claims without the prior consent of the Writer such consent not to be unreasonably withheld or delayed. The Publisher is hereby irrevocably appointed the true and lawful representative of the Writer so far as may be necessary to defend and/or institute claims to establish or maintain copyright in the Work.

   In the event of any material breach of any of the above warranties and agreements the Publisher shall be entitled without prejudice to its other rights to suspend payment of royalties hereunder and to pay same into a separate interest-bearing account pending final resolution of such matter in an amount reasonably related to their probable loss.

3. The Publisher shall have the right to make and publish and to authorise others to make and publish new adaptations orchestrations and arrangements of the Work and new lyrics or translations in any language to the music of the Work as the Publisher shall think fit IT BEING AGREED that no major or substantial alterations may be authorised by the Publisher hereunder without the prior written consent of the Writer. The entire copyright and all other rights whatsoever in such modifications and new matter shall be vested in the Publisher for the Term.

4. The Publisher shall use all reasonable endeavours to procure the promotion of the Work it being agreed that if at any time following the expiry of two years from the date hereof the Writer shall serve notice on the Publisher enquiring whether any such promotion has taken place and if within three months from receipt of such notice the Publisher shall fail to provide evidence of such promotion, whether or not as a result of the Publisher's endeavours, then all rights hereby granted to the Publisher shall forthwith revert to the Writer. For the purpose of this agreement 'promotion' shall mean the commercial release for sale to the public of a recording of the Work or inclusion of the Work in a film, television commercial or commercial video production.

5. The Publisher shall pay royalties (excluding performing and broadcasting fees) to the Writer in respect of the Work as follows:

(i) 12.5% per copy of the marked retail selling price of all printed editions of the Work sold in the United Kingdom by the Publisher and paid for to the Publisher (pro rata in the case of collective editions)

(ii) 65% of all net licence fees computed at source and received by the Publisher in respect of the manufacture for sale to the public of recordings of the Work save that such royalty shall be 50% in respect of recordings procured by the Publisher ('Cover Recordings')

(iii) 65% of all sums computed at source and received by the Publisher in respect of synchronisation rights and any and all other uses of the Work (excluding performing and broadcasting) not specified hereunder

(iv) 65% of any and all net royalties received by the Publisher specifically in respect of the Work arising from the imposition of any levy on blank tapes or audio equipment provided that if the Writer shall receive any portion of such levy direct then the Publisher shall only be required to pay the balance necessary to bring the Writer's share of such levy to an aggregate of 65%.

   'Sums received' shall mean all sums received by or credited to the Publisher or its sub-publishers and licensees outside the United Kingdom who may, at the Publisher's absolute discretion, be affiliates associates subsidiaries or parents of the Publisher, less only normal bona fide arms-length collecting society commissions and deductions of any amounts paid to arrangers adaptors and translators subject to local rules and practices or, if none, as agreed by the Writer. The Publisher will use its best endeavours to receive promptly in the United Kingdom from such sub-publishers and licensees any and all sums not retainable by such sub-publishers and licensees hereunder.

6. General performing fees and broadcasting fees shall be divided equally by the PRS between the Writer and the Publisher subject to any allocation for orchestral arrangements or lyrics in accordance with the rules of PRS for the time being in force.

The Publisher further undertakes to pay to the Writer 30% of the 6/12ths total publisher share of all such fees received by the Publisher or its overseas sub-publishers and licensees specifically in respect of the Work. The Writer hereby certifies that for the purpose of PRS rule 1(o) the Publisher is to be treated as exploiting the Work (otherwise than by publishing) for the benefit of the persons interested therein to the extent indicated in the said rule.

7. (a) All copies of the Work (whether sheet editions, mechanical reproductions or otherwise) distributed free for the purpose of propagating and popularising the Work shall be free of all royalties or payments to the Writer

(b) In calculating the Publisher's receipts Value Added or any similar tax forming part thereof shall be deducted therefrom. All payments hereunder are exclusive of VAT which shall be payable in addition to the principal sum upon presentation of a VAT invoice in respect thereof.

8. (a) Royalty statements shall be made up to June 30 and December 31 in each year to include all sums received by the Publisher in that period and sent to the Writer within 90 days thereafter accompanied by a remittance for the amount so found due

(b) All royalty statements and other accounts from the Publisher to the Writer hereunder shall be binding upon the Writer unless specific objection in writing stating the basis thereof is given to the Publisher within three years from the date rendered

(c) If the Publisher shall be unable to procure the remittance to the United Kingdom of monies accountable hereunder to the Writer from any country then it shall at the written request of the Writer and subject to the laws of that country open an interest bearing bank account in the name and under the control of the Writer in such country and pay the Writer's share of such monies into such account and notify the Writer of details thereof.

(d) The Writer shall have the right to appoint a professional accountant to examine and inspect all books and records of the Publisher pertaining to the Work not more than once in any 12-month period during normal office hours on reasonable prior notice. In the event that a deficit in excess of 10% of total monies in any accounting period is found by such inspection to be outstanding then the Publisher will forthwith pay the cost of such inspection, such cost not to exceed the amount found to be outstanding for payment, together with such amount and interest thereon at 3% above the Bank of England minimum lending rate.

9. The Writer hereby grants the Publisher the right to use the Writer's name, approved likeness and biographical material solely in connection with the publication or exploitation of the Work.

10. The Writer, for himself his heirs and successors in title with the intent that this clause be binding upon them hereby represents warrants undertakes and agrees that he or they will not at any time hereafter assert any moral right in the Work, save for the right of the Writer to be credited as author, or commence or maintain any claim or proceedings in relation to the Work against the Publisher its licensees or successors in title or save as aforesaid perform any of such acts against any other person without the prior written consent of the Publisher. The Writer shall promptly in his name and at the Publisher's request and expense institute or defend any suit action or proceedings which the Publisher shall deem appropriate or necessary for the protection of any moral rights in relation to the Work and if the Writer fails so to do the Writer hereby irrevocably authorises and appoints the Publisher to do any of such acts in the Writer's name. The Writer shall nonetheless fully co-operate with the Publisher in the commencement or defence and maintenance of any such suit action or proceedings and shall hold the Publisher harmless from and against any and all claims costs liabilities and expense arising out of or related to any breach of the Writer's representations, warranties undertakings and agreements contained in this Clause 10.

11. (a) The Writer will on demand at the Publisher's expense execute and sign any documents and do all acts which the Publisher hereafter may reasonably require for the purpose of confirming or further assuring the Publisher's title to the rights assigned or intended to be assigned hereunder.

(b) All notices required to be served hereunder shall be in writing sent to the addressee at his last address notified in writing to the other party by recorded delivery post and shall be deemed served on the date on which it is deposited at the Post Office. Proof of deposit shall be deemed proof of service.

(c) No waiver of any term or condition of this agreement or of any breach of any part thereof shall be deemed a waiver of any other terms or conditions hereof or of any other breach of any part thereof.

(d) Neither party shall have the right to assign transfer or charge this agreement or any of its rights or obligations hereunder without the prior written consent of the other provided that the Publisher may assign this assignment to any third party purchasing all or substantially all of its assets or with whom the Publisher may merge without however relieving itself of its primary liability hereunder it being understood that nothing contained herein shall be deemed to restrict the Publisher's right to licence or assign its rights in the Work to third parties.

(e) The illegality or unenforceability of any part hereof shall not affect the legality or enforceability of the balance hereof.

(f) The provisions hereof constitute the entire agreement between the parties and this agreement may not be modified altered or changed except in writing signed by both parties.

(g) The Writer hereby warrants and undertakes that he has taken independent legal advice as to the terms and conditions hereof.

(h) This agreement shall be construed in accordance with the laws of England whose courts shall have exclusive jurisdiction.

AS WITNESS WHEREOF the parties have hereunto set their hands the day and year first before written

Signed and delivered by the Writer as his Deed:

....

In the presence of:

....

Signed for and on behalf of the Publisher by

....

In the presence of:

....

2. Recording Contract

This is a one-off recording agreement with an independent production company. It lists the royalties you would get (fairly normal) if the company released your records itself and also what you would get if (as is more likely) it licensed your records to a record company (any AP1 company would be a reasonable definition if the producer objects to 'major')

AN AGREEMENT made this .... day of .... between:

....................of .... (hereinafter called 'the Artist') of the one part and
....................of................ (hereinafter called 'the Company') of the other part

WHEREBY IT IS AGREED AS FOLLOWS:

1. The Artist hereby agrees to render his recording services to the Company for the making of audio and audio-visual recordings and hereby grants and assigns to the Company all copyright and any and all other rights in all the Artist's performances and recordings thereof made hereunder for the Universe ('the Territory') and for the full term of copyright therein and grants to the Company all consents and licences to permit the Company fully to exploit any such recordings made hereunder by any means and in any and all manners. The Artist hereby waives any moral right which he may have against the Company or its licensees. The Artist hereby grants to the Company the right to use his name, approved likeness and biographical material solely in connection with the making and exploitation of recordings hereunder.

2. The Artist shall attend at such times and places as the Company shall reasonably require and render to the best of his ability whether alone or with other artists performances of not less than three musical works. The choice of such musical works, producers (who shall be engaged by the Company) and recording studios shall be specified by the Company but giving due consideration to the wishes of the Artist. The term of this agreement ('the Term') shall commence upon the date hereof and expire upon the date of acceptance by the Company of fully equalised edited two-track stereophonic mixed down tape or disc recordings of the Artist's performances of such musical works which are satisfactory in the reasonable opinion of the Company for the manufacture of records (such recordings being referred to herein as 'the Recordings') together with the original multi-track recordings from which the Recordings were produced. Save as a result of any default by the Artist, the Term shall not extend beyond 6 months from the date hereof. The date of acceptance by the Company shall be deemed to be 45 days following receipt by it of the Recordings together with label copy, any necessary consents and clearances and current Musicians Union numbers of all performers thereon, unless the Company shall give notice within such period of its failure to accept together with the reason(s) therefor.

3. In the event that the Company shall enter into a third party licence agreement in respect of the Recordings then the Company shall pay to the Artist a royalty equivalent to 50% of the Company's 'Net Receipts' which shall mean all fees royalties or other sums received by the Company solely in respect of the Recordings including any so-called synchronisation payments (but excluding any sums payable in respect of the phonographic performance rights or video performance rights in the recordings) less any and all proper and reasonable costs incurred by the Company in the making of the Recordings including without limitation the following:
   All costs of tape, equipment, musicians, and singers and any other costs incurred directly in the recording of the Recordings save for costs of the Company's in-house studio and in-house engineer,
   Royalties and fees payable to any producer, mixer or remixer of the Recordings,
   All reasonable costs incurred by the Company in the conclusion of any licence agreement in respect of the Recordings, it being agreed however that all recording and pre-production costs excluding manufacturing costs but including any sums paid by the Company at its discretion in respect of rehearsals, clothing, hair-styling, choreography, car hire and per diems and any amount by which the agreed recording budget for the Recordings, if any, shall be exceeded through the actions or at the behest of the Artist without the prior written consent of the Company, shall be fully recoupable against all income, save for mechanical royalties payable in respect of the musical works embodied on the Recordings, becoming due to the Artist hereunder, which shall be recouped 'off the top' before the balance of any royalties or advances are divided between the parties hereto as provided for above.

4. In the event that the Company shall manufacture distribute and sell records itself derived from the Recordings then the Company shall pay to the Artist a royalty equivalent to 16% in respect of UK sales and 12% in respect of non-UK sales ('the Royalty') based on 90% of all sales less only bona fide returns calculated on the published price to dealers of records after tax and the packaging deductions listed below and after deduction of any and all reasonable and proper costs incurred by the Company as set out in this Clause and Clause 3 hereof. The term 'records' as used herein shall mean any and all forms of physical embodiment of sound with or without visual images manufactured and/or distributed for sale to the public by any means now or hereafter known.

5. The following packaging deductions shall be applied to the Royalty: 10% for 7" or 12" singles in special sleeves, 15% for single-fold vinyl albums in plain inner bags, 20% for double-fold and gatefold- albums and singles and for CDs in 'jewel cases', 25% for boxed sets, 30% for DVD's
   The Royalty in respect of the following categories of records shall be 50% of that stated under Clause 4 hereof: Low price and budget records under 75% of the full price, multi-album packages, audio-visual CDs up to 10,000 units on a format by format, territory by territory and release by release basis, television-advertised records (solely in respect of sales in the country where television advertising takes place), soundtrack albums, compilations and mini-albums
   The Royalty shall be 50% of that stated under Clause 4 hereof or 50% of the Company's net receipts whichever shall be the greater in respect of records sold by mail order and through record-clubs on a royalty basis by a bona-fide third party on arms-length terms, records sold to charities, libraries or military bases and so-called premium records.

No Royalty shall be paid in respect of deletions, scrap records and records for which the Company shall receive no payment, picture and/or non-standard shaped discs, free and promotional records actually and solely promoting the Recordings.

The Royalty shall only be paid during the life of copyright of the Recordings in the country of sale and shall be reduced pro rata in respect of records embodying the Recordings and other recordings.

6. Mechanical royalties shall be borne by the Company or its licensees it being agreed however that in respect of sales in the USA and Canada of Recordings embodying musical works in which the Artist has an interest as copyright owner the mechanical royalty payable shall, to the extent of that interest, be limited to 75% of the minimum statutory rate at the date of first release thereof subject to a maximum of 12 times such rate for albums and three times such rate for singles save that the Company will use reasonable endeavours to obtain higher rates and more favourable provisions in respect thereof from any licensee(s) in the USA & Canada in which case such more favourable rates and provisions shall apply. The Artist hereby grants to the Company an all-media worldwide synchronisation licence in respect of music videos free of charge for promotional use in respect of any such musical works and at a one-off non-recoupable fee of £100 in respect of the commercial exploitation of such videos. In all other countries the Artist will procure the grant to the Company of a mechanical licence for such musical works at the prevailing rate.

7. (a) The Company shall account to the Artist all sums due hereunder within 30 days following the Company's receipt thereof from third parties.

(b) The Company shall be entitled to retain reasonable reserves against records shipped but unsold which reserves shall be liquidated within 2 accounting periods of creation thereof (3 in respect of USA & Canada sales) by equal instalments or as liquidated by the Company's licensees.

(c) The Artist shall have the right to appoint a professional accountant to audit the books and records of the Company relating to sales of records hereunder not more than once in any 12-month period upon reasonable prior notice in normal office hours. No statement may be objected to by the Artist more than three years after such statement was rendered.

8. The Company shall originate and pay for all artwork in connection with the sale and exploitation of records derived from the Recordings and the Artist shall be entitled to use any such artwork for merchandising purposes under exclusive licence from the Company on payment of 50% of the cost thereof subject however to any limitations upon the Company's control thereof under any licensing agreements concluded by the Company for the Recordings hereunder. However the Company shall have no so-called 'merchandising rights' hereunder save in respect of the sale and exploitation of records derived from the Recordings.

9. The Artist hereby undertakes not to re-record any musical works embodied in the Recordings for any other party within the period of five years from the date of first release thereof by the Company or its licensees hereunder.

10. In the event that the Company shall produce or procure at its discretion but after consultation with the Artist, the production of a promotional video in respect of any or all of the Recordings then 50% of the cost to the Company thereof shall be treated as an advance to the Artist against income from such promotional video and the remaining 50% against income from any other sources.

11. The Artist undertakes to assist the Company upon reasonable prior notice in the promotion of records derived from the Recordings including without limitation attending at photographic and/or publicity receptions and radio and television appearances, the reasonable and approved cost to the Artist thereof to be reimbursed to the Artist by the Company.

12. The Artist hereby warrants and represents that he is over 18 years of age and has taken full independent legal advice from a solicitor experienced in the music industry as to the terms hereof and that he is free to enter into this agreement and to grant the rights granted herein and the Artist hereby agrees to indemnify the Company against any claims demands or expenses made against the Company as a consequence of the breach of any of the Artist's warranties hereunder which claim, demand or expense has been adjudicated by a court of competent jurisdiction or agreed pursuant to a settlement made with the consent of the Artist.

13. (a) The Company shall be free to license or assign any or all of its rights hereunder.

(b) Unless otherwise stated herein the Artist's consent where required herein shall not be unreasonably withheld or delayed and shall be deemed given within 5 working days of his receipt of written request therefor unless approved or rejected prior to such date.

(c) The Artist undertakes not to render his recording services to any other party during the Term without the prior written consent of the Company, such consent not to be unreasonably withheld.

(d) This agreement shall be construed in accordance with the laws of England whose courts shall have exclusive jurisdiction.

....
The Artist   The Company

3. Artist/Manager long-term agreement

Here is the sort of general management agreement which you may well wind up with. These terms are reasonably favourable to you. When the deal is first offered it may not contain these limitations on the amount the manager can spend without asking you, the length of time he goes on getting his commission or the extent of the earnings he gets commission on. These are the least 'standard' sort of agreements and both the wording and the terms vary enormously. Many management contracts are much longer than this but they are generally only covering, in more detail, the same points as this one. There might be an additional clause stating that he can renew the term of the agreement for another period (not more than about another 2 years) if you've earned, or else he's advanced you, a stated large sum of money by the time the agreement ends. There is no catch here. If you've made that much money (net) (excluding any income in the 'pipeline') then you're obviously succeeding and good management is so important that this will almost certainly have been partly down to your manager. If you haven't earned that amount, then you are free to leave or re-negotiate unless he has such faith in you that he's prepared to pay you that amount anyway just to keep you. It is worth bearing in mind that many artists have happy (and very long) relationships with their management. Some of the accounting provisions (which are common to most music business agreements) in this and the recording agreement are abbreviated and are more fully set out in the publishing agreement.

AN AGREEMENT made this .... day of ....between
........................of ....hereinafter called 'the Artist' of the one part and
........................of ....hereinafter called 'the Manager' of the other part

WHEREIN IT IS AGREED AS FOLLOWS:

1. The Artist hereby appoints the Manager to act and the Manager hereby agrees to act as the sole and exclusive manager throughout the Universe of the Artist in connection with all his activities in the entertainment industry including but not limited to:
(a) the performance of musical works in concert, for broadcast via radio television or otherwise, and the recording of performances in films or other audio-visual media and any other media
(b) the recording of musical works and the exploitation thereof by means of broadcast, sale or in the form of records, audio-visual devices or otherwise
(c) the composition and exploitation of musical works by any means
(d) merchandising and sponsorship.

2. This appointment shall be for a period of 3 years ('the Term') from the date hereof IT BEING UNDERSTOOD that in the event that upon the expiration of one year from the date hereof the Artist shall not have entered into an agreement reasonably acceptable to the Artist with a so-called major record company then the Artist shall be entitled to terminate this agreement forthwith.

3. The Manager agrees to use his best commercial endeavours to enhance and develop the career of the Artist in the entertainment industry and generally to render all services customarily rendered by a manager in such industry and in consideration of his services the Manager will be entitled to a fee equal to 20% of all gross monies (subject to Clause 5c hereof and exclusive of VAT or any similar tax) received by the Artist or by a company controlled by the Artist on his behalf during the Term and arising from any of the Artist's activities in the entertainment industry whether as a result of an agreement or arrangement negotiated by the Manager or otherwise and of all gross monies received by the Artist after the expiry of the Term but arising from an agreement entered into or subsequently negotiated during the Term, or in substitution of any such agreement, provided however that the Manager shall not be entitled to a fee in respect of:
(a) the exploitation of records featuring the performances on master recordings of the Artist recorded after the expiry of the Term or prior to the commencement of the Term if already exploited
(b) the exploitation of musical works written by the Artist after the expiry of the Term or prior to the commencement of the Term if already exploited

Notwithstanding the foregoing the Manager shall not be entitled to a fee on any monies advanced to the Artist for recording or video costs, tour support, or any third party producers mixers or remixers advances.
(c) The Manager's fee in respect of income from live concert performances shall be calculated on the net income therefrom i.e. gross income less all bona fide expenses incurred in connection therewith
(d) The Manager's fee shall be reduced to 10% three years following the expiry of the Term and shall cease to be payable 10 years following the expiry of the Term.

4. (a) The Artist hereby appoints the Manager to collect and receive all monies payable to him during the Term arising from his activities within the entertainment industry prior to or during the Term subject to the terms hereof and the Artist shall irrevocably direct all third parties to make payments accordingly. All such monies shall be paid into a specially designated account in the Artist's name but under the Manager's control and the Manager shall keep the Artist's monies in such account strictly separate from the Manager's income or that of any other artist.
(b) The Manager shall keep accurate and up to date books of account showing all monies received by him on the Artist's behalf and the Artist shall have the right to inspect such books and records upon reasonable notice during normal office hours.
(c) The Manager shall be entitled to deduct his fee and any expenses to be reimbursed to him pursuant hereto from monies collected on the Artist's behalf and shall send a statement as at 1st. Jan., lst. April, 1st. July and 1st. October in each year of the Term showing all monies received by him and paid or retained by him during the preceding 3 month period to the Artist within 60 days thereafter and shall pay the balance of all sums due to the Artist simultaneously therewith
(d) Notwithstanding the above if at any time the Manager shall hold monies in excess of £5,000 he hereby agrees to pay over the excess on demand after deducting his fee and any expenses properly incurred by him hereunder
(e) After the expiry of the Term the Artist shall render statements and keep books and records of account in respect of receipts by him after the Term in the same manner as set forth in (a) and (b) hereof and the Manager shall have the same right of inspection thereof as is granted under (b) hereof
(f) All payments to the Manager hereunder are exclusive of VAT which shall be paid by the Artist in addition thereto upon receipt of a VAT invoice from the Manager therefor.

5. The Artist shall bear any commission payable to any so-called 'booking agent' in respect of live performances or to any agent appointed by him in respect of his acting or other activities within the entertainment industry.

6. The Artist hereby grants to the Manager power of attorney to sign agreements for one-off live appearances on his behalf but any other offers of work shall be referred to the Artist for approval and signature of agreements in respect thereof, and the Manager shall not incur any one item of expenditure in excess of £750 without the prior written consent of the Artist, not to be unreasonably withheld or delayed.

7. In the event that the Manager shall become insolvent or is adjudicated bankrupt or shall make any composition with his creditors or in the event that .... (key man) shall cease to be a director of the Manager then the Artist shall have the right to terminate the Term forthwith.

8. The Manager shall be solely responsible for the Manager's normal office expenses. Any other expenses reasonably and necessarily incurred by the Manager specifically in connection with the performance of the Manager's obligations hereunder shall be reimbursed by the Artist within 30 days of the Artist's receipt of the relevant invoices. If the Manager or any employee of the Manager shall travel on the Artist's behalf (in which event the Manager or such employee shall enjoy the same standard of

accomodation, form of travel etc. as the Artist) the Artist shall reimburse the Manager's or such employee's travel, accommodation and subsistence expenses.

9. (a) Any notice to be served by either party hereunder shall be in writing to the last address of the other party notified in writing by recorded delivery and the date of service thereof shall be deemed to be the date upon which such notice was delivered to the Post Office

(b) The Artist shall be solely responsible for his personal tax and national insurance payments and arrangements

(c) The Artist hereby warrants that he has taken independent legal advice on the terms hereof from a solicitor specialising in the entertainment industry and confirms that he has read and understands the terms hereof

(d) This agreement represents the sole agreement between the parties hereto. Any amendment or modification hereto shall be in writing and signed by both parties.

(e) This agreement shall be construed in accordance with the laws of England whose courts shall have exclusive jurisdiction.

Signed by   Signed by

....
The Artist   The Manager

4. Artist Venue Agreement (through an agency)

An Agreement made this.........day of.....................between.....................
(hereinafter referred to as "the Management") of the one part and.....................
(hereinafter referred to as "the Artiste") of the other part

WHEREBY IT IS AGREED as follows:-

1. THAT the Management engages the Artiste and the Artiste accepts the engagement to appear as known at the following venue from the date(s) for the period and at the salary set forth below

Date(s) ....

Venue ....

Salary ....

2. IT is agreed that the Artiste shall arrive at .... and perform his/their usual and known act for a period of .... hours divided into .... sessions as arranged with the Management terminating not later than ....

3. THE Artiste shall not without the written consent of the Management perform at any other public place of entertainment within a radius of   miles of the venue during a period of .... weeks prior to and..........weeks following this engagement.

4. THE salary shall be payable by .... to ....

5. THE Management undertakes to provide adequate dressing room facilities for the Artiste.

AS WITNESS the hands of the parties hereto the day and year first before written.

....
for and on behalf of
  the Management

....
The Artiste

Here is the sort of agreement submitted to an Artist or to his manager for him to sign for a specific booking or series of bookings. ('Management' here means the owners of the venue, not the artist's manager.)

This form of agreement is quite normal and acceptable. The ideal form of payment is 'by cash to the Artiste on the night', preferably before you perform, but normally afterwards. If a singer or group wishes to take more than just a couple of roadies/sound engineeer to a venue (i.e. wives, girlfriends, hangers-on) it's just as well to check by phone beforehand.

The Clause in this particular form of agreement which you must watch out for is Clause 3. The radius is often about 15 miles, and if you are playing at different London suburbs every night for a week it is quite unreasonable for the management of one venue to make you agree to this, especially when you are comparatively little-known and the venues are private functions and are several miles apart. In such a case, in law this would probably amount to a 'restraint of your trade' and be unenforceable. But it's much better to try to have it deleted before you perform, to save misunderstandings and bad feelings. It really only exists for public concerts where a good turnout would actually be noticeably affected by your being billed to play at another local venue at around the same date.

Another clause which is often included is one in which you undertake that you will not deal directly with the venue for around the next two years and thereby cut out the agency. As we have said this is quite understandable if it was through the agent that you came to know of the venue in the first place.

5. Simple agreement to perform at a venue

If you are securing engagements yourself and are dealing with a venue which is not regularly booking acts, or where the management is a bit casual as to paperwork, they may ask you to write and confirm a phone booking, in which case the following is really quite adequate in most cases; typed in duplicate, signed by you and sent to the management of the venue. You could add that a cancellation fee of, say, 50% is payable if cancelled less than a month before, but you risk putting yourself in a position where they could expect you to pay them if you suddenly discovered you couldn't make it.

```
                                        Artists address

                                        date


       Dear ...............

       This will serve to confirm that..............(the artist)

       is booked to perform at....................on...........

       ............(date) from...............until..............

       with suitable breaks for a fee of £............... payable

       in cash on the night.

       If you are in agreement with this please sign in the

       place provided below, and return one copy to me.


       Yours sincerely,




       .............................
       (the Artist)
       read and agreed




       .............................
       (the Management)
```

6. PRS/MCPS JNWF (Joint Notification of Works Form)

Here is an example of PRS/MCPS notification form (the precise wording and layout may vary from time to time) completed in respect of a normal song assigned by two UK co-writers to their respective UK publishers. The publishers would each complete this, either in hard copy or else directly on-line to MCPS.. If you do not have a publisher you as a PRS member could register your songs yourself, and it is now possible to do this on-line as well. The MCPS Member Services Dept. will be pleased to help you. The 'duration' and 'instrumentation' are not usually filled in for a straightforward three minute song, but should be shown if the piece is much longer. The signature of the writers is no longer needed. PRS as you will see, generally pay 50% to the writer and 50% to the publisher, whereas the publisher generally collects 100% of royalties paid by MCPS. The societies don't need to know how much of all this the publisher is going to pay you under your agreement with him, so it is not mentioned here. If you want MCPS to ask you or your publisher before granting the first licence for the release of a recording (maybe to ensure that your record of your song comes out first) the box on the right should be ticked.

If a song of yours becomes successful before you've signed it to a publisher then it might be worth registering it yourself as controlled by you (perhaps using a trading name – written by John Smith, published by John Smith Music). By doing this, if anyone else tries to register a claim to the same title and includes you in the writers then in theory (though not always in practice) MCPS will spot this and will have to contact you to ask if this is OK. However when you subsequently sign the song to a real publisher you'll need to remember to tell MCPS this, or they'll think it's a 'duplicate claim' between your real publisher and John Smith Music. If this happens, your real publisher won't be able to claim royalties straightaway on your behalf and you'll then get your share later than necessary.

I LOVE YOU

...ndary Title ....
...tion .... Description ....

Title for Advertising 'Jingle' ....
Product .... Agency ....
Script Title .... VT/Radio No. ....

Writer(s) names (if appropriate, indicate registered pseudonym only) Publisher(s) name(s) (or unpublished)	Share of Royalties		Writer/ Publisher designation (see a)	Chain of Title (see b)	Enter your CAE number, if known, alternatively part of your address	For Office Use
	Performing	Mechanical				
WINNER, OSCAR	25 %	%	C/A	✳		
WARD, NOVELLO A.	25 %	%	C/A	o		
HONEST MUSIC LTD.	25 %	50%	OP1	✳		
HIT MUSIC LTD.	25 %	50%	OP2	o		
	/	%				
	/	%				
	/	%				
	/	%				

Country of Original Publication .... Publication date ....

Tick box for:
Amended Registration: (see note 13) ☐
Dramatico-Musical Work ☐
for PRS: BMI Licence (see note 14) ☐
for MCPS: Authority not given for First Recording ☑

Writer & Publisher Designations: Indicate appropriate combinations - 'C' for Composer, 'A' for Author, 'Ar' for Arranger, 'SA' for Sub-Author; 'OP1' for 1st Original Publisher; 'OP2' for 2nd Original Publisher (etc); 'SP1' for 1st Sub-Publisher; 'SP2' for 2nd Sub-Publisher (etc).
Chain of Title (Most important - usually to be completed by publishers). Use Various symbols (✳, ∅, X, etc) to link the chain of title of various interests, where known, to the agreements. If other writer/publisher details are unobtainable, please show 'UNKNOWN' on a separate line for EACH party.
...mation supplied will be used for registered purposes under the Data Protection Act 1984.

...separate line indicating the appropriate ...ment type 'ESA', 'General Catalogue', 'Part ...ngue', 'Administration' or 'Specific' ...er to Publisher	Publisher to Publisher	Chain of Title (see b)	AGREEMENT DETAILS (Complete for all published works) TERRITORY DETAILS Territory Assigned (Unless unpublished for the world)	Start date	End date	Manufacture or Sales Please specify
...ECIFIC		✳	WORLD	1. JAN 2000	31. DEC. 2009	

...rumentation ....
Comments/ SINGLE BY 'THE STARS' ON
Performance Details HIT RECORDS HSCD 1
Commercial/Library Recording Details and Numbers.

...undersigned assigns to The Performing Right Society Limited (PRS) the performing right as defined by the Articles of the Society and agrees to the division of the royalties indicated.
...ature of Publisher .... Name of Company HONEST MUSIC LTD. Date 20. DEC. 1999
...ature(s) of Writer(s) 1 .... 2 .... 3 .... 4 .... 5 .... 6 ....
...h Writer hereby certifies that, for the purposes of PRS Rules, the Publisher is to be treated as exploiting the work(s) for the benefit of the person(s) interested therein. (Delete if inapplicable.)

PRS JOINT NOTIFICATION (WORKS) FORM **mcps**

Stock No. JNWF/A4/191

Finally by way of illustrating how valuable it is to read and understand the small print in contracts, here is a contract which no-one in their right mind would ever sign. Some of the clauses are obviously ridiculous, but in most cases the jargon is exactly what you would expect to find in a perfectly reasonable contract – it has simply been changed around slightly (e.g. clause 5). In point of fact if you were to sign such a contract you could not be held to it purely because it is so unfair to you and ambiguous, but remember, just because a contract looks OK at first there could easily be something hidden away in it which makes it very unfavourable.

An Agreement made this   day of   between   and Dishonest Records Ltd.

WHEREAS the Artist is desperate to secure a recording contract of any sort and WHEREAS the Company is totally unscrupulous.

NOW IT IS AGREED as follows:

1. THIS agreement shall be for the period of 10 years or the life of the Artist whichever shall be the greater, during which time he shall render no services to any other party for any purpose whatsoever. The Company guarantees the Artist not less than £1,000,000 (one million pounds) within each year of this agreement and should this sum not be reached then this agreement shall continue until such figure is reached, in which event the company may renew it for a similar term.

2. THE Company shall have the right to re-name the Artist eg. Madonna, Led Zeppelin, The Beatles, etc. and the Artist hereby indemnifies the company against any legal action by third parties resulting from the use of such names.

3. SUBJECT to the Company giving not less than ½ hour's reasonable notice, the Artist shall attend at such times and places as the Company shall decide, and failure to honour this or any other undertaking made by either party hereunder shall import the determination of all the Artist's rights under this or any other agreement, in addition to any remedy which the Company may (or may not) have at law. The Company shall use whatever methods it finds necessary to ensure that the Artist performs to the best of his ability.

4. THE royalty payable to the Artist shall be 1% of the retail selling price of Master Tapes rising annually till it reaches 1½% of the wholesale selling price less taxes and other deductions which the Company may decide to make based on 90% (the figure customary in the industry) of all records returned as faulty or distributed free to any club operation.

5. IN the event of the Company releasing the Artist's performances on the so-called "normal", "full-price", records then the royalty shall be 50% of the normal rate and if the Artist be a duo, then the total royalty payable shall be halved before being divided equally between the Artist and the Company.

6. THE Artist hereby authorises the Company to pay any sum due to him into a numbered Swiss bank account, the number of which shall not be divulged to the Artist for reasons of security.

7. THE Artist shall be solely liable for all expenses incurred by the Company in the production, manufacture, distribution and advertising of all Recordings produced by the Company during the term hereof, and in the event of the Artist becoming bankrupt then this agreement shall be binding upon not only his successors but also his friends, relatives and the Official Receiver.

8. IN the event of the Company being unable to get money due to it out of any foreign country then the Artist undertakes to go and get it personally.

9. THE Artist warrants that he has not taken any independent legal advice on the terms hereof. The Artist warrants that he clearly understands this agreement even if he doesn't and further undertakes not to discuss the terms hereof with any other party particularly Private Eye and certain Sunday newspapers.

IN WITNESS WHEREOF etc. etc.

INSTANT GUIDE TO ROYALTIES

A summary of the royalties and terms which can be expected from Publishers, Record Companies, Managers and Agents. Royalties, record prices, calculations of fees etc. vary substantially between one company and another, one country and another, and from one year to the next, so remember that these calculations of actual money you might receive, and the others in the book, are only a very rough guide to what you might get in any particular situation.

PUBLISHING CONTRACTS

Printed Music (including downloads)

10-12.5% of the UK retail selling price for all UK sheet music sales of individual songs (pro-rata in music books) but if the books are not actually produced by your publisher he'll pay you the same rate as on record royalties from what he gets from a specialist company – say 60-85%

Record Royalties: 60-85% of all record royalties from UK (known as 'mechanicals'), which the record company pays to MCPS at 8.5% of the published price to dealers (around 2/3rds of the retail price – 'the rsp') less VAT. On a 70/30 deal with the publisher you might get around 15p per single where you wrote all the mixes 100%, and from around 3p-3.5p per track generally for a 14-track album depending on length of the tracks, so you'd get around £3-3,500 upwards per track for 100,000 albums (this is based on a PDP for a full-priced album of £8. (Bear in mind that the PDP may be up to £1 more, in which case the figures would need to be increased by up to around 10% or just over). It would be much less for budget compilations (e.g. well below 1p per track for a 40-track £4.99 rsp album). As a very rough guide royalties on long-form music videos work out to approximately the same as normal price albums but sales are very much lower.

Same percentages for overseas mechanicals from an 'at source' deal, or around 40-50% from a 'receipts' deal where overseas publisher pays say 70% to your UK publisher who pays say 70% of that to you. A track on a US album should bring in roughly the same rate of royalties but if you're on a receipts deal you might be down to around 2p per track on a full-price album and if controlled composition clauses apply (see definition) it might be only around 70% of that.

Same percentage for Internet downloads which will be at roughly same rate as record royalties in UK though nowhere near as many 'sales' or uses. You'll usually get a slightly lower share on 'covers' (records not recorded or produced by you which your publisher goes out and gets).

Performing/broadcasting royalties

60-85% in total of performing royalties (join PRS as soon as you are eligible and get 50% of 'PRS' money direct instead of through the publisher, including the foreign performing fees which you wouldn't get at all if you're not a member) + anywhere from about 20-70% of the publisher's share as well, depending on your status as a writer (i.e. 70% of his 50% share + your 50% from PRS = 85% of the total performing royalties (this bit is recoupable by the publishers but your 50% writer share worldwide should be payable directly to you via PRS even before your publisher has recouped any advances he's paid you.

PRS pays out from under £1 to over £10 per minute for UK radio broadcasts, depending on the audience size and/or advertising revenue of the radio station, up to around £150 for your 3-minute song on network TV. Do remember that 'sampling' operates with local radio, unless your song was recorded locally (i.e. specifically used on your local station) in which case tell PRS if you don't get paid. Otherwise remember that if your song isn't actually a hit (or maybe only in the clubs) and you don't get plays on national radio, you may miss out on samples on local radio and the income could be very low.

Overseas 'PRS' royalties – again PRS pay you 50% of the total earned anywhere in the world, which comes to them from the foreign performing right societies, but your share of your publisher's share depends on whether your deal is at-source or on receipts again.

Miscellaneous and synchronisation fees and royalties:

60-85% of miscellaneous (i.e. of everything else the publisher gets).

Your publisher can get roughly a minimum of around £30,000 for a year's use in a network UK television commercial on a recent UK hit + minimum £10,000 for a commercial on network radio, £10,000 for satellite & cable, £10,000 for cinema and roughly another £12,000 if they want to include the Republic of Eire television and then more (hard to quantify) for use on an Internet commercial or the website of a particular brand/manufacturer or in association with a webcast etc. depending on international success of the song and territories the use is aimed at and whether the product is international. Usually these figures would be rounded down substantially (in fact very substantially) if the user wants all these media. You'd get much more for a really big song, but much much less for a 'dormant' song where you and the publisher are happy to get it used at all. Similar amounts in other major countries, but less than you might think for an international campaign (say £150-200,000 for television for a year in the whole of Europe for a well-known song or recent hit, unless it's really big).

Around £10,000-20,000 for use of a song in a film + another £3,000 or so for a 'video buyout' but again this varies hugely according to the importance of the song and film and could be substantially lower than the bottom of this scale or higher than the top. Lots of other smaller audio-visual and so-called 'new media' uses are possible.

You get 60-85% of this, probably nearer 60% if your publisher went out and got the deal (rather than waiting for an agency or film company to ring and ask)

An international number 1 hit can easily bring in £500,000 or more from all these sources over say 3-5 years (more if it takes off in USA and/or Japan).

Notes on deals:

1. Royalties are paid on 100% of records, videos, downloading direct to home and printed music sales etc., (very few records will be royalty-free even if large numbers of records are given away or sold very cheaply to supermarket chains etc.)

2. You never pay a publisher to print or record your song.

3. A 'blanket' contract should not last more than five years and ideally should include a provision for you to have back songs 2-3 years after signing them or maybe a year or two after the end of the term of a blanket agreement, if nothing has happened – i.e. no record release and no film or advertising use. Otherwise your publisher should get to keep it for around 3-5 years under an admin deal or 12-20 years under a blanket writer deal.

4. You can get by without a publisher, but you'd have to collect through the societies and couldn't improve on an 80/20 'at source' publishing deal (in your favour) outside the UK. You'd certainly give yourself a lot of work and may even actually end up with less overall.

RECORD CONTRACTS

UK royalties:

Even for an unknown act around 16-18% of the published price to dealers (i.e. the wholesale price). Maybe around two-thirds of this for foreign sales.

Full-price UK album – your royalty at 16% would be just under £1.25-£1.30 in total, but more like 90p after deductions and reductions i.e. say £90,000 for 100,000 sales. (This is based on a conservative PDP price of £8 but as we've said it's possible that the PDP may be as much as £9.00, and so you'd have to increase these figures by up to 10% or just over). If the record company is offering a deal without these deductions then the basic royalty may be only 14-15% but will amount to roughly the same amount.

No. 1 single – your royalty is around 40-45p, but again this is before deduction of packaging allowances, free goods etc. which might knock around 30% off, i.e. on a royalty of 16% of PDP (could be a bit less) you get around 25p per single. (say £25,000 for 100,000 sales). If the record company gives away or sells cheaply a lot of records to chain stores etc. then it could be less. Then all the costs and advances mentioned above have to come off this before you get what's left, if anything.

Other income:
PPL income (from broadcasts of your recordings) will be divided equally – this can be a 5-figure sum for a number 1 hit. You should be able to collect your share directly through PPL or via PAMRA or AURA (phonographic performance royalties for broadcasts and performances of your recordings).

For uses of recordings in commercials, films etc. the fees are generally very much the same as the fees for the songs used in them unless it's a big song and an unknown artist, or unless it's very much cheaper for the user to re-record it rather than pay the fee (see under Publishing Contracts). In that case your record company will not ask too much. Of course if the agency or their client really want you (the famous artist), and not just someone who sounds like you, to be

appearing to endorse their product then you should receive a great deal more. In any event, whether you like the product or not, you should have approval of uses for commercials)

Deductions:
Unless you've done a deal based on the kind of thing BMG started offering (a lot less deductions but a lower overall royalty percentage etc.) it's likely that all recording costs, royalties to producer, costs of remixes, even tour support and other money (but not general PR and advertising budget) plus half the cost (anywhere from £20-100,000) of making promo videos comes out of your artist royalties under your agreement with your record company. Remember, if your first album's big but the second album bombs, you won't get any more artist royalties on the first till they've recovered their losses on the second and so forth.

Reductions:
1. Royalties are usually paid on 90% or less of actual sales.
2. Royalties usually less 20% packaging deductions including 'normal' formats like CD and even possibly the Internet where there are obviously no packaging deductions at all (though these might be described as 'facilitation' or something similar).

Notes on deals:
Try to get a commitment to make at least one album, but there's no particular benefit in being offered a 5-album deal as the second and subsequent albums, and the budgets and advance royalties that go with them will all be at the label's option which they won't take up if the first album flops.

Remember you should continue to be paid the same royalties on sales and uses of your records after you've long since gone to another company.

Don't sign away your publishing or merchandising rights under the record contract even for what look like reasonable fees (not least because the record company would be able to offset income from one against losses on another before you were paid anything at all even if they could get the same deal from a specialist company for merchandising as your manager could).

Remember the label generally doesn't absolutely guarantee to release your records (an independent producer simply can't) but should guarantee to record a certain number of songs per year or give you the money to do it (at least half the money for each album on signing or taking up the option with maybe 25% on delivery of the album and 25% on release) and should agree to give back the UK rights after say 6-9 months of your delivering the record and 'row' (rest of the world) if the local licensees/distributors don't release it within a few months of the UK release date (or else at least they should agree to license it to a company you nominate if you can find one).

Whether you write your own material or not there will be 'controlled composition' clauses (see Glossary)

Management and Agency contracts

The manager's commission will usually be 20%. This will probably be based on gross earnings on publishing and recording deals but on net earnings from live performances (i.e. after costs of putting on the show/tour etc.). The methods of calculation vary enormously.

An agent's commission ought to be around 15% of fees for gigs he secures for you. In your early career you'll probably collect and pay his commission to him. Later he'll do all the negotiations, collect the fee, deduct his commission and then pay you.

Acts playing music for dancing, Fifties/Sixties/Seventies theme parties, cabaret etc. should get £50-100 per person minimum or more depending on the venue, distance travelled, duration and time the gig ends. A top-flight band with no record deal could easily make

£1,000; £2–4,000 upwards for an act who have had chart hits, even if the line-up isn't original. A dance act with a UK hit could make £1,000-2,000 or more per PA at clubs etc. A really big act on a big US tour can gross £3-500,000 or even more per performance, but may not make a cent after deducting all expenses.

Acts (if they're not yet well-known) playing well-known clubs and touring as support for top acts however will probably have to pay for the privilege – maybe £150 or so to the club per performance and £500-£1,000 per night to be on someone else's tour.

Merchandising can be big business. A relatively big act can still get a guaranteed £50,000 or so advance from a merchandiser for a tour, against a share of around 30% of the retail price, less taxes and less 25% which goes to the venue. A merchandiser might hope for a spend of around £4 per head at live concerts, so... for the right sort of acts (which generally means 'rock') you could be looking at as much as around £10,000 for the artist just for one 10,000-seater concert. The more eye-catching your name and logo the better, however if you haven't registered your name/logo it's likely that you'll get much much less, as there's a lot less protection against counterfeit goods.

Notes

1. As soon as you have a manager and start to earn through him, you need your own independent accountant (not one recommended by your manager, preferably).
2. Don't give away too much control of your career for too long to a non-professional manager and be absolutely sure he can't claim 20% of your first number 1 hit under his old agreement!
3. Look twice at any 'guaranteed' large earnings. You may never get them.
4. If you're in a band and then leave, you're almost certainly still bound as an individual to all the contracts you or your manager have signed. If you join a band who already have contracts you will

probably be required to become bound by them as well.

5. Most management contracts cover all aspects of the music and entertainment business down to writing articles and books and opening supermarkets. A manager will expect to start receiving your income and keeping a share even on deals such as publishing which you may already have but try to limit or resist this if possible.

6. Don't give him power of attorney to commit you to any expenditure over a few hundred pounds at most or to sign away your publishing, recording or merchandising rights without consultation and approval.

7. Try to negotiate at the start that his share of your income ceases as soon as possible (no more than around 3-5 years at full rate and another 5-10 at half rate) after he ceases to be your manager, especially with a 'local' manager. Also try to ensure that he doesn't get commission on any albums you make or songs you write after he ceased to be your manager (which he might try to do if you remain signed to the record company or publisher who he introduced you to).

Finally ... do get a lawyer to check and if necessary nit-pick before signing anything more than simple agency agreements, but remember that unless the deal's utterly dreadful the lawyer will only push as hard as you want him to. It's worth the money and he may even get the people you're signing with to pay his fee as an advance ... do take away and look at all agreements before signing. If someone expects you to sign it there and then, it may be unenforceable later, but do you really want the hassle of arguing about it? ... do ask questions, even if you're afraid they might sound a bit silly ... don't sit there being cool and hip and not understanding a word they're talking about ... do try not to sign the first deal you're offered if you can see, having read this book, that it's not a good one.

Don't be led to think that the first company to offer you a deal is doing you a huge favour by signing you up. Very few people will do you a favour that might cost them money – even if you have contacts in the business. Unless your contact is the managing director of the company they're with then you can't really expect them to do you a favour anyway. Ultimately it's down to having enough faith in yourself to believe that you really can make a good living (or a fortune) in the music business and that if they don't sign you it's their loss. That way you'll almost certainly get a better deal, if not from them, then from someone else. Keep your head screwed on, and good luck.

He's certainly got his head screwed on!

USEFUL ADDRESSES

The best suggestion for further reading is to keep up with what's being written in the newspapers and magazines comprising the British musical press. Some are available from most newsagents, others you might get locally only on order or by subscription. The following list includes some magazines plus addresses.

The following lists also include some of the firms of solicitors and accountants who specialise in the music business, some of the various organisations which may be of help to you, and also a list of some of the UK television stations and programme producers. There are now so many local radio stations in the UK that a complete list would be pages long. You are probably familiar with your local ones and the addresses of others around could be supplied by the BBC or in our 'Useful Addresses' section or elsewhere.

NEWSPAPERS AND MAGAZINES:

BBC Music Magazine
Room A1004
Woodands, 80 Wood Lane
London W12 0TT
(0208 8433 3283)

Billboard (UK address)
5th Floor
189 Shaftesbury Avenue
London WC2H 8TJ
(0207 420 6003)

Blues & Soul
153 Praed Street
London W2 1RL
(0207 402 6869)

Classic FM Magazine
38-42 Hampton Road
Teddington
Middx. TW11 0JE
(0208 267 5000

Clubscene
PO Box 11
Bathgate
Lothian EH48 1RX
(01506 636038)

Country Music People
225a Lewisham Way
London SE4 1UY
(0208 692 1106)

DJ
121 Kingsway
London WC2B 6PA
(0207 721 8182

The Face
Exmouth House
Pine Street
London EC1R 0JL
(0207 837 7270)

Folk Music Journal
5 Hanborough Close
Witney,
Oxon OX29 4NR
(01865 880 283)

Future Music
30 Monmouth Street
Bath
Avon
BA1 2BW
(01225 442244)

Guitar
Link House
Dingwall Avenue
Croydon CR9 2TA
(0208 686 2599)

Guitarist
see Future Music

Hip Hop Connection
See Future Music

Jockey Slut
1a, Zetland House
8–26 Scrutton Street
London EC2A 4HJ
(0207 613 3773)

Kerrang!
EMAP Metro
Mappin House
4 Winsley Street
London W1R 7AR
(0207 436 1515)

Metal Hammer
99 Baker Street
London W1U 6FP
(0207 317 2600

Mixmag
see Kerrang

Mojo
EMAP Metro
see Kerrang

Music & Media
50-51 Bedford Row,
London WC1R 4LR
(0207 7822 8302)

Music Business International (MBI)
Ludgate House
245 Blackfriars Road
London SE1 9UR
(0207 620 3636)

Music Week
See MBI

New Musical Express (NME)
Kings Reach Tower
Stamford St
London SE1 9LS
(0207 261 5813)

19
See NME

Q
EMAP Metro
see Kerrang!

Sleazenation
See Jockey Slut

Smash Hits
EMAP Metro
see Kerrang!

Songlink International
23 Belsize Crescent
London NW3 5QY
(0207 794 2540)

Songwriter Magazine
PO Box 46
Limerick
Ireland
(0353 61228837)

Sound on Sound
Media House
Trafalgar Way
Bar Hill
Cambs CB3 8SQ
(01954 789888)

The Stage
47 Bermondsey Street
London SE1 3XT

Studio Sound
See MBI

Time Out
251 Tottenham Court Road
London W1A 0AB
(0207 813 3000)

Tip Sheet
7a, Spring Street
London W2 3RA
(0207 262 6666)

Top of the Pops Magazine
Room A1136
80 Wood Lane
London W12 0TT
(0208 433 3910)

The Voice
8th Floor, Bluestar House
234-244 Stockwell Road,
London SW9 9UG
(0207 737 7377)

SOME MUSIC BUSINESS SOLICITORS:

Bray and Krais
70-71 New Bond Street
London W1S 1DE
(0207 493 8840)

Clintons
55 Drury Lane
London WC2B 5SQ
(0207 379 6080)

Collyer Bristow
4 Bedford Row
London WC1R 4DF
(0207 242 7363)

Davenport Lyons
1 Old Burlington Street
London W1S 3NL
(0207 437 8216)

David Wineman
121 Kingsway
London WC28 5NX
(0207 400 7800)

Denton Wilde Sapte
5 Chancery Lane
Cliffords Inn
London EC4A 1BU
(0207 320 6516)

Edmonds Bowen & Co.
4 Old Park Lane
London W1Y 3LJ
(0207 629 8000)

Field Fisher Waterhouse
35 Vine Street
London EC3N 2AA
(0207 861 4000)

Gentle Jayes
26 Grosvenor Street
London W1X 0BD
(0207 629 3304)

146

Harbottle & Lewis
14 Hanover Square
London W1R 0BE
(0207 667 5000)

Lea & Co. Bank Chambers
Market Place
Stockport
Cheshire
SK1 1UN
(0161 480 6691)

Leonard Lowy & Co.
500 Chiswick High Road
London W4 5RG
(0208 956 2785)

Magrath & Co.
52-54 Maddox Street
London W1R 9PA
(0207 495 3003)

Nicholas Morris
70-71 New Bond Street
London W1Y 9DE
(0207 493 8811)

Robin Morton & Co.
27 Sandyford Place
Glasgow G3 7NG
(0141 248 7676)

Olswang
90 Long Acre
London WC2E 9TT
(0207 208 8888)

P. Russell & Co.
Gable House
18-24 Turnham Green
Terrace
London W4 1QP
(0207 742 8132)

Russells
Regency House
1-4 Warwick Street
London W1R 5WB
(0207 439 8692)

Schilling & Lom
Royalty House
72-74 Dean Street
London W1V 6AE
(0207 543 2500)

Searles
The Chapel
26a Munster Road
London SW6 4NE
(0207 371 0555)

Sheridans
14 Red Lion Square
London WC1R 4QL
(0207 404 0444)

Simkins Partnership
45-51 Whitfield Street
London W1P 6AA
(0207 907 3000)

Spraggon Stennet Brabyn
225 Kensington High Street
London W8 6SD
(0207 938 2223)

Taylor Joynson Garrett
Carmelite
50 Victoria Embankment
London EC4Y 0DX
(0207 353 1234)

Teacher Stern Selby
37-41 Bedford Row
London WC1R 4JH
(0207 242 3191)

Tenon Statham Gill Davies
56 New Cavendish Street
London W1G 9TF
(0207 487 5565)

Theodore Goddard
150 Aldersgate Street
London EC1A 4EJ
(0207 606 8855)

SOME MUSIC BUSINESS ACCOUNTANTS

Arram Berlyn Gardner
100 Grays Inn Road
London WC1X 8BY
(0207 400 6000)

Baker Tilly
2 Bloomsbury Street
London WC1B 3ST
(0207 413 5100)

BDO Stoy Hayward
8 Baker Street
London W1M 1DA
(0207 486 5888)

Bowker Orford
15-19 Cavendish Place
London W1M 0DD
(0207 636 6391)

Brebner Allen & Trapp
180 Wardour Street
London W1V 4LB
(0207 734 2244)

Carnmores Royalties Consultants
Suite 212-213
157-168 Blackfriars Rd
London SE1 8EZ
(0207 261 1660)

Deloitte & Touche
1 Little New Street
London EC4A 3TR
(0207 303 3858)

Entertainment Accounting International
26a Winders Road
London SW11 3HB
(0207 978 4488)

Ernst & Young
Becket House
1 Lambeth Palace Road
London SE1 7EU
(0207 928 2000)

147

**Freedman Frank &
Taylor**
Reedham House
31 King Street West
Manchester M3 2PJ
(0161 834 2574)

**Gelfand Rennert
Feldman & Brown**
1b Portland Place
London W1B 1GR
(0207 636 1776)

Harris & Trotter
65 New Cavendish Street
London W1G 7LS
(0207 467 6300)

O J Kilkenny
6 Lansdowne Mews
London W11 3BH
(0207 792 9494)

KPMG
1 Puddle Dock
London EC4V 3PD
(0207 311 3350)

Macnair Mason
18 Bevis Market
London EC3A 7ED
(0207 469 0550)

Martin Greene Ravden
55 Loudoun Road
London NW8 0DL
(0207 625 4545)

Prager & Fenton
Midway House
27-29 Cursitor Street
London EC4A 1LT
(0207 831 4200)

Price Waterhouse
Coopers1 Embankment
Place
London WC2H 6RH
(0207 583 5000)

RSM Robson Rhodes
186 City Road
London EC1V 2NU
(0207 251 1644)

Saffery Champness
Lion House
Red Lion Street
London WC1R 4GB
(0207 7841 4000)

**Sedley Richard
Laurence Voulters**
1 Conduit Street
London W1S 2XA
(0207 287 9595)

Sloane
36-38 Newton Road
Westbourne Grove
London W2 5SH
(0207 221 3292)

SOME TELEVISION STATIONS & PRODUCTION COMPANIES

Anglia TV
Anglia House
Norwich
Norfolk
NR1 3JG
(01603 615151)

BBC Midlands
Pebble Mill Road
Birmingham
W. Midlands
B5 7QQ
(0121 414 8888)

BBC North
Woodhouse Lane
Leeds
W. Yorks
LS2 9PX
(0113 244 1188)

BBC NE
Broadcasting Centre
Newcastle-upon-Tyne
Tyne & Wear
NE99 2NE
(0191 232 1313)

BBC NW
Oxford Road
Manchester
N60 1SJ
(0161 200 2020)

BBC N. Ireland
Ormeau Avenue
Belfast
BT2 8HQ
(01232 338000)

BBC Scotland
Queen Margaret Drive
Glasgow
G12 8DG
(0141 339 8844)

BBC South
Havelock Road
Southampton
SO1 0XQ
(01703 226201)

BBC South West
Seymour Road
Plymouth
Devon
PL3 5DB
(01752 229201)

BBC TV Centre
Wood Lane
London W12 7RJ
(0208 743 8000)

Big Eye Film & TV
Lock Keepers Cott.
Century Street
Manchester M3 4QL
(0161 832 6111)

Border Television
TV Centre
Carlisle
Cumbria CA1 3NT
(01228 25101)

The Box
11-13 Young Street
London W8 5EH
(0207 376 2000)

**British
SkyBroadcasting (BSB)**
Unit 2 Grantway
Isleworth
Middx TW7 5QD
(0208 805 8230)

Carlton UK
101 St. Martins Lane
London WC2N 4AZ
(0207 240 4000)

Channel 4
124 Horseferry Road
London SW1P 2TX
(0207 396 4444)

Channel 5
22 Long Acre
London WC2E 9LY
(0207 550 5555)

Chrysalis TV
46-52 Pentonville Road
London N1 9HF
(0207 502 6000)

GMTV
TV Centre
Upper Ground
London SE1 9TT
(0207 827 7000)

Grampian TV
Queens Cross
Aberdeen
Grampian
AB9 2XJ
(01224 846846)

Granada Television
Quay Street
Manchester M60 9EA
(0161 832 7211)

HTV TV Centre
Culverhouse Cross
Cardiff
S. Glamorgan
CF5 6XJ
(01222 590590)

HTV West
TV Centre
Bath Road
Bristol
BS4 3HG
(0117 972 2722)

Landscape Channel
Hye House
Crowhurst
E. Sussex
TN33 9BX
(01424 830900)

**London Weekend
Television**
(see GMTV)

Meridian
TV Centre
Northam
Southampton
Hants.
SO14 0PZ
(01703 222555)

MTV
17-19 Hawley Crescent
London NW1 8TT
(0207 384 7777)

Music Box
30 Sackville Street
London W1X 1DB
(0207 478 7300)

Music Choice
57-61 Clerkenwell Road
London EC1M 5LA
(0207 024 8700)

RTE
Donnybrook
Dublin 4
Ireland
(00353 1208 3111)

Top of the Pops
Room 385
Design Building
Wood Lane,
London W12 7RJ
(0208 576 9917)

Tyne Tees
TV Centre
City Road
Newcastle-upon-Tyne
NE1 2AL
(0191 261 0181)

Yorkshire Television
TV Centre
Leeds LS3 1JS
(0113 243 8283)

MISCELLANEOUS USEFUL ADDRESSES

AIM (Association of Independent Music)
Lamb House
Church Street
London W4 2PD
(0207 994 5599)

AMIA (Association of Music Industry Accountants)
66 Chiltern Street
London W1U 4JT
(0207 535 1400)

ASCAP
8 Cork Street
London W1X 1PB
(0207 439 0909)

AURA (Association of United Recording Artists)
See under MMF

British Academy of Composers & Songwriters
26 Berners Street
London W1T 3LR
(0207 636 2929)

British Association of Record Dealers (BARD)
1st Flr. Collonade House
2 Westover Street
Bournemouth BH1 2BY
(01202 292 063)

British Music Rights
20 Berners Street
London W1T 3lr
(0207 306 4446)

British Phonographic Industry (BPI)
25 Savile Row
London W1X 1AA
(0207 851 4000)

British Video Association
167 Great Portland Street
London W1N FD
(0207 436 0041)

Broadcast Music Inc. (BMI)
84 Harley House
Marylebone Road
London NW1 5HN
(0207 486 2036)

Christian Copyright Licensing
PO Box 1339
Eastbourne
E. Sussex BN21 1AD
(01373 417711)

Commercial Radio Companies Ass.
77 Shaftesbury Avenue
London W1V 7AD
(0207 306 2603)

Country Music Association (CMA)
Third Floor
18 Golden Square
London W1R AG
(0207 434 3025)

International Federation of Phonograph Industries (IFPI)
54 Regent Street
London W1B 5 RE
(0207 878 7900)

Mechanical Copyright Protection Society Ltd. (MCPS)
41 Streatham High Road
London SW16 1ER
(0208 769 4400)

MMF (Music Managers' Forum)
7 Russell Gardens
London W14 8EZ
(0207 751 1894)

Music Publishers Association (MPA)
Third Floor, Strandgate
1-20 York Buildings
London WC2N 3BW
(0207 262 5797)

Musicians Union
60-62 Clapham Road
London SW9 0JJ
(0207 582 5566)

National Band Register
Second Floor
65 George Street
Oxford OX1 2BE
(01865 798795)

Performing Right Society Ltd. (PRS)
20-33 Berners Street
London WC1P 4AA
(0207 580 5544)

PAMRA (Performing Artists Media Rights Assoc.)
161 Borough High Street
London SE1 1HR
(0207 940 0400)

Phonographic Performance Ltd. (PPL)
1 Upper James Street
London W1F 9DE
(0207 534 1000)

Phonographic Performance Ltd. (Ireland)
PPI House,
1 Corrig Avenue
Dun Laolaire
C. Dublin
Ireland
(00353) 380 5977)

PRS (Performing Right Society)
29-33 Berners Street
London W1T 3AB
(0207 580 5544)

RAJAR (Radio Joint Audience Research)
81 Oxford Street
London W1D 2EJ
(0207 903 5350)

School of Performing Arts and Music
PO Box 7874
London SW20 9XD
0207 222 8873

Video Performance Ltd.
1 Upper James Street
London W1F 9DE
(0207 534 1400)

Worshipful Company of Musicians
1st Floor,
74-75 Watling Street
London EC4M 9BJ
(0207 489 8888)

GLOSSARY OF TERMS

Here's an alphabetical list of some of the words and phrases which you may come across in the music business. If a term is not defined here you may well find it in the general index. Forgive us if there are some you already know and completely take for granted – it's possible that someone else may not.

A & R

Artist and Repertoire. The A&R manager of a label is the man or woman to see with your demos. They decide which artists get signed to the company's roster and what tracks they should release (or acquire and promote, in the case of publishers)

Advances

Payments made to writers and artists or expenses paid out by a company on your behalf or to promote your music or recordings, which should not have to be paid back (non-returnable) unless, possibly, to buy yourself out of a contract but which will be recovered by the company from royalties due to you (i.e. you don't get anything until the royalties you would have got equal the advance payment).

Album deal

A deal with a record company whereby they undertake to make (or give you the money to make) and release at least one album. More likely to be offered to rock acts than dance acts.

AP1, AP2A, AP2

These are the licensing schemes offered to actual mainstream record labels by the MCPS to collect the songwriters' and publishers' royalties for the songs they use on their records. AP1 covers not only the major labels but most labels who've had several hits- they pay on what they sell once they've sold it. AP2A is for smaller labels who pay on how many they press but don't have to pay in advance. AP2 is for everything from quite established small but successful labels right down to very small specialist labels pressing 500 CDs of each album (which is why MCPS charges publishers about three times as much to collect from AP2 as from AP1 companies). There are lots more AP schemes- for record clubs, cover mounted albums on magazines, 'premium' albums advertising something etc. and although they're not 'mainstream' record sales they can bring in a great deal of money.

Arrangers

The term used of writers who make arrangements or adaptations of traditional music. It also refers to people within the business whose job it is to take down music from records for printing, who prepare scores for recording sessions, broadcasts, bands and so forth. There are far less than there used to be years ago, but it's a very specialised skill and as you can imagine such people are skilled musicians in their own right.

Arms-length

Meaning particularly a deal between an international publisher or record company- they guarantee that if your song or record is licensed to one of their own affiliated companies overseas then at least the terms are no worse for you than if it had been a totally separate UK company doing the deal with those overseas companies. The same applies where a UK management company signs a writer/ artist to a recording/ publishing deal with their affiliate.

A-side Protection

A guarantee in your agreement that if you only wrote produced or mixed the feature track (radio edit) on a single your royalties won't be 'diluted' by the inclusion of other 'throwaway' tracks or mixes some of which might be longer than yours and therefore attract a higher share of the mechanichal royalties on sales of the record.

Ayants Droit
The owners of the rights to songs, recordings, merchandise etc. Most often used in publishing to refer to the original (usually foreign) owners.

Black Box
Not just a successful Continental dance act from a while ago, but the term for income which some collecting societies have 'left over' or unallocated (see 'non-member') after making payments to their members and sister societies abroad and which is then divided amongst their own members. Estimates of the amounts involved and the ways they are calculated vary wildly, but are often highly exaggerated.

It's fashionable for writers to ask for shares in the proportion that the earnings on their songs bear to the publisher's total earnings. As this would enable you to calculate what the publisher's total earnings from these sources were, this is usually resisted. Some mechanical right societies will send publishers separate statements for individual writers or original publishers if requested. These are called 'editions' and you could ask for a share of 'black box' based on these, though if the society makes a charge, as

some do, then it may simply not be worth it. Your publisher shouldn't have a problem with giving you your specified share of income from these.

Blankets
The term used for exclusive agreements under which all the songs you write or recordings you make for a period of time will go to the one company. Remember that once that period's over, the company will usually go on owning those songs or recordings for much longer. Publishing companies may be prepared to do a deal just for one song but record companies will almost always want a blanket agreement.

Bonus
Generally refers to an amount paid to a songwriter or artist which will not be recouped from his royalties (i.e. not an advance). These are very much less common than advances and you should not expect to be offered bonuses. The term 'chart bonus' however (a payment made when your single or album reaches a certain position) will usually just mean an additional advance.

Bootlegged Records
Bootleg recordings are usually ones made illegally at live concerts, especially where otherwise unrecorded material was played. Pressing

plants in the UK work together with the BPI and MCPS to try to spot anyone trying to duplicate unauthorised recordings of an artist. Bootleggers themselves often escape the punishment of the law and it's the sellers who attract attention. However, if caught in the act of recording, bootleggers risk not only prosecution but loss or damage to their equipment and even physical assault. One ground-breaking band in the early Eighties avoided the problem by recording every single concert they gave and making available tapes of the most recent 24-hours' worth of live material. It goes without saying that they were not signed to a major label, as no such label would have had the administrative capacity to deal with such a project but, although this wasn't their aim, it was an excellent marketing ploy and it got around some of the bootlegging problem.

Breakers

Records 'bubbling under' the charts with sales increasing but not yet enough to push the record into the charts. Not applicable to the UK, where most records, after five or six weeks of advance promotion enter the charts at their highest position on the strength of advance orders then drop down, sometimes dramatically. In the USA there is an entirely separate chart published by Billboard of records by artists who have never made the charts but which are looking like entering the charts in the near future.

Bullet

Mark shown against records making good progress up the USA *Billboard* trade magazine's weekly charts.

CAE numbers

These are the code numbers allocated to every writer or publisher member of a collecting society. Every writer member of PRS, including the authors of this book, has his or her own number. The use of this number by the collecting societies, especially in conjunction with the ISWC codes (see below) should ensure that the writer is correctly identified as the person who should receive royalties on his or her works.

Collecting Societies

In the UK there are two main writer/publisher societies. PRS basically licenses all forms of public performances of songs (broadcasts, live concerts, music played on the Internet etc.). MCPS basically licenses the reproduction of songs on all forms of sound-carrier (records, tapes, music downloaded from the Internet etc.). The administration for both is now shared by the two societies. A totally separate company, PPL, collect royalties for record companies, artists and musicians when recordings, rather than just the songs, are performed and broadcast, and its sister organisation VPL does the same for videos. Thus broadcasts of records on television and radio etc. involve PRS and PPL. There are affiliated societies to all of these in most other countries.

Compilation shows

Musical shows in which the music used was not written for the show but 'interpolated' into it at a later date. Many successful ones are based on the lives of well-known artists of the past (usually dead ones to avoid legal problems) as diverse as Buddy Holly, Roy Orbison, and the famous French diva Edith Piaf.

Writers and publishers, as with musicals, get a share of the box office receipts from each performance of the show, but whereas the publisher always collects directly for musicals where the music was written for the show, compilation shows are sometimes licensed by PRS, sometimes by the publishers. Although the Copyright Tribunal has set the tariff for shows like this, it's not entirely clear whether such shows should come under the PRS's rules or not, so PRS allows publishers to license the use of their songs directly as long as they don't ask less than the PRS would have asked. In practice the usual rate is about 5% of the gross box office receipts (which should be payable weekly and no more than a week or so after the relevant performance). This could easily amount to tens of pounds per song per week.

Container Allowance

Permits record companies to deduct a further percentage (usually around 20% for CDs) before paying artist royalties. It is meant to recompense record companies for the cost of manufacture of jewel cases for CDs, plastic cases for cassettes, cardboard sleeves for vinyl etc. though these usually cost next to nothing to produce nowadays. Especially high deductions are usually made for any new format on which your album is released. In some cases, as with CD when it was first introduced, the mechanical royalties payable to publishers and songwriters are also reduced for a limited period, to allow for high development and manufacturing costs at the start. They are subsequently reduced, but usually not quickly enough.

Contract Year

Used in contracts for a year commencing with the date of the contract and not January 1 (unless of course that happens to be the date of the contract anyway). It makes sense for contracts to be dated (or effective from) half year or quarter days, as this makes it much easier for collecting societies to know whether to pay a new publisher or the-previous one.

Controlled Compositions

The system whereby USA record companies try to ensure that their copyright and artist royalties together do not exceed a certain amount on records where the artist is also the writer. The artist's contract will state that, if his publisher holds out for more than a certain royalty per track, generally 75% of the statutory US royalty rate when the record was first delivered or released there, then the excess will be deducted from the artist royalty. Your publisher may have the right to comment on such clauses, but in prac-

tice he won't be able to do so without prejudicing your negotiations as an artist with the record company, even, in some cases, if you signed the publishing agreement first and therefore that should really take precedence. In the UK the record companies are not able to negotiate such deductions with the copyright owners of the songs and as a writer you or your publisher will always get the full statutory rate

Counterfeits

These are records or videos illegally re-recorded from the original releases or copies of the Master Tapes and pressed up to look exactly like the genuine article, but without any royalties having been paid. Some are sold at a discount to unsuspecting or opportunist dealers, and it is virtually impossible even for the record or video companies concerned to tell them apart from the real thing. Others are sold on street corners and are usually just re-recorded from discs or tapes and the quality, even with digital recordings, can be appalling.

Covers

A recorded version of a song other than the original recording. Under most publishing agreements you get a slightly lower royalty on covers. These may be described as all recordings where you

yourself were not involved as artist, producer, mixer or remixer, or they may have to be recordings specifically 'fixed' by the publisher, which in a lot of cases these days could include your own recording remember unless it's specifically excluded.

Cross-collateralisation

This applies to virtually all advances paid to you by anyone in the music business and is the real sting in the tail. If a publisher or record company pays a separate advance for each year or each album, all the royalties will be added up and until (as at any accounting date) your royalties exceed the whole of what they've paid in advances or costs 'on your behalf' they won't pay you any royalties for an artist, recording costs will be recouped too, so all the earnings from a million-seller can be wiped out by the cost of the follow-up if it bombs.

Just about the one cost that shouldn't be deducted from your artist royalties is the payment of mechanical royalties for the songs on your records which the record company will be obliged to pay your publisher (however, see 'Controlled Composition Clauses') and, in the case of publishing your publisher will not expect to receive and deduct your writer share (50% worldwide) of performing fees. However if you are signed as a writer to your record company's publishing arm, then you really should be very careful (especially if it's a small company) not have your artist royalties and your publishing royalties cross-collateralised so that all those recording costs are also deducted from songwriting royalties.

Crossover

Apart from being a hi-fi term, this is mainly used to describe records from the specialist charts, rock, club, country, classical, independent etc. which go on to become hits on the main charts.

Cue sheets

Lists, prepared by film, television and other audio visual production companies, of all the musical works in the production. Against each piece of music should be the writer, publisher, length of the use and whether it is vocal or instrumental, visual or background. Visual means it should be audible to the characters on the screen and sometimes attracts a higher fee for the use. Cue sheets are sent to PRS and other performing right societies so that when the film or programme is broadcast, they know how to divide up the royalties. Often every separate piece of specially written music is listed eg. Singer enters the room: 32' IB, Singer calls his agent: 10' VV Singer leaves the room: 1'15' IB and so

on ... (IB meaning 'instrumental background' – i.e. no vocals and not audible to the people on the screen and VV meaning 'vocal visual' i.e. sung and audible to the people on the screen).

Custom Pressing

Generally refers to pressings made by one record company's pressing plant for the benefit of its company in another country or for another record company.

Cut-off Periods

Some record companies, publishers and other bodies operate cut-off periods whereby your statement of money earned from say July 1 to December 31 may actually be cut-off at the end of November and therefore not include some big Christmas sales which you may have been expecting. You will of course get these royalties in the next Jan-June statement, which itself may be cut-off at the end of May.

Dealers

The usual term for record shops. There are over 5,000 in the UK of varying sizes, and many 'outlets' such as petrol stations and supermarkets, where impulse buying keeps sales up on budget LPs and cassettes. Some acquire their stocks from 'one-stops' who keep stocks of product from most record companies. Some of these actually

decide which records should go to certain outlets and 'service' them exclusively, usually with middle of the road records. By using one-stops some retail outlets can receive records from different companies at only slightly more than the normal dealer price, thus saving time and avoiding delivery charges of some record companies which are added to small orders. In the USA similar companies are known as rack jobbers.

Delivery

The term used for the final completion of an album to the satisfaction of a record company and for handing over of new songs or demos to a publisher. Highly relevant to songwriter/artists as frequently the rate on which they're paid US mechanical royalties (even decades later) is the date of delivery of their album to the record company.

Direct Injection

Plugging an electric instrument, e.g. bass guitar, straight into the mixing desk in a recording studio, instead of recording it into a microphone in front of a speaker in the studio. These days, as you probably know, apart from vocals and acoustic drums virtually everything is direct injected.

Doubling

Playing more than one

instrument at a session, performance etc.

Drop-in
Re-recording part of a track of a recording in a studio, commencing part of the way through without having to start from the beginning.

Dubbing
Re-recording from one recording medium to another, eg master tape to CD. Broadcasters pay small dubbing fees for the use of the song and the recording when they re-record music onto the soundtracks of their programmes.

Electronic Press Kit
Usually on DVD this is one of the terms to describe the material on you (a compilation of tracks, interviews etc.) sent by your record company to the press and media to promote you.

Exported Records
Sometimes treated as regards royalties as local sales and sometimes as sales in the country of destination. Small quantities are usually treated as local sales for calculating mechanical royalties for the songs involved. The artist contract may well say that exports are treated as foreign sales, which may well be at 50% of the royalty you get for UK sales, or it may even spell out the royalty rate applying to any exports of your recordings.

Fiduciary Duty
This is the 'good faith' which a manager in particular has to show to you in doing the best deals he can for you in respect of publishing, recording, merchandising etc. even if the deals are with companies which he has an interest in. If that's the case there's no reason not to sign with him provided you and your lawyer are happy that these deals really are on 'arms-length' terms, meaning that they're every bit as good as you could get if you were doing each one completely individually. Remember you also have a fiduciary duty, for example to the record company to finish your album on time (as long as the time scale was reasonable) and not to get completely stoned then spend the summer in Ibiza and finally start writing the rest of the songs for the album eight months later.

Fixer
Someone who acts as an agent for session musicians and brings the required musicians together, usually for broadcasts or recordings or for UK tours for foreign artists.

Freebies
These are generally records distributed free to members of the public who subscribe to record clubs, mail order organisations and the like. The usual principle is 'buy a certain number, get one free, or at a very low price'. If the free album happens to be the only one by you then it's unfair that you don't get paid artist royalties. If the other albums in the offer are all by you, then it doesn't matter. The songs on freebies are licensed at special rates by MCPS so you will get royalties for your song from your publisher. As an artist you may get no royalties from

albums given away with newspapers etc. but as a songwriter you will still be paid at a set rate, though such albums tend to devalue music – it's harder to justify £12 or more for an album if you can get an album full of hits for nothing just by buying a newspaper.

Ghosting

The practice (increasingly unusual) of having experienced musicians playing behind a band on stage without being seen, or playing instead of a group at a recording session just in case the regular group members should make a mistake, which could be costly in studio time wasted. As the general standard of musicianship improves and as more boy/girl bands make no pretence of playing instruments, it is becoming less common.

Grading

The practice of some performing right societies of paying less than normal royalties for a performance or broadcast of an arrangement of a public domain song depending on the amount of new material contained. This is becoming much less common.

Grand Rights

This has no legal or clear definition but is taken to mean the 'Dramatico-Musical Performance right'. In the UK it is the right to license a performance of a musical or of a number of songs from the same musical, generally live on stage (meaning songs that were originally written specifically for that musical). On the Continent the definition is taken to cover compilation shows (see definition) which in the UK are not considered grand right uses even though royalties are paid for these shows on a percentage of box office basis.

Graphic Rights

Generally refers to the right to reproduce the actual music and lyrics of a song, not as a hard copy, but on magnetic media, for example in video karaoke, or on CD Rom or CDI, DVD etc. Where these can be downloaded and printed out then of course they are very likely taking sales away from printed music and songbooks. It's hard to regulate this on the Internet, but for karaoke etc. in the UK there has been an additional 2% of the price added onto the normal mechanical royalty for the songs included.

Hyping

Really just exaggerating the merits of a record or artist, but usually this refers to chart-rigging – record companies either buying their own records from shops which they believe are making 'returns' to the chart compilers or sending quantities of free copies of records to those shops in the hope that they will try harder to sell them or else in the hope of a 'you scratch my back ...' relationship with the shop concerned. Every few years these activities have been exposed and have made the national press. A record company doing this risks heavy penalties including having its

Sid – do we have 2000 copies of 'Why don't you lerv me no more?'

records removed from the chart, but it's hard to prove exactly who was employing the person 'buying in' the records (the label? the manager? the publisher? even the artist's family!).

ISWC/ISRC

These stand for International Standard Work Code and International Standard Recording Code, and are gradually being introduced so that all collecting societies around the world can allocate money for uses of songs or recordings to the correct parties and lessen the chances of the money going astray because a work or record was wrongly identified.

Jingles

Mostly written by specialist writers for specialist publishers or directly for advertising agencies or the facility houses which make commercials. Some are taken from Production Music libraries (see 'Library Recordings') and licensed at around £1,000 or so for the song and the recording for a year's use

on UK network television for a commercial (for the song and recording), where each might have cost at least around £20,000 if the client/agency had used a commercial hit song and record. However, in recent years the use of existing hits for advertising jingles has been enormous and often prompted the original song or record to be re-released and make the charts again, though not where a parody lyric is used.

A one-year UK network use of a past hit would usually be worth £30,000 upwards for the song and, if the original hit recording is being used, the same sort of fee for using that too (although if the agency doesn't necessarily want the recording by the hit artist then the fee for this could be much lower, as it would only cost them about £5,000 or less to re-record the song. Incidentally if a parody lyric is made, the writer of that shouldn't get a share of the broadcasting fees, so if your song is used in a commercial, try to make

sure your PRS royalties, or a share of them, are not accidentally being paid to the person who made the recording of it that's on the commercial.

Key Man Clause

This is a clause in your agreement that says that if the particular person who signed you and enthused about you leaves the company, then you can give notice if you wish to terminate the agreement. It's much more likely to be agreed to by smaller companies and by management than publishing or recording companies.

Lease Tape Deal

An agreement under which an independent producer of a Master Recording licenses it to a record company. The artist would usually be signed to the independent producer, who would pay him his royalty out of what the record company pays to him under the lease. The producer may give the artist a split of around 50/50 up to about 70/30 of profits instead of a royalty. These days of course it's likely that the recording won't be on tape at all, but on some form of digital medium.

Library Recordings

A recording in the catalogue of a Production Music Library, formerly known as background or mood music libraries. These days a number of

former 'pop' writers write and produce albums for library companies, though most production music is still composed by specialists in this field. Their music is used by producers of films, television, commercials etc. instead of commissioning their own music or using existing 'commercial' songs which can be much more expensive. The rates they pay are laid down by the MCPS. The writers are usually not signed exclusively to one publisher, but album by album, though most have a regular publisher.

The terms of acquisition of such music (they are hardly ever songs, with words) are virtually the same as those for the ordinary songwriter but new writers would probably only get a 50/50 split of the all-important synchronisation fees and just their 50% writer share worldwide of performing fees, + an advance to help pay for the cost of making the album. The library publishers, although they produce records and tapes, do not release them for sale to the public as a rule. Pressings of library recordings are sent free of charge to potential users, who then only pay when some of the music is actually used. There are a small number of specialised production music library publishers in the UK. It is also sometimes possible for the potential

user to download some of the music directly into his computer from a central database, complete the appropriate MCPS licence form, receive an invoice and make payment without recourse to a disc or paperwork.

Long form video
Music videos other than promo videos for singles, usually either live or else compiled from individual promo videos and sold to the public.

Long-stop
One term used to describe the date upon which a 'contract year' terminates no matter what (eg. if an album is to be released within a year of the start of an agreement but is released after that year ends, the company doesn't have to take up its option (and usually pay a substantial advance) for the next year/next album until the first album is released, or a few months after. Without the long-stop – say two or three years from when the agreement began, that first 'year' could continue forever.

Masters, Master Tapes
Finished recordings of sufficient quality for records to be pressed up from them. Sound quality has improved so much through digital technology that even home-made demos can usually be remixed in a studio into finished masters.

Matching Offer
This is a provision, usually in recording or songwriting agreements, under which you agree to give your existing record company or publisher, at the end of your deal with them, the right to match any offer from a new record company/publisher for your services. It's always easier for your current company to come up with a new deal for you (better royalty splits etc.) firstly because they know how much you've been earning (though you can always tell your new publisher/record company this) and secondly because they can pay an advance based on their ability to recover part of it (if you let them) from money you've already earned under the first deal but which hasn't reached you yet (pipeline income).

If a new record company/publisher comes up with a much better offer (in the light of the above) then as long as that company is trustworthy (some that are not will make 'offers you can't refuse' then simply not honour them) it's worth looking seriously at changing over to them. However there really is a 'trust' in the music business between certain artist/writers and their record companies, publishers, and managers which goes beyond advances and promises of fortunes to come. If you do have to give your existing company the right to match an offer from an new one you should reasonably expect to give it up to around 10 working days to match the offer in writing.

M.D. (Musical Director)

Co-ordinator of the music in plays, musicals, television programmes, films, recording sessions, etc. and generally the leader of the band or orchestra performing.

Mechanicals

The royalties payable to the owners of the copyright in a song on a recording and earned by the sales or uses through downloading direct to home of the recordings.

Merchandising

Term used to describe the making and selling of any non-musical goods associated with the name, logo or image of an artist.

MIDEM

An annual gathering in winter in the South of France for music industry executives from around the world to make contacts and finalise deals for songs and recordings etc. as well as debate matters of international importance to the music industry. The biggest such gathering in the UK is 'In The City' which is usually in Manchester though it has moved around. There are other similar gatherings in the Western

Hemisphere such as SBSW (South By South West) in Texas. These events also tend to showcase newly-signed acts and occasionally unsigned acts, so it's well worth asking your record company if there's any possibility of you appearing there.

Midi Files

Actually stands for Musical Instrument Digital Interface and is of course the normal method of synch'ing up drum sounds and keyboards from the computer in a studio. Midifiles are the diskettes or other files containing the information, and in some countries the files used to record tracks or specially prepared backing tracks on diskette are duplicated and sold or hired out to other acts to play along to live. In the USA it was considered that these should be treated just like normal audio discs for royalty calculation, but in the UK, MCPS has attempted to standardise the royalty payable.

Min/Max formula

This is a method of calculating the amount which a publisher, record company etc. should pay as an advance to take up an option for additional songs, albums etc. Generally it is a certain percentage of the amount earned during the first period or by the first album (including earnings in the pipeline) at the time

the option is due, subject to a minimum of maybe 75% of the advance paid for the first period/album and a maximum of maybe 150% of that advance.

Non-Member

Usually used to describe the status of a songwriter vis-à-vis a performing right society. A non-member writer will not be able, even through his publisher, or his publisher's sub-publishers, to collect performing fees in many countries of the world, no matter how much his songs earn in those countries. Non-member shares generally end up as so-called 'black box' money.

Non-needletime

A certain small amount of broadcasters' time on air is given over to the playing of music which does not require a licence from PPL (see 'Collecting Societies' earlier). This includes production music from library publishers, demo recordings and other recordings the rights in which are owned by companies which are not members of PPL and which therefore don't qualify for payment. For them it's a way of getting some airplay on which PRS royalties are nevertheless paid for the broadcasting of the songs even though nothing, or just a nominal amount, is paid for the use of the recordings.

On hold

Where songs are submitted by writers and publishers to an artist to record, the artist or their management is likely to ask for a hold on the song if they like it. This means they don't want you to pitch it to anyone else till they've had a chance to record it. Of course songs can be on hold for years till they finally get onto an album and it can be tricky knowing when to say 'time's up'. Unless you desperately want the artist holding it to record your song, your publisher would normally start pitching it again once you know that the first artist has finished their album and not used it.

Orchestrations

Copies of songs arranged for the whole or part of an orchestra. These are very expensive to produce, and whereas they were once even considered essential to launch a new mainstream pop song they are now very rarely made by publishers themselves, although bands and orchestras sometimes make their own, with the publishers' permission and some small private firms are also licensed by publishers to make and sell small quantities, generally for brass bands and dance bands.

Overrides

Percentage points given to someone on songs or recordings in return for some assistance. A common example would be a publisher producing a master tape of an artist/songwriter and approaching a record label with it. The label, if it wants to sign the artist then they may insist that the publisher actually sells them his tracks in return for what it cost to record them + an override royalty of say 2-4%. The label will be asked to pay this direct to the publisher and generally deduct it from your artist royalty on these particular tracks under your agreement with them. If it's subsequently remixed then the override may be reduced.

Parallel Imports

Records coming into one country from another at a lower price to the dealers than the locally released copies of the same record. Under EU rules imported records and tapes can be sold in UK record shops, and if, because of the prevailing exchange rates for example, the imported records are cheaper, then it's these that will be selling, and your artist royalty rate may be a lot lower on these imports than it would have been on the UK release. It's actually quite normal and reasonable however that in some cases a record company in one country will prefer to test the market in another country with a few exports before doing a licensing deal with a company in that second country under which the local company will press and release the recording there on their own label. As a writer your local publisher (or the local mechanical rights society) may or may not collect copyright royalties on imported discs for often they have been paid in the country of export.

Parody

Generally humorous versions of songs, but can also refer to any alteration of the lyric of a song for use in an advertising campaign etc. For reasons mentioned in the Songwriting Section parodies are referred to in the USA as derogatory treatments of songs. Some have been very big hits in the past.

Pay for Play

The practice of some venues charging bands to play there, rather than the other way round. It may be expressed as a charge to use the house PA system, whether you want to or not, (and in small venues you probably don't). Alternatively you have to pay in advance for a certain number of tickets which it's then up to you to sell.

Payola

An American term for the practice of record companies, publishers etc. bribing disc jockeys or radio producers to broadcast certain records. Broad-

casting authorities and companies set rules to determine where reasonable business relations, lunches and small gifts end and payola begins.

Per diems
Living expenses paid to artists by managers or record companies generally whilst recording or touring at so much per day.

Performing Fees
The more general term for all royalties received through PRS and its affiliated performing right societies including broadcasting royalties and royalties for digital diffusion of songs.

Pipeline income
Generally refers to money which a publisher, record company etc. knows has been earned (perhaps it has been received by a

foreign subpublisher or licensee, or by MCPS from a record company) but which hasn't actually been received yet by your publisher or record company and therefore isn't actually due to be paid to you in the next accounting. It's sometimes possible to negotiate regular payments every March 31 and October 31 based on the amount of the last half-year's royalties taking into account pipeline income.

Pirates
Not to be confused with Bootleggers. Pirates abound in countries where copyright is not rigidly enforced. The pirate usually gets a record or video and makes further low quality copies from it without authority. Pirate record labels are usually blank except for the artist's name and song titles. Videos are more

often counterfeits – looking just like the original. In some countries books, including songbooks, are also pirated and counterfeited. Piracy is bad in Eastern Europe, Russia and the Indian sub-continent, but is particularly rife in the Far East.

Play List
Associated with radio stations. The producers who put together the programmes and other station executives meet regularly to hear new record releases and decide whether to give them airplay in their programmes and also decide which records should be removed from the previous list. The principle daytime shows which are largely composed of songs from the play list, or the current charts in the absence of a play list are sometimes known as strip shows, because of the way they are put together. There are still plenty of plays to be had by non play-listed tracks though usually not at peak times. The emergence of Radio 2 (playing admittedly older records) and more importantly the decline in audience ratings for Radio 1 in the early years of the 21st C. have tended to mean that new singles no longer have to rely on whether they get airplay on one or two major radio stations to (almost) guarantee them success (or failure).

Power of Attorney

This is the right, given by artists to record companies and managers and by writers to publishers, to take action against infringers and other unlawful users and to sign contracts on their behalf though it shouldn't include any agreement for a writer/artist's long-term services (anything more than about a guaranteed maximum of six months). Under some management agreements it goes much further and allows the manager to spend unlimited (but recoupable!) sums of money on behalf of the artist and to negotiate and sign, without reference to the artist, long-term record and publishing deals. Power of attorney should be limited in artist agreements to certain types of agreement and managers should not be able to commit the artist to any expenditure above a certain limit.

Premiums

Releases which are designed to promote a product, usually by being given away free in return for the public sending in a number of vouchers from a food product suchlike. Artists and writers should have the opportunity to say no to these if they object to them (particularly if they're advertising cigarettes or alcohol), though there is usually a lot of money to be made from premiums.

Pressing and Distribution (P & D) Deals

These are agreements under which independent record companies can have their records pressed up and distributed to UK dealers under one agreement with a specialised pressing plant/distribution company, who will normally take around 30% of the PPD (published price to dealers) of the records they handle.

Pressing Plant

A record and tape factory. The major companies have generally sold off their own pressing and distribution affiliates, and these functions are performed by independent pressing plants, used by indie and major labels alike.

Promo copies

Record companies will send out a certain number of copies of a new release for promotional purposes free of charge and will not pay artist royalties on these even if they wind up supplying large quantities free or very cheaply to chain-stores to encourage sales. They are however only allowed 1,500 free of mechanical royalties to writers/publishers before they have to start paying the full mechanical rate.

Promoter

Person or company arranging tours and engagements for artists.

Public Domain

No longer in copyright.

Racking

The sale of records and tapes on racks in supermarkets, petrol stations etc.

Recoupment

A record company or publisher will usually pay an 'advance' to an artist/writer which they will then expect to 'recoup' from his share (his share notice, not their overall income) of royalties and fees or other income they collect in respect of his recordings/songs. Recording advances will usually include all recording costs and will usually be recouped much later than publishing advances.

Release Sheets

Also known as 'dealer mailings' these are simply sheets sent to every record shop in the country by most major record distributors every week telling the retailers what records are being released and any good reason why the retailer should be sure to order a supply (i.e. previous record was number 1; forthcoming tour by artist in certain areas etc.).

Returns

Two meanings. One, unsold records returned by the shop to the distributor. Two, information as to uses of songs, i.e. a BBC return (to the PRS) will show songs used in a particular programme.

Ripping

Making an MP3 or other

similar format of a CD, generally for the purpose of e-mailing it to friends or putting it onto the Internet on a P2P site (usually illegally)

Rolling advance/Roll-over advance

This is a method of paying advances whereby as soon as the initial advance is recouped by the publisher, label or whoever (usually including your share of any money that their sub-publishers or licensees overseas have received but not yet paid to your UK label and publisher and hence to you), then an identical sum becomes payable again and so on up to maybe a year or so from the end of the deal (if it carried on right to the end of course, the payer could find himself paying another big advance a few months before the deal ends, leaving him with no more time to recoup it).

Sleeper

A record which becomes a hit months or years after its initial release with no further publicity from the record company.

Split copyright

A song where more than one publisher controls a share usually because the co-writers of the song are under contract to different publishers. This was almost unknown till the Seventies. Now it's more or less standard and cre-ates problems when, for example, the song is wanted for use in a film or commercial or even for printing in a songbook. All writers and publishers must clear their individual shares before it can be used. This is even more complex where, for example, a song was written by five members of one act, but included a sample of a song written by five other writers. All of them must agree before it can be used. Incidentally if, in this example, the film company only wanted the part of the song which didn't include the sample, it would not be unusual for the sample writers and publishers to be involved anyway (another reason for not using samples unless they're really really likely to make or break your record).

Sub-Publishing

Most publishers acquire world rights in a song from a writer and then appoint other publishers outside the UK and Eire to administer the rights there in return for a share of the local royalties. Only the so-called 'major' publishers plus a couple of big 'independent' publishers, notably peermusic, actually have their own people operating in all the major territories of the world. Otherwise in general Fred Smith Music (UK) may have a subsidiary called Fred Smith Music in, say, Brazil, but actually it's really being run by, for example, Universal Music or peermusic in Brazil. As regards Ireland it's quite normal (but not unknown) for a UK publisher to collect money through the collecting societies rather than to appoint a sub-publisher in Ireland, but an independent Irish publisher with an international hit may sometimes appoint a sub-publisher for the UK.

Tax Exiles

The high rate of UK tax can be especially harsh on those who earn a large sum of money in a relatively short time and this causes a regular flow of writers, musicians and singers from the UK to take up residence in countries with more favourable tax laws. Some, like the USA, are good places in any case to further your career. Others, like the Channel Islands, are not. Writers, whose earnings from hits tend to be spread over a longer period than recording artists, tend to be less affected by this problem. Your accountant will advise you as to whether it's worth leaving the country. If you are a 'tax exile' you can still spend most of the year in the UK but you mustn't, under any circumstances, exceed the limit of many days a year in the UK. This is the reason The Rolling Stones were unable to tour the UK a few years back – a change in the rules meant that they'd have lost money by being in the UK for too much of the year.

Terms

Used in contracts in the singular to describe the length of an agreement and in the plural to describe the actual royalty rates and conditions ('Term' in the singular meaning the length of time that you're tied to the company exclusively)

Test pressings

As you would assume, these are a few copies of a pressing supplied in advance to the record company to ensure that the sound is as expected before a pressing plant goes ahead with duplicating large numbers. You should get to hear the test pressing if at all possible as it may sound significantly different from the original master you heard in the studio.

Video buyout

The practice of film companies and other audiovisual producers wishing to clear the rights in a song or recording they want to use without ever again having to go back to the copyright owner to ask for rights for another new form of CD Rom or DVD for example, and without having to pay royalties on sales of videos etc. Sometimes limited buyouts of 50-100,000 copies worldwide are granted

but these are obviously very hard to 'police'.

Publishers and record companies are naturally reluctant to grant rights in 'all media which may hereafter be invented' or a similar phrase, as one of these could take the place in the market of normal audio CDs etc. at some future time but film companies generally demand this so it's not unreasonable for a publisher or record company to agree to it. As you can imagine DVD's of films are generally regarded as 'videos' for the purpose of working how much a song or recording should be worth.

White labels

Pressings, generally 12" vinyl pressings of dance tracks for distribution to DJs and specialist record shops. To maintain the artist and label cred, these contain minimal information about who has put them out. Some do get sold, but the object of the exercise is to create the interest and test the market before the official

release rather than necessarily to make money. On the subject of credibility, it's interesting that Cliff Richard released a record in the late Nineties under the name 'Black Knight' and the record was critically acclaimed until it became known that it was really by Cliff Richard (phenomenally successful though he may be) at which point it was 'dropped' by the media for no other reason than the fact that Cliff Richard was, by that time, not considered 'hot' and 'current' enough to justify playing his records. Needless to say if your white labels are broadcast there's a good chance you won't get paid unless there's enough information for whoever is making the programme returns to PRS to recognise what the track is, but then the object is to get the club-goers to like them and try to buy them, and if they do then you'll probably get a commercial release and won't mind losing a bit of money on the white labels themselves